Brave Men's Blood

The Epic of the Zulu War, 1879

One of the battlefield memorials at Isandlwana bears the following inscription:

Not theirs to save the day but where they stood, falling, to dye the earth with brave men's blood for England's sake and duty – Be their name sacred among us – neither praise nor blame Add to their epitaph but let it be simple as that which marked Thermopylae. Tell it in England those that pass us by, here, faithful to their charge, her soldiers lie.

The memorial marks the last stand of the Natal Carbineers. Since, throughout the Anglo-Zulu War, neither side held a monopoly of courage or sacrifice, the title *Brave Men's Blood* has been used here to reflect the suffering of all the protagonists, whatever their nationality.

Ian Knight

Brave Men's Blood

The Epic of the Zulu War, 1879

Greenhill Books, London
Stackpole Books, Pennsylvania

To 'Makhanda',
who opened a road for me to the blue haze
of distant hills, and adventure.

Greenhill Books

OTHER BOOKS BY IAN KNIGHT

The Anatomy of the Zulu Army: From Shaka to Cetshwayo, 1818–1879

'By The Orders of the Great White Queen':

Campaigning in Zululand, through the Eyes of the British Soldier

Fearful Hard Times: The Siege and Relief of Eshowe, 1879 (with Ian Castle)

Go to your God like a Soldier: The British Soldier Fighting for Empire, 1837–1902

Nothing Remains But To Fight: The Defence of Rorke's Drift, 1879

The War Correspondents: The Anglo-Zulu War (with Professor John Laband)

Warrior Chiefs of Southern Africa

Zulu: The Battles of Isandlwana and Rorke's Drift

The Zulu War: Then and Now (with Ian Castle)

OSPREY MONOGRAPHS:

Queen Victoria's Enemies 1–4

The Zulus

The Zulu Warrior

British Forces in Zululand 1879

The Zulu War (with Ian Castle)

Colenso and Spioenkop

Rorke's Drift

The Boer Wars

This edition of *Brave Men's Blood* first published 1996
by Greenhill Books, Lionel Leventhal Limited, Park House,
1 Russell Gardens, London NW11 9NN
and
Stackpole Books, 5067 Ritter Road, PA 17055, USA

Co-published in South Africa by Book Services International SA
Pty Ltd, P.O. Box 782395, Sandton 2146, Transvaal.

© Ian Knight, 1990
Typography and design © Lionel Leventhal Limited, 1990

British Library Cataloguing in Publication Data
Knight, Ian, 1956–
Brave Men's Blood: The Epic of the Zulu War, 1879
1. Zulu War, 1879 2. Zulu War, 1879 - Campaigns
I. Title
968.4'045

ISBN 1-85367-248-3

Library of Congress Cataloging-in-Publication Data available

PUBLISHING HISTORY
Brave Men's Blood was first published in hardback in 1990 by
Greenhill Books and is reproduced now complete and unabridged.

Designed and edited by DAG Publications Limited, London
Printed by Redwood Books, Trowbridge, Wiltshire

CONTENTS

PREFACE

The 1879 Anglo-Zulu War is perhaps one of the best known of the so-called 'Colonial Small Wars' fought during Queen Victoria's reign, and it might fairly be asked what point is there in going over the story again. Yet most popular histories of the war, even very recent ones, have persisted in using only a fraction of the source material available, namely official and unofficial contemporary British accounts. Even when these were fair and well-informed, they were necessarily one-sided, and their uncritical use has led to the perpetuation of a number of errors and myths. This is all the more surprising, considering the detailed and thorough academic work which has been done in the field since the Centenary in 1979, and which has let new light into many hitherto ignored aspects of the war, often challenging accepted truths. I am thinking particularly of John Laband's work on the Zulu army, Paul Thompson's work on the various African troops raised in colonial Natal, and their joint work charting sites in the field. Jeff Guy's work on the economic and political structure of the Zulu state has given us a much clearer picture of the balance of power within the kingdom, and the factors which drove it into conflict with the expanding British frontier in southern Africa. Yet these aspects have been resolutely ignored by popular historians, with a resulting lack of balance and depth. This work is intended purely as a narrative military history of the war for the general reader yet I hope it will present a more complete picture of the campaign, drawing, as it does, on much of this new work.

It is to be hoped that many of the illustrations in this book will be new, even to established students of the campaign. Great care was taken to search through sources hitherto overlooked by writers on the war, and the collection of photographs herein is the most comprehensive yet published. Wherever possible, particular attention has been paid to establishing the accuracy of original captions, to avoid perpetuating errors of identification. This is especially true of the Zulus, where careless or inaccurate captions have been accepted in the past without question. It is worth mentioning that photography in 1879 was a slow and difficult process, the more so in remote areas like Zululand, where the photographers had to undergo considerable discomfort to record scenes at the front.

It was impossible to take 'action photos' of battles in progress, and as a result most contemporary photographs show posed groups, or views of historical sites taken some months after the event. Cameras seldom ventured into Zululand during the days of the independent Zulu kingdom (although John Dunn hired one to record King Cetshwayo's 'coronation' in 1873). So most of the portraits of Zulu personalities were taken after the war. As a general principle, however, I have tried to choose photographs taken as close to 1879 as possible; most of the portraits of British officers were taken during the campaign itself. To bring the battle scenes to life, I have drawn on contemporary sketches and engravings. During the early part of the war, particularly, when British newspapers had few correspondents 'on the spot', these owed a good deal to the imagination of the engraver at home, but many of the later ones, particularly those by experienced artists such as Charles Fripp of *The Graphic* and Melton Prior of the *Illustrated London News* were both accurate and atmospheric. I have tried to use only those which seem to me to have the latter qualities.

Finally, I have tried to standardize Zulu spellings in accordance with correct orthographic practice (e.g., 'Thukela' instead of the old 'Tugela'), and given each man's patronym in deference to Zulu custom: hence Shaka ka ('the son of') Senzangakhona, Cetshwayo kaMpande, and so on.

Many people have contributed their time and knowledge to this project and none more so than that great Natal expert on the Zulu people and their history and culture, Mr. Sighart 'SB' Bourquin. During the years I have known him SB has been unfailingly generous, both with his personal knowledge and his remarkable collection of photographs and artifacts. He has been my guide and mentor on several trips to the battle sites and I feel rarely privileged to have shared those times with him, for he has made Zululand and its past accessible to me in a way that no one else could. Without him this book could not have been written. SB's friend and colleague, Ken Gillings, has also been an invaluable guide, and I treasure the memory of our joint expedition to King Cetshwayo's grave. John Laband too has been most generous, in sharing the fruits of his research, and providing hospitality. I have leaned heavily on the topographical approach he and Paul Thompson pioneered for the *Field Guide to the War in Zululand* for my maps. My thanks are also due to Mobbs Moberly of the University of Natal Press for giving me permission to use their approach, and to Helena Margeot and Raymond Poonsamy for finding the time in their busy schedule actually to produce the maps. Needless to say, all responsibility concerning troop dispositions on these maps is entirely mine. Rick Scollins also kindly drew the campaign map and those of the battle of Rorke's Drift. Michael Barthorp, that acknowledged master in the field of uniform history, helped me date some suspect photographs, and Kenneth Griffith not only allowed me to use material from his collection, but gave me some timely and helpful advice.

Jennie Duggan and her staff at the Killie Campbell Africana Library in Durban were indefatigable in searching their collections on my behalf, as were Gillian Berning at the Local History Museum, also in Durban, and Mrs Wanless at the Africana Museum in Johannesburg. My thanks are also due to the staff of the National Army Museum in London, and the Curators of the various Regimental Museums listed in the picture credits. Ian Castle struggled across the battlefields with me in the wet and miserable January of 1989 – 110 years on – and later read the manuscript. Keith Reeves, as ever, was most generous with material from his collection and advice, as were Bryan Maggs, Tim Day, John Young and Brian Best. George Rice and especially Claire Colbert helped me out with the seemingly endless task of photographic copying. Mr. Shele Ngubane of Durban showed me how traditional Zulu costume and shields were made, and Judy and Stan Cooke took my largely unannounced impositions on their hospitality in their stride.

Several debts are of a more personal nature. My parents, John and June Knight, have been unflinching in their support of this and other projects over the years, and my good friend Felicity Baker has been a continual source of encouragement.

My thanks to them all.

Below: General Marshall's reconnaissance to the battlefield of Isandlwana, May 20th 1879. On the ruined wagon-park, the troops harness-up undamaged vehicles and remove them, whilst others rummage through the debris and marvel at the evidence of the fight.

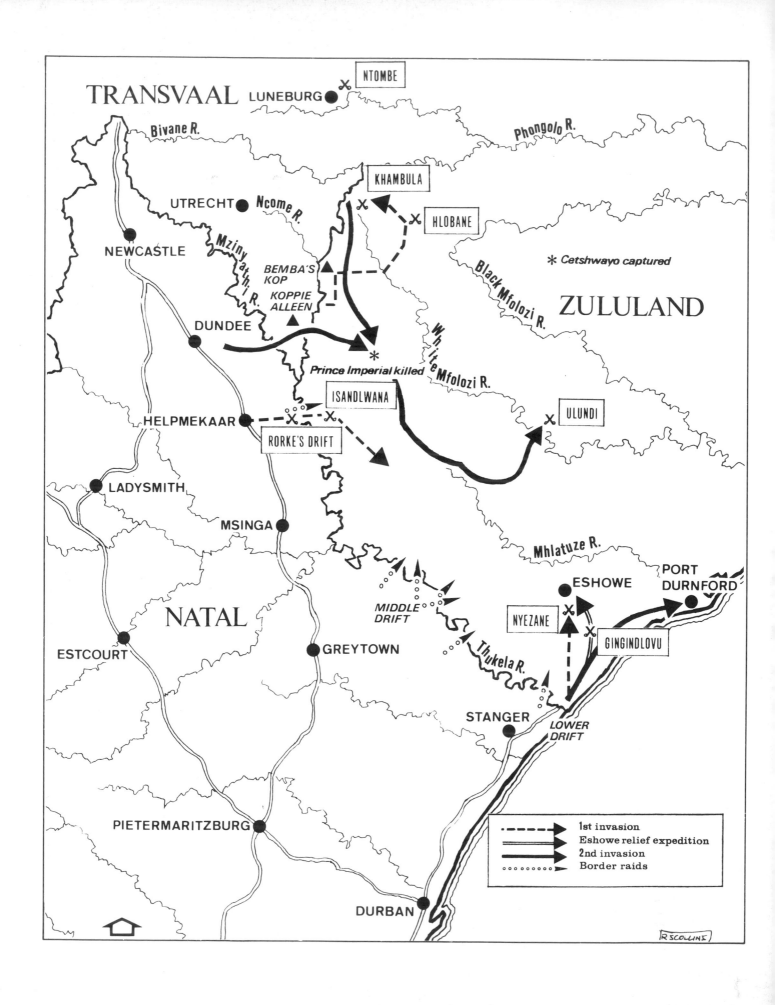

TRANSVAAL

LUNEBURG · ✗ NTOMBE

Bivane R.

KHAMBULA

UTRECHT · *Ncome R.* ✗ ✗ HLOBANE

NEWCASTLE

Mzinyathi R.

Black Mfolozi R.

* *Cetshwayo captured*

ZULULAND

BEMBA'S KOP ▲

KOPPIE ALLEEN ▲

DUNDEE ●

White Mfolozi R.

Prince Imperial killed

ISANDLWANA

HELPMEKAAR ● ✗ ✗ ULUNDI ✗

RORKE'S DRIFT

LADYSMITH ●

Phongolo R.

MSINGA ●

Mhlatuze R.

PORT DURNFORD

ESHOWE ● ✗

MIDDLE DRIFT

NYEZANE ✗

NATAL

GINGINDLOVU ✗

ESTCOURT ●

GREYTOWN ●

Thukela R.

STANGER ●

LOWER DRIFT

PIETERMARITZBURG ●

	1st invasion
	Eshowe relief expedition
	2nd invasion
	Border raids

DURBAN ●

R SCOLLINS

King Cetshwayo kaMpande, a splendid portrait by Carl Sohn, commissioned by Queen Victoria in 1882. After his capture at the end of the Zulu War, the King was sent into exile in Cape Town. In 1882, however, he was allowed to visit England to petition for his return to Zululand. He had a brief audience with Queen Victoria at Osborne House, and was a great favourite with the London crowds. His mission was partially successful; he was restored to a portion of his former territories, but this only provoked conflict with factions that had thrived in his absence, and he was defeated in the subsequent civil war. (By gracious permission of Her Majesty the Queen; Local History Museum, Durban)

Perhaps the most famous image of the war; C. E. Fripp's dramatic painting of the last stand of the 24th at Isandlwana. Fripp saw the closing stages of the war as the 'special artist' for The Graphic, and several engravings based upon his sketches are included in this book. His eye for detail and atmosphere is excellent, although this tableau owes a good deal to the conventions of Victorian battle painting; the heroic back-to-back stand, for example, and the sentimentality implicit in the juxtaposition of the upright sergeant and the young drummer boy. The inclusion of a Regimental Colour is a touch of artistic licence, too, since neither battalion's Colours were out on the firing line during the battle. Yet the background detail accurately suggests the carnage of the camp's last moments. (Peter Newark's Military Pictures)

rather than the larger isihlangu war-shield, but this charming sketch captures the appearance of Zulu dress and weapons in the days before European influence. (Peter Newark's Military Pictures)

Below: Reviving the spirit of their ancestors; a group of Zulu warriors at the Zulu War Centenary commemoration in 1979. A century of involvement in South Africa's industrial economy has meant that traditional costume is seldom worn today, except on important national occasions like this one. Nevertheless, these men evoke something of the appearance and spirit of their forebears. (Author's collection)

THE ROAD TO WAR

*The origins or European interest in the region. The contact between white and black during the eighteenth century: the competition for natural resources. The emergence of the Zulu empire under **King Shaka** in the 1820s, and the nature of the Zulu state. The arrival in Natal of the British and the Boers, and the **Boer/Zulu War** of the 1830s. The British annex Natal; the interaction between Natal and Zululand, and the reconstruction of Zulu power under King Mpande. Political and economic reasons for Natal/Zulu friction. **Cetshwayo** is crowned King of the Zulus, and re-asserts monarchial authority; Missionary opposition to his rule and settler insecurity. The **Confederation** policy; the annexation of the Transvaal in 1877 brings Britain and Zululand into conflict over the disputed border. Sir Henry Bartle Frere is convinced of the necessity of a war with the Zulus; British military plans and preparations. Border incidents are seized upon as a casus belli; the **Ultimatum**. War begins in January 1879.*

'Mpande did you no wrong, and I have done you no wrong, therefore you must have some other object in view in invading my land'.
King Cetshwayo kaMpande

Top left: *Orlando Norie's watercolour of the final stages of the battle of Khambula; a sortie by the 1/13th disperses the Zulu left horn. (Somerset Light Infantry Museum, Taunton)*

Below left: *The 1st Battalion, 13th Light Infantry, on the march in Zululand, flanked by scouts from the Natal Native Horse. The 1/13th served throughout the war in Wood's column. Watercolour by Orlando Norie. (Somerset Light Infantry Museum, Taunton)*

Right: *Cetshwayo kaMpande, b. c.1832, d. 1884, the last fully independent king of the Zulus (1873–79). It was King Cetshwayo's misfortune to be ruling his people at a time when their way of life was under threat from British economic and political expansion in southern Africa.*

At about 8 pm on 22 January 1879, Lieutenant-General Lord Chelmsford returned to his base camp beneath the distinctive mountain of Isandlwana in Zululand. He had ridden out before dawn that morning at the head of perhaps a third of his force, to investigate reports that a large Zulu army was in the vicinity. He had spent a frustrating day chasing enemy patrols, but making no major contact. Throughout the day he had received a confusing series of messages from the camp, indicating that fighting was taking place. But Lord Chelmsford was not unduly worried; he had left more than seventeen hundred men in the camp, including six companies of British regulars, and two cannon. Now, in the inky blackness of a moonless African night, broken only by the smouldering ruins of gutted tents and wagons, their bodies lay strewn about him. As the General's command picked its way slowly over the camp site the men tripped over the fresh corpses of friends and colleagues to whom they had said goodbye such a short time before. There was little choice but to spend the night on the battlefield, but few could sleep. The stench of death and the fear of attack stretched nerves to breaking-point and the hours passed in a series of alarms. To spare his men a full view of the horrors Lord Chelmsford had them roused before daybreak. Some awoke to find they had been lying across mutilated bodies in the long grass, or that their greatcoats were caked with bloody mud. Wearily, the column began the march back to the border post at Rorke's Drift, where a dull glow above the hills suggested further terrors.

Lord Chelmsford's fall from grace had been as swift as it had been dramatic. He had crossed into Zululand at the head of his invasion force at that same Rorke's Drift only eleven days previously. Seldom had a British General embarked on a Colonial campaign after such thorough preparation, and seldom had one been so spectacularly defeated. The magnitude of the disaster was incomprehensible. 'There were', as one witness put it, 'no wounded, no missing, only killed.' More officers were killed at Isandlwana than at Waterloo, and more men than at the Alma or Inkerman. 'I can't understand it,' someone heard the General say, 'I left a thousand men there.'

And more lay ruined upon the devastated field than the thousands of bodies slowly desiccating in the sun. With them lay the hopes of the British High Commissioner in southern Africa, Sir Henry Bartle Frere, that the Zulu War which he had instigated without the sanction of the Home Government would be brought to a swift and successful conclusion with a minimum of fuss. With them, too, ironically, lay the prospects of the very independence the Zulu had fought to preserve. For although Britain would later renounce Frere's policies in an outburst of public indignation, it was honour bound to exact a high price for its humiliation first.

Yet neither the British nor the Zulu nation had been long in southern Africa, and their paths had moved quickly to confrontation. During the fifteenth and sixteenth centuries, the great age of exploration and intervention which marked the emergence of the European empires, the southern half of the African continent was regarded as little more than a nuisance, an obstacle to be by-passed on the long voyages to the apparently limitless wealth of the Indies. Few knew about the affairs of its interior and fewer cared. On Christmas Day 1497 the great Portuguese explorer and navigator Vasco da Gama had given a name to the stretch of green hills fringed by crashing surf which he had discovered several hundred miles north-east of the Cape of Good Hope: *Terra Natalis*. But da Gama was no colonist. He sailed on and it was not until 1652 that the Europeans came to stay. The Dutch East India Company built a small harbour at the Cape to service its ships on the long haul to the east. They evicted the indigenous inhabitants, the semi-nomadic Khoi people, dug an earthwork fort and marked out some gardens where fresh vegetables could be grown. But the interior held no prospect of profit to them and they resolutely turned their back on it. In time their frontier farmers, swollen by a trickle of stern religious refugees

from Europe, would develop a hardy independent spirit and grow tired of the restrictions imposed on them by Company officials. They gradually spread eastwards along the fertile coastal downlands in search of pastures new.

Then, in the middle of the eighteenth century, along the banks of the Great Fish River, they were brought up short with a shock. For the land beyond the Great Fish was already occupied by a black African people who for generations had been drifting in the opposite direction. Although the two cultures were in many ways very different, they were in one crucial respect similar; they were both pastoralists, and that put them in competition for the same natural resource – land. The interaction between black and white on the Eastern Cape Frontier was characterized by bloodshed, a theme which was to become depressingly familiar across southern Africa. Of Natal still little was known. Lying beyond the Frontier tribes, cut off inland by the barrier of the Drakensberg, and from the sea by shoals, reefs and breakers, it remained largely impenetrable. Only those lucky enough to survive the misfortune of ship wreck, and the long overland trek to safety, could provide any insights into the land and its people.

Yet momentous events were to occur in Natal, beyond the reach of European influence. Some experts have suggested that black Africans first lived there as long as fifteen hundred years ago, and certainly archaeological deposits have been found dating to the sixth century. Sometime in the sixteenth century, however, a new human wave washed gently over the landscape. These were a linguistic and cultural group

Below: *An African home-stead (umuzi; pl. imizi) in Natal or Zululand during the nineteenth century. The dome-shaped huts are typical and the presence of milk pails and a fresh hide suggest the extent to which cattle domin-ated the Nguni lifestyle.*

Below right: *A remarkable study of an impi (an armed force), apparently taken dur-ing the 1860s. It is not clear whether these men are war-riors in the Zulu king's army or retainers of a powerful Natal chief, but all are carry-ing the full-size war-shield (isihlangu) and are wearing ceremonial regimental regalia. This picture gives a unique impression of the appearance of a Zulu army early in the century.*

Right: Frederic Augustus Thesiger, 2nd Baron Chelmsford, the commander of British troops in South Africa during the closing stages of the Ninth Cape Frontier War and Zulu War.

known as the Nguni, a series of related clans, each one a collection of families claiming descent from a common ancestor. Like their cousins on the Cape Frontier these people were pastoralists, and it is impossible to make sense of what was to follow without understanding the extent to which cattle dominated their lives. Although meat was eaten only on special occasions, cattle provided milk products, chiefly curds called *amaSi*, which were a staple diet, and hides for clothing and shields. Wealth and status were measured in cattle, which therefore governed all social relations. A young man could not leave his father's homestead until he married, and he could not marry until he had sufficient cattle to provide *ilobolo*, the guarantee of future standing and good treatment demanded by a bride's family. While unmarried he was required to give service to the clan chief, whose own political power was regulated by his ability to control the wealth of his chiefdom. A chief could take cattle from those judged guilty of a crime, or distribute beasts captured in wars waged by the unmarried men at his disposal. The more cattle a man had the more wives he could afford to support, and the more his household grew. Thus, in a very real sense, the expansion of Nguni society was dependent on its environment's ability to support cattle.

And Natal was very good cattle country. Geographically it is a coastal strip perhaps eighty miles wide, dropping down in a series of rolling terraces from the foothills of the Drakensberg to the Indian Ocean. The off-shore winds provide a high rainfall, and the resultant river systems have cut wide, often spectacular valleys on their way to the sea. The

summers are hot and wet and the winters cool and dry, with considerable variation across the country, from the humid sub-tropical coastal lowlands to the fresh inland heights. Although there were several large natural forests, and some of the hot valley floors were covered in thorn-bush, most of the area was carpeted with a variety of sweet and sour grasses which matured throughout the year. This, coupled with the comparative absence of the tsetse fly, meant that as the Nguni spread out over the hills their cattle multiplied and their people thrived.

But there were ecological limits. The coarse grasses were easily damaged by over-grazing and, if not bound together by a natural covering, Natal's red soil was easily washed away by the torrential summer downpours. The result was soil erosion which stripped many hills to their skeletal boulders, and scarred the landscape with *dongas*, deep run-off gullies. By the middle of the eighteenth century the suggestion is that the population of humans and cattle in Natal was approaching a saturation point. The result was a friction between clan groups who sought to bring more and more land under their control to fulfil their grazing needs. Slowly, tentatively at first, the friction broke into violence as clans sought to dominate their neighbours and gain access to their resources. Then, in the early years of the nineteenth century, the tensions within Nguni society exploded in a cataclysmic upheaval still known as *mfecane*, 'the crushing'.

In no sense were the Zulus the instigators of the *mfecane*, but they contributed largely to it and were finally to emerge as the clear winners. In 1816 they were a small clan of a couple of thousand souls who had already accepted domination by the much stronger Mthethwa. But in that year their chief, Senzangakhona, died, and the Zulus were forced to accept the Mthethwa candidate for their throne, Senzangakhona's illegitimate son Shaka. Shaka was to prove perhaps the most important single individual to emerge in the history of black South Africa, a military genius whose iron will shaped the destiny not only of Natal, but of thousands of square miles beyond. A dynamic and ruthless warrior, Shaka introduced a number of revolutionary battlefield innovations which changed the nature of Nguni warfare. Hitherto, battles had had a strongly ritualistic content. The opposing armies would meet at an appointed time and place, accompanied by a crowd of non-combatants, and open the proceedings by taunting one another. The main weapon was a light throwing spear, which was easily deflected by an oval shield of cow-hide. Moral ascendancy, not massacre, was the order of the day, and one side usually backed down before casualties became too heavy. Shaka changed all that. He introduced a new spear, with a long, wide blade and a stout haft, specifically designed for stabbing, together with a much larger shield which covered his warriors from chin to ankle. He trained them to use the two together, battering the enemy with the shield then running him through with the spear. To bring his men to contact as quickly as possible, he taught them a

tactic known as the *impondo zankomo*, the 'beast's horns'. One body of warriors, known as the *isifuba*, or 'chest', would rush down on the enemy, while flanking parties, the *izimpondo*, or 'horns', would rush out to surround it on each side. A fourth body, the 'loins', was kept in reserve, ready to plug any gaps that might develop in the attack.

Most of Shaka's enemies soon crumbled before such sophisticated brutality. In a series of brilliant campaigns from 1817 to 1820, he defeated the major clans between the Phongolo and Thukela rivers, including his old patrons the Mthethwa. This area was to become the heart of the Zulu kingdom. From 1820 he began raiding south across the Thukela, dislodging the powerful clans who lived there, sending them fleeing over the Drakensberg into the interior, or squeezing them south on to the fringes of the Cape Frontier. His rise was meteoric; oral tradition has it that when he first assumed the Zulu throne, Shaka could muster no more than 400 warriors: within two years it had risen to 4,000 and by 1824 when the major phase of expansion came to an end his army numbered 15,000. His nation was a conglomerate of all those clans he had conquered or who had offered allegiance, held together by a strong state apparatus controlled by Shaka himself.

Yet if Shaka's revolution were a purely African one, it could not help but attract the attention of the outside world, and draw to it the elements that ultimately would ensure its destruction. In 1805 the British came to the Cape, inheriting the Dutch possessions in one of the rapid shifts of political fortunes which marked Bonaparte's progress through Europe. No less

Right: The Zulu fighting formation was likened to the horns of a buffalo; the 'horns' rushed out to surround the enemy flanks while the chest charged head-on.

Right: The idyllic settlement of Port Natal (Durban) in the 1840s. British territorial claims were based on Shaka's grant of the port – the only viable harbour in the region – to British traders.

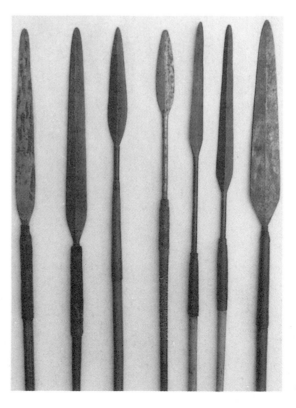

Left: A selection of Zulu spears, several dating from the 1879 War. The weapon with the heavy blade (right) is typical of Shaka's prototype stabbing spear; those at the left are later variants; those in the middle are for throwing.

parsimonious than their predecessors, they were equally as reluctant to commit themselves to an expensive colonial policy, but they were inexorably drawn into the complicated and messy Frontier entanglement. Here, from the 1820s on, they came to learn about Shaka from the stories of black refugees fleeing his wars in the north. Bureaucracy remained determinedly disinterested, but free enterprise was intrigued. In 1823 the first whites set out to establish contact with the interesting King of the Zulus, to see whether the tales told of palisades of ivory were true.

These pioneers were an unprepossessing bunch, hunters, traders and adventurers lured by the prospect of a wild life beyond the reach of European mores. Whites were not unknown to the Nguni who remembered them in the past, apparently cast ashore by the waves like *abeLungu*, pallid sea-creatures.

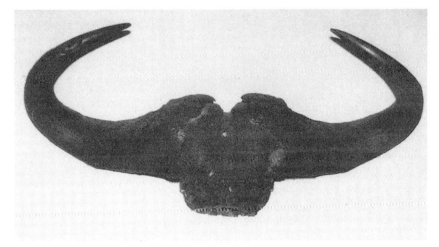

Shaka was intrigued by them and the glimpse of the outside world they afforded him. They, in turn, were over-awed by him, and the extraordinary power he seemed to wield over his subjects. In response to their importuning Shaka granted them a tract of land south of the Thukela, which included Port Natal, the only viable harbour on the coast. Here the *abeLungu* set themselves up as clan chiefs, marrying Zulu girls, accumulating retainers, quarrelling, scheming, interfering in Zulu politics, and generally enjoying the privileges Shaka had decreed their white skins entitled them to, until accident, disease or violent death overtook them. Shaka remained amused by them, but considered their numbers far too small to pose a threat; until, perhaps, the very end. In late September 1828, Shaka fell victim to a palace *coup*, and was assassinated by his half-brother Dingane. Many Zulus believed that he cursed his attackers as he died: 'You will not rule when I am gone, for the land will see white people and locusts come!'

Mentioning both in the same dying breath could scarcely be more significant.

The change of monarch ushered in a new era in the history of the kingdom. Shaka's rule had lasted just twelve years, and his system of government had been a very personal one. Without so dynamic a leader, the precarious balance of power within the kingdom would be exposed, and, as King Dingane soon discovered, the presence of the whites was already upsetting the equilibrium. There was a permanent tension between the apparatus of the state and the clans that composed the nation. True, many of the clans had been heavily defeated and impoverished by Shaka, and their power broken, while the ruling lines

of others had been overturned and replaced by the king's appointees. But many more had joined Shaka as allies, and the extent to which they commanded the loyalty of their clan manpower and cattle made them important and wealthy men. These were the so-called *izikhulu* (sing.; *isikhulu*), the 'great ones' of the nation, who sat on the *ibandla*, the national council which advised the king. There was always a danger that the *izikhulu* might use their power to secede or ferment revolution. Shaka, the strong man, intimidated them by force and seldom a day went by without several executions, often on the flimsiest of pretexts, at his court. And to some extent their power was undermined by the central apparatus of the state administered through *izinduna* (sing.; *induna*), state officials appointed by the king himself. The most important of the state institutions was the army.

In the days before the *mfecane* young men of the same age were banded together in guilds known as *amabutho* (sing.; *ibutho*) for the ceremonies necessary to initiate them into manhood. The ceremonies bound them with strong ties which lasted throughout life. Until they married the men of the *amabutho* were considered the property of the chief and were required to give him occasional service, building royal homesteads, taking part in hunts, mustering for war. Once they were married the men transferred their allegiance to their families and were lost as a labour resource to the chief. It is thought that the Mthethwa were the first to realize that the *amabutho* could be used as battlefield units, and Shaka went one step further, turning them into a regimental system. Each *ibutho* was recruited from across the nation regardless of clan loyalties, thus reducing the risk of subversion. Shaka extended the traditional chief's right to regulate the rate at which the *amabutho* married so that he alone could grant them permission. By artificially prolonging the period before marriage, he thus maximized the time the men were at his disposal. Shaka seldom allowed a regiment to marry and disperse before the men were in their forties, but this was not as uncomfortable as it sounds, because Zulu moral codes allowed for limited sexual activity outside marriage. Marriage marked a profound difference in status for the men concerned; they ceased to be *izinsizwa*, youths, and became at last *amadoda*, men. This change was demonstrated by means of the *isicoco*, a fibre ring sewn into the hair on top of the head and plastered with black gum.

The *amabutho* were quartered at royal homesteads known as *amakhanda*, literally 'heads', sited strategically around the kingdom as centres of royal authority. Each *ikhanda* was an ordinary homestead, an *umuzi* (pl.; *imizi*) writ large, a collection of dome-shaped thatched huts arranged around a central cattle pen and surrounded by a stockade. At the top end was a fenced-off area, the prerogative of the *isigodlo*, the king's household, where he or his representative lived. The strength of individual *ibutho* varied, but they were on average a thousand strong, and they were sustained in the *amakhanda* at the king's expense. Each one was

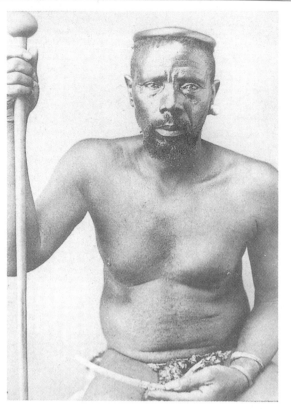

Left: A typical induna, *or state official, in King Cetshwayo's reign; Mgwazeni kaMbonde, an important man within the Zungu clan, and brother of Cetshwayo's mother. He wears the* isicoco *headring of a married man.*

given a herd of cattle with carefully matched hides, which provided not only meat and *amasi*, but also hides for war-shields. Each regiment therefore had a uniform shield-colour, with junior regiments carrying black shields, senior ones white shields, and all manner of combinations and variations between. The warriors also had lavish and distinctive ceremonial costumes. Every-day clothing for a man consisted of an *umuTsha*, a thin belt of hide with strips of dressed skin hanging at the front, and an oblong of hide, an *ibeshu*, low on the buttocks. When warriors mustered in full regalia, however, their bodies were almost completely covered in the bushy part of cows' tails. These were attached to garters worn below the knees and to armbands above the elbows, and to a necklace in such a way as to fall in dense bunches to the waist at the front and the knees at the back. Padded headbands of leopard or otter skin formed the foundation for extravagant headdresses. Flaps of monkey skin hung down over the side of the face, and some younger regiments wore stiff strips of white cowhide standing upright above the temples, with cows' tails attached to the tips. The long black tail feathers of the *sakabuli* bird were worn on each side of the head, and black and white ostrich feathers were worn in different combinations. Senior regiments wore one or two blue crane feathers, and only those especially favoured by the king might wear the waxy scarlet and green breast feathers of the lourie. In theory, warriors were supposed to provide their own costumes, but the rapid expansion of the army in Shaka's day far outstripped the ability of Zululand's wildlife to clothe it. Many of the rarer pelts and feathers were traded from

Right: A magnificent and very rare study of a group of warriors in full ceremonial regalia, c.1870. The men are wearing identical headdress of a type typical of an unmarried ibutho *(regiment); a white cow-hide headdress called* amaphovela, *leopard-skin headbands and bunches of black* sakabuli *feathers.*

Right: Nineteenth-century domed huts, typical of both ordinary homesteads and the amakhanda, *the royal barracks. These particular huts are reconstructed on the site of King Cetshwayo's Ulundi (oNdini) homestead, which was destroyed by the British in 1879.*

Left: A senior warrior in typical costume; note the otterskin headband around the headring, and crane feathers. The shield is a dancing shield; his regimental shield would have been larger and white in colour.

enjoyed royal patronage, survivors of the devastation began to emerge from hiding and seek the traders' protection. In Shaka's day their numbers remained few, and the king firmly regulated the whites' activities, but Dingane had scarcely assumed the throne when the first political dissidents fled his regime and made for Port Natal. Dingane was as keen as Shaka to enjoy the advantages that the British presence brought him, but the early years of his reign were marked by his attempts to persuade the traders to send back his erring subjects. The very real danger to the unity of the kingdom became apparent as early as 1829 when Chief Nqetho, an important *isikhulu* and leader of the powerful Qwabe clan, simply gathered up his followers and fled across the Thukela before Dingane could stop him.

Then, in the 1830s, the Zulu position deteriorated with the arrival of a new group of whites in Natal. These were the Boers, descendants of the old Dutch frontier farmers at the Cape, who had found British rule so irksome that they had simply packed their possessions into their ox-wagons, and trekked off into the interior in search of a promised land to call their own. Their progress, as Dingane well knew, was characterized by conflict with local African groups in which the Africans always came off worst. This new threat was too much. When Boer envoys arrived at his royal residence to discuss a treaty, Dingane had them murdered. He then dispatched his armies to attack their camps in Natal. At first he left the British at the Port unmolested, but when they sided with the Boers his *amabutho* razed their settlement. Unfortunately for the Zulu kingdom, despite some initial successes the resulting war was a catastrophe. The Zulu army was shattered by Boer firepower at the battle of Blood River in December 1838, and under such pressure the bonds which held the nation together began to split. Dingane's brother, Prince Mpande kaSenzangakhona, went over to the Boers. Seizing their chance, the Boers offered to install Mpande as king, and at a battle in the Maqongqo hills in January 1840 Mpande's warriors routed those of Dingane. The king was murdered shortly after.

Dingane's attempt to rid himself of the white problem had been a calamity. The Boers did crown Mpande, but they laid claim to a large portion of his country, extending to the Black Mfolozi River, and thousands of cattle in compensation for their losses. The struggle had ended in civil war, in which both sides had had to make extravagant promises to secure the support of the *izikhulu*. There was now no chance of preventing the whites dominating Natal, and of turning the clock back to the days when the Zulu monarchs functioned at the centre of a self-contained universe. In a very real sense the war marked the end of Shaka's state, and the future fortunes of Zululand and Natal would become inextricably intertwined. Mpande and his successor would try to re-establish monarchical authority, but the result would be an increase in tension which would contribute ultimately to war with the British.

neighbouring tribes and distributed by the king. After a successful campaign the king would also distribute plundered cattle to those warriors who had distinguished themselves, together with highly prized badges of bravery, a heavy brass armband known as the *ingxotha*, or a necklace of interlocking wooden beads. Thus the relationship between the king and his *amabutho* was mutually supportive; the king depended on the warriors for a non-sectarian labour force, and the warriors depended on the king for sustenance and potential advancement.

The problem with such a system was that it required the king to maintain a monopoly of patronage. If the warriors found an alternative way to better themselves, the king's control over the *amabutho* might weaken, and power slip away from the centre towards the *izikhulu*. And with the coming of the whites just such an alternative existed. When Shaka had first granted land to the traders it had been virtually depopulated by his raids. But once it became clear that the whites

Above: A Zulu regiment parades before Prince Hamu kaNzibe, c.1873. Mpande's reforms restored the Zulu army to something of its glory; note the regimental uniformity of the shield colours.

Not that the trekkers had gained everything they had bargained for. Natal's great attractions to them had been its fine pasturage and its emptiness. Now that the spectre of Dingane had been lifted however, Africans flooded in and settled large areas which the Boers had earmarked for their own farms. Most of these were survivors of the pre-Shakan clans, but many were Zulu subjects for whom white rule offered an alternative to the *amabutho* as a route to wealth and wives. The Boers were seriously alarmed and proposed relocating them in large reserves in the very south of Natal. But this was not far from the Cape Frontier, and the British were ever-sensitive to disturbances on that particular doorstep. The Colonial authorities, indeed, had never recognized the Boer claim to independence, and were further worried by their apparent attempts to establish diplomatic links with rival European powers. Justifying their actions on the grounds that Shaka's original land grant had been to British subjects, the authorities moved to occupy Port Natal. The trekkers, to whom the prospect of British rule was anathema, put up a fight, but an amphibious landing covered by broadsides from a British war-ship dispersed them. In December 1842 Great Britain formally annexed Natal. Most of the Boers, who had come so far and endured so much precisely to escape the British, abandoned Natal in disgust and trekked back across the Drakensberg into the Boer republic of the Transvaal.

This unexpected turn of events was a blessing to Mpande. The Boer claims for reparations lapsed, and an Anglo-Zulu accord of 1843 established the Rivers Thukela and Mzinyathi (Buffalo) as the country's southern borders. The king, whose carefully cultivated façade of indolence and incompetence concealed the shrewd mind of a political survivor, set about rebuilding the state. To reduce the chances of further challenges within the Royal House, he carefully eliminated any potential rivals in his own family. Then, to stem the flow from the *amabutho*, he made service among them more attractive. The warriors were not required to spend all their time in the *amakhanda*, and were allowed to spend long periods with their families. Furthermore, they were allowed to marry at an earlier age. To ensure that this left him with sufficient manpower Mpande created *amabandla amhlope*, 'white assemblies', regiments of married men carrying white shields who served in the *amakhanda* for a period and brought their wives with them. By careful management of the women in his *isigodlo*, Mpande linked himself by marriage to the families of prominent *izikhulu*. And by trade with the whites, he secured a number of goods which furthered his personal wealth and prestige. Chief among these were firearms, which Mpande demanded in return for licensing white traders and hunters who wanted to operate in his territory.

Yet it was some time before the flow of people from Zululand to Natal slowed. In 1845 the newly appointed Colonial administration estimated that there were between 60,000 and 100,000 blacks in

Natal. By 1861 there were 140,000 and by 1872 305,000. Even allowing for the healthy rate of natural increase made possible by the lower rates of *ilobolo* prevailing there, this was a major influx. In contrast, the white population was slow to grow. There were between one and two thousand whites in the Colony in 1848, with the 'native trade' beginning to replace hunting, which had already decimated the area's game as the main economic activity. By the 1870s successive waves of immigration had brought that figure to only 20,000. Small towns grew up at the Port – renamed Durban in 1835 – and at the old Boer camp at Pietermaritzburg, but most settlements remained hamlets of a few huts, and roads were little more than wagon tracks following trade routes. Entrepreneurs found that cattle-ranching and sugar-cane cultivation were viable, but, curiously, Natal developed with an acute shortage of both land and labour.

In an attempt to hold back the best land for white use Natal officials designated only 2,000,000 acres of the Colony's total acreage of 12,000,000 for black reserves, known as locations. This, of course, was quite insufficient to contain them, and many blacks squatted illegally on land set aside for whites. Since the Colony was poor and under-developed, however, wage rates were low, and many blacks preferred to subsist by their own efforts rather than by working for whites. One solution was taxation, which forced blacks to work to raise the money to pay them, but this particular device had its limitations where means of enforcement were feeble, and the white population was heavily outnumbered. As it was, taxation was one reason why, in the 1870s, some blacks, disillusioned

with white rule, actually began to move back to Zululand.

At least one Natal official, whose views were to be of crucial importance in coming events, was convinced that Natal's backwardness was the fault of independent Zululand. Theophilus Shepstone was born in England in 1817, but grew up in the Cape, where his family were missionaries. Fluent in several African dialects, he was known to the blacks by the rather self-important name of *Somtsewu*, the 'white father'. In 1846 he had come to Natal. As Secretary for Native Affairs, he was to have a profound influence on the development of Natal's policy towards the Africans for nearly thirty years. Like many of his generation, he believed implicitly in the moral superiority of white civilization, and he was deeply convinced of his own insight into the 'native mind', and the authority he believed that vested in him. He also had a vision of the development of Natal which saw it as the gateway to central Africa, with Durban importing European trade goods and sending them in the wake of the expanding imperial frontier to the Zambesi and beyond, receiving in return cheap migrant labour from the limitless pool of the north. The most serious obstacle to this plan, in Shepstone's view, was the Zulu kingdom, which not only sat squarely across the routes, but also apparently dumped its surplus population in Natal, and maintained a standing army which could be nothing but a threat.

Shepstone, of course, had no legitimate reason to interfere in the affairs of a neighbouring sovereign state, but such was the inter-dependency of Natal and Zululand that the succession crisis which developed in

Below: *The magazine at Fort Napier, overlooking Natal's provincial capital, Pietermaritzburg.*

Right: *Sir Theophilus Shepstone, Natal's Secretary of Native Affairs, and one of the principal architects of the Zulu War.*

Below right: *'Chief' John Dunn and his izinduna, photographed at King Cetshwayo's coronation in 1873. Dunn made himself extremely influential within the kingdom by his advice on matters concerning Natal, and by bolstering Cetshwayo's power with firearms.*

the latter overspilled its borders and provided him with an opening. Unlike Shaka and Dingane, Mpande had been careful to remove any potential threats within his household when he had come to the throne, but, also unlike them, he had proved extremely fertile and fathered a large number of sons. Nguni tradition was decidedly muddy on the question of succession, and of course a ruling monarch risked signing his own death warrant if he nominated an heir too soon. Mpande's sons therefore grew to manhood without knowing which of them would succeed him. Two, in particular, fully intended to do so; the Princes Cetshwayo and Mbuyazi. Since the king refused to choose between them, both began courting *izikhulu* and collecting a faction. Then, in late 1856, Mbuyazi emulated his father's road to power by crossing to Natal, and seeking the support of the whites. Cetshwayo mustered his warriors, set off in pursuit, and caught him at 'Ndondakusuka on the Zulu bank of the Thukela. In the bloody battle which followed, Mbuyazi's faction was completely destroyed.

Such a resounding victory clearly made Cetshwayo the prime contender, but he could not afford to move too soon. The king still controlled all ceremonial functions and only he could grant permission for the *amabutho* to marry. Cetshwayo could not hope to win the nation's support until he was an *indoda*, a man. And Mpande refused to commit himself and recognize Cetshwayo as his heir. Shortly after 'Ndondakusuka, no doubt with his father's connivance, another of Mpande's sons, Mkhungo, slipped across the border and appealed to Shepstone for sanctuary. Mpande hinted that Mkhungo was his choice as successor and began to cultivate the friendship of missionaries to foster closer links with Natal. This engendered in Cetshwayo a lasting distrust of missionaries, and instead he turned to white traders for support. One, in particular, gained his confidence. John Dunn was born to a settler family at the Cape in 1833 and three years later his parents moved to Natal. He had enjoyed an adventurous youth as a transport rider and hunter, and had offered his services as a mercenary to Mbuyazi, but had scarcely escaped 'Ndondakusuka with his life. He had made his peace with Cetshwayo, however, and the two became close personal friends. The prince found in Dunn an honest and perceptive adviser on the world of the white man; he also found him an invaluable source of firearms which Dunn imported in their hundreds via Mozambique.

In 1861 Shepstone tried to play the Mkhungo card, but blundered badly. A rumour spread through Zululand that he was about to invade and install the prince as King. Shepstone visited Cetshwayo at his father's royal homestead of kwaNodwengu, *The Place of the Irresistible One*, on the rolling Mahlabatini plain, and tried to gain concessions regarding land and the passage of free labour. In an angry meeting Cetshwayo shouted him down and Shepstone was forced to acknowledge him as the heir apparent. For a month or two there were fears of invasion on both sides of the Thukela, but the incident blew over.

It did, however, have one long-term serious consequence. When they heard of the crisis the Transvaal Boers sent a message to Cetshwayo offering to intervene. Exploiting divisions within the Zulu Royal House had proved a profitable tactic for them in 1839, and now they were after a specific reward. The 1843 pact between Mpande and the British had specified the Thukela and Mzinyathi as Zululand's southern boundaries, but it had not mentioned a border in the north-west of the country where it abutted the Transvaal. In 1848 Chief Langalibalele kaMthimkhulu of the Hlubi clan had broken away from the kingdom and moved to Natal, leaving a triangle of land on the upper Ncome (Blood) River largely depopulated. Mpande had given the Boers permission to graze their cattle there, and gradually the area had become lightly settled with Boers whose republican sympathies had caused them to move out of Natal when the British took over. Now they sought more lasting grants in the area. Cetshwayo apparently toyed with the idea, and the results of the negotiations would become a matter of bitter controversy when the border dispute became a direct cause of the war with the British.

In the meantime, however, Mpande, Cetshwayo and Shepstone continued their subtle power plays. In 1867 Mpande finally admitted defeat and gave permission for Cetshwayo's age-grade, the *uThulwana*, to don the headring and marry. It was a public recognition of his son's fitness to succeed him, but, although Cetshwayo began to take control of the apparatus of state, Mpande continued to rule, in name at least, for another five years. Then, in September or October 1872 he died. He had been on the throne for 32 years and had consolidated the kingdom at a time when it was under threat from powerful external forces. He was the only one of Senzangakhona's sons to die peacefully of old age, and he was buried in the traditional manner, wrapped in the fresh hide of a slaughtered black bull, at the top of the cattle kraal at kwaNodwengu.

The great prize was within Cetshwayo's grasp at last. He was now about forty years of age, tall, with a heavy build which struck observers as regal rather than fat. He was inclined to be taciturn, and his interest in the affairs of his kingdom was deep and genuine, but the years of waiting had made him passionate, ruthless and suspicious when it came to matters of his own authority. Even at this stage he feared an internal challenge. There were two main dangers, both important *izikhulu* from the north of the country. The first was Hamu. Hamu was biologically a son of Mpande, although his mother had previously been a wife of Mpande's brother Nzibe, who had been killed fighting in one of Shaka's wars. Mpande had then taken the widow into his own household, but the complicated Zulu laws of genealogy meant that Hamu was legally Nzibe's son. This technicality ruled him out as a legitimate candidate, but many believed he had his eye on the throne, and his people, the Ngenetsheni, had waxed fat and powerful a long way

from the centre of royal authority. The second was Chief Zibhebhu kaMapitha of the Mandlakazi people. The Mandlakazi were descended from a brother of Senzangakhona and were thus a section of the Royal House itself; Zibbebhu was Cetshwayo's cousin. He was a dynamic and ambitious man who had already made himself wealthy by trading with whites on his own account. He, too, was perhaps not content to remain a provincial *isikhulu*.

Considering how best to strengthen his position during the long period of national mourning for Mpande's death, Cetshwayo played into Shepstone's hands. He sent a message to the Natal authorities asking them to bestow their recognition of his title by attending his coronation. Shepstone, acting on his own initiative, accepted with alacrity. Cetshwayo's installation was fixed for the end of August 1873, but in the event Shepstone arrived late and missed the spectacular Zulu ceremonies. Instead he crowned Cetshwayo himself on 1 September, in a farcical ceremony which many Zulus resented and many in Natal found ridiculous. But even so, Shepstone had his price. In return for his support he raised the question of the disputed territory which might have provided both a route for migrant labour from the north, and a dumping ground for Natal's surplus blacks. He also asked Cetshwayo to allow more missionaries into the country. The king would not budge on the disputed territory, nor would he allow more missionaries in, though those already there might stay. He did, however, allow Dunn to act as labour agent and secure workers from Thongaland, a tribute kingdom to the north. In return Shepstone

publicly read out a number of laws at the coronation. The wording of these was ambiguous and their intention remains unclear; they were mostly concerned with limiting gratuitous bloodshed and execution without trial. Shepstone was later to claim they were promises of good conduct binding on the king himself, though Cetshwayo probably saw them as a reinforcement of monarchical authority. In any case, the king was dissatisfied with the whole proceeding, while Shepstone and his party departed elated; he had been given an implicit right to interfere in Zulu policies at last.

With Shepstone back across the border, Cetshwayo settled into his throne. The *amabutho* were ordered to build a new and fitting royal homestead. He picked a spot on the Mahlabatini plain, opposite old Nodwengu, and called his residence oNdini or Ulundi, from the common root *Undi*, meaning 'the heights', one of the Zulu names for the Drakensberg. It was certainly a most impressive complex, with an outer circumference over two thousand yards round, and a thousand huts arranged in rows of three around the central enclosure which covered ninety acres. A feature of the *isigodlo* was a European-style building of wattle and daub, where the king entertained important visitors. Once it was complete Cetshwayo summoned the royal cattle from *amakhanda* across the country, and reviewed the nation's wealth – there were more than 100,000 of them, though the grand round-up was to have tragic consequences. Some among them had contracted bovine pleuro-pneumonia – lungsickness – from beasts introduced from Natal, and when the huge herd was redistributed it took the disease to every

Opposite page; top: King Cetshwayo's principal residence, Ulundi (oNdini); it was destined to be burnt by the British at the end of the 1879 War.

Opposite page, bottom left: King Cetshwayo's attempts to revitalize his army led to conflict with Natal; this man wears a typical young man's full-dress uniform, and carries the large isihlangu shield. His appearance is similar to that of the iNgobamakhosi ibutho.

Opposite page, bottom right: A warrior in 'war dress', an abbreviated form of the regimental regalia actually worn into battle, since the full uniform was too valuable and too constricting. He carries an umbumbuluzo a slightly smaller war-shield intoduced by Cetshwayo in the 1850s. Both shields were carried in 1879. Compare this man's dress with the one next to him.

Above: Chief Mahubulwana kaDumisela (standing, in cloak), one of the principal izinduna of the abaQulusi in 1879, and their senior military commander. Standing next to him is Mfunzi Mpungose, chief messenger of the Zulu Royal House. Photograph c.1882.

corner of the kingdom. Within two years perhaps half of them would be dead.

In other respects, too, the kingdom was less healthy than it appeared. With the decline in the exodus to Natal, and the relaxing of the *amabutho* system under Mpande, Zululand's population had risen steadily in the years of peace, so much so that in some parts of the country pasture was exhausted and tracts were becoming uninhabitable. Furthermore, many of these people were no longer serving the king in the *amabutho*, which made it difficult to manage the population. Many *izikhulu* had accumulated a degree of regional autonomy in the unsettled political climate since 1856, and some had gone so far as to raise their own *amabutho*. Cetshwayo was determined to restore the central authority of the state. One solution would have been a military expedition. This would have allowed the king to call up the army, it would have won new wealth in terms of captured cattle and it would have boosted Cetshwayo's prestige. In 1874 the king therefore proposed a raid on the Swazi, the only independent African group left on Zululand's border. The *izikhulu*, recognizing a threat to their independence, would have none of it, and the *ibandla* over-ruled the king. So, significantly, did Shepstone to whom Cetshwayo had written informing him of the plan. Nevertheless, the king refused to be thwarted and set about revitalizing the *amabutho* anyway. This inevitably resulted in friction which a growing party in Colonial Natal, opposed to his regime, eagerly publicized.

The first incident was 'the marriage of the *inGcugce*'. The *inGcugce* was a female age-guild, a non-military equivalent of the *amabutho*. As part of his plans to tighten up the marriage laws, Cetshwayo directed two regiments of men in their late thirties to take wives from the younger *inGcugce*. But many of the *inGcugce* girls had already promised themselves to men in younger *amabutho*, and some refused to obey the command. Cetshwayo lost patience and gave the girls several months to find husbands in the designated regiments, failing which they would be 'married to *uNkhata*', *the bewhiskered man* – the rock of execution. In the event only a handful of girls were killed, and a salutory lesson about the king's authority was learned, but the incident was to have a sequel which clearly highlighted the tensions within the kingdom. Two years later, at the First Fruits ceremony in 1878, the annual gathering of the nation, the iNgobamakhosi and uThulwana *amabutho* quarrelled. Quarrels between regiments, who were intensely competitive, were not unknown, and this one had been sparked off by resentment on the part of some iNgobamakhosi warriors who had had to give up *inGcugce* lovers to the older uThulwana. But the iNgobamakhosi were the first regiment raised by Cetshwayo and he had a particular affection for them; the uThulwana were a 'white assembly' who were quartered at Ulundi itself, and included many of the *abantwana*, the royal princes. Cetshwayo himself had served in their ranks, but now they were commanded by Prince Hamu

Left: Zulu spiritual beliefs were dominated by the isangoma, or diviner, who was in touch with the spirit world, and could 'smell out' the perpetrators of evil. So attached were the Zulus to these beliefs that Christianity made little headway among them. Note the gnu's tail switches which were badges of their profession.

kaNzibe. Hamu resented the challenge issued by his brother's 'boys', and the uThulwana were the first to reach for their spears. By the time the king's representatives prised them apart more than sixty warriors had been killed. Cetshwayo is said to have wanted to execute Hamu, but he dared not move against him, and the Prince returned to his own territory under a cloud.

Word of these incidents reached Natal as highly coloured rumours spread by the missionaries. By the 1870s missionary frustration was intense. There were about twenty missions in the country belonging to rival Norwegian, British and German groups and they were conspicuous by their lack of success. Unlike Natal, where there were several *kholwa*, or Christian African settlements which enjoyed a high reputation, the Zulus refused to be prised from their traditional beliefs. Most Zulu converts were outcasts and misfits, distanced from the institutions of their own culture and despised by the majority of the population. The missionaries blamed the king for this, believing that he was deliberately obstructive; certainly Cetshwayo had no room for a philosophy which preached an authority above his own while its advocates attempted to meddle in his affairs. With a vested interest in damning his regime, the missionaries began a concerted campaign against Cetshwayo in the Natal press, where they found a section of opinion willing to listen to them.

Insecurity was a characteristic of the white population in the Colony. King Dingane's terrible massacres of the Voortrekkers were within living memory, and had been recalled by the invasion scares of 1856 and 1861. Their fears had been confirmed in

1873 when an attempt to curtail the arms trade to Natal blacks had provoked a minor uprising. Chief Langalibalele of the Hlubi, who had fled Zululand twenty years before, had refused to hand over his arms and had tried to cross the Drakensberg into the sanctuary of Basotholand. A force of Colonial volunteers had tried to head him off, and in the ensuing scrimmage three volunteers and several levies were killed. Langalibalele was soon brought to book, and his clan effectively broken up, but the affair had left a lasting impression, which rumours of a new and aggressive policy across the Thukela preyed upon. While a few colonists actually wanted a war with the Zulus, many would have slept easier in their beds had the threat of the *amabutho* been removed.

To this sentiment did Shepstone appeal. The Secretary of Native Affairs was increasingly determined to see his view prevail in Zululand, encouraged by an unexpected economic miracle sweeping South Africa. For seventy years the region had been a drain on Imperial resources, the reluctant price to be paid for the strategic necessity of the Cape. But then, in 1867, in a place called Griqualand West, just north of the Cape's borders, diamonds had been discovered. Within a few years the economy had been radically transformed. Diggers had flooded into the region, bringing with them investment capital which stimulated the transport and communication networks, put money into the coffers of hitherto destitute colonies, and created a ferocious demand for cheap black labour. At last it seemed as if Shepstone's dreams of a wealthy and thriving Natal feeding the expansion and exploitation of imperial Africa might become a reality. And the political implications of the new economic geography were enormous. Southern Africa was still a patchwork of small, often antagonistic units: the British colonies of the Cape and Natal, the Boer republics of the Orange Free State and the Transvaal, and a host of independent African kingdoms in between. If the new mineral wealth was to be used to its best advantage an infrastructure that cut across national boundaries would have to be set up. Roads, railways and telegraphs would have to connect the major areas of growth, and migrant labour would have to travel vast distances as efficiently as possible. The backward administration and determinedly isolationist outlook of the Boer republics would be a serious obstacle, as would any African state which refused to accept the new role demanded of it.

The British solution to these problems, conceived by the head of the Colonial Office, Lord Carnarvon – probably with Shepstone's advice – was Confederation. This was simply an attempt to bring all southern Africa's disparate states under one authority

Below: Mbilini kaMswati (right), the young exiled Swazi prince whose raids were one of the causes of the Zulu War, and who was one of the most agressive Zulu leaders on the northern frontier.

Below right: SigcwelegcwelekaMhlekehleke, the commander of the iNgobamakhosi ibutho, who fought at Isandlwana and Gingindlovu.

– British, of course – to ensure their mutual development. As a by-product it might even have brought stability to a region notorious for its festering conflicts. The Cape and Natal, being British possessions, could simply be brow-beaten into accepting the scheme, but there was always a risk that more forceful means might be necessary against those reluctant to give up their sovereignty. 'I hope', said Lord Carnarvon in 1877, 'it does not mean we shall have great pressure put upon us to annex Zululand. This must and ought to come eventually, but not just now.' But once started, the juggernaut of Confederation would move swiftly into confrontation with King Cetshwayo.

The Transvaal was the first to be drawn into the scheme. This was the most republican and anti-English of the Boer republics, but its population was small and so independent-minded that they refused to pay taxes, with the result that its administration was bankrupt and unable to prosecute a war it had undertaken against Chief Sekhukhune's Pedi tribe. Citing the threat from the Pedi and the continuing border dispute with the Zulu as justification, Britain stepped in to save the Transvaal burghers from the shambles they had made of their own affairs. The man Carnarvon chose to do it was none other than Shepstone, who resigned his post in Natal and in April 1877 raised the Union Flag at Pretoria. The Boers, for the most part, greeted him with sullen resentment.

Shepstone's new position as Administrator of the Transvaal now involved him directly in the border dispute. Hitherto he had been opposed to the Boer claims because he had his own plans for the region, but now he found it expedient to champion their cause. The atmosphere had become increasingly tense since Cetshwayo's accession. Keen to reassert his power at home, the king was not inclined to give up his authority over a slice of territory to which he believed he had every right. He accepted that Mpande had allowed the Boers to graze cattle there, but neither Mpande nor he had ever given away lasting title to the district. In 1875 the Transvaal had attempted to beacon off the area they claimed, and to evict the Zulus living there. These were mostly abaQulusi, who were not a clan as such, but descendants of the occupants of an *ikhanda*, ebaQulusini, which Shaka had located in the area, and who had subsequently settled nearby when they married. There was still an *ikhanda* there, and the abaQulusi considered themselves a royal section. The tussle thus became a very important one for Cetshwayo's prestige. The danger of violence was very real and the tension was further aggravated by the activities of a freebooter named Mbilini kaMswati.

Mbilini was actually the eldest son of the Swazi King Mswati, but not, alas, his legal heir. When Mswati had died in 1865 Mbilini had tried to seize his throne, but failed to win sufficient support within the kingdom. A year later he fled to the Transvaal, where the Boers tried their old trick of playing him off against his rivals in an attempt to win influence. Mbilini proved unprofitable, however, and his Boer supporters abandoned him, so in 1867 he *konza*'d (paid allegiance to) Cetshwayo. Cetshwayo allowed him to settle in the Ntombe river valley in the heart of the disputed territory. Mbilini was a young man, not yet married, but he wore the headring as a sign of his rank. Despite an apparently pleasant personality, he was really, according to those who knew him, a 'hyena'. Once installed in the Ntombe valley, he began a series of raids on both European and Swazi homesteads in an attempt to restore his fortunes and win supporters. Cetshwayo denied having any control over him and gave the Boers permission to kill him, which they singularly failed to do.

In October 1877 Shepstone met a Zulu delegation on the Blood River to discuss the whole border question. Among the Zulu representatives was Mnyamana kaNgqengelele, Chief of the Buthelezi clan, an *isikhulu* of the highest rank who was also Cetshwayo's prime minister; his presence was an indication of the seriousness of the meeting. Shepstone tried to browbeat the Zulus into accepting the Boer position, and the *izinduna* were shocked by his sudden change of face. Asked Sigcwelegcwele kaMhlekehleke, the passionate commander of the iNgobamakhosi:

'Is it so, then, Somtseu, that after two men have been friends, and then one of them dies and leaves his son fatherless, the one who lives on ought to be harsh to the son of the deceased? This Cetshwayo, whom you have come to trouble and not to help, is Mpande's son, and Mpande used to be your friend.'

It was an accusation of betrayal which stung Shepstone, the more so because it exposed the sham of his pretensions as a benefactor of the Zulus, and the meeting broke up amid bitter recriminations. Many Zulus saw that meeting as a turning-point in their relations with the British, the first serious step to war. Cetshwayo reacted to its failure by instructing the abaQulusi to build a new *ikhanda* only five miles from the disputed German settlement at Luneburg. He recalled them shortly afterwards, but his message was clear.

Meanwhile, a new British representative had arrived in southern Africa, sent out by Carnarvon with the express intention of implementing Confederation. Sir Henry Bartle Edward Frere was in his sixties and had just retired from a long and distinguished career in the Indian Civil Service, where he had acquired a reputation as a man of sound judgement, able to act upon his own initiative. The job of High Commissioner for southern Africa lacked the prestige of many of Frere's previous positions, but Carnarvon was persuasive and Frere approached the task with considerable dynamism. His assessment of the complex situation was vigorous and thorough, and he did not shirk the responsibility of adopting a forward policy if he felt it were required. It did not take him long to become convinced that a confrontation with the Zulus was necessary. Not only was Shepstone telling him so, but he had the evidence of a wave of black unrest before him.

Right: Sir Henry Bartle Edward Frere and his staff, at Pietermaritzburg in 1878. Standing behind Frere (in uniform) is Captain Henry Hallam Parr, who served in the Zulu War and wrote a book about his experiences.

By the late 1870s many of the African groups south of the Limpopo were in a sorry state. In 1877 a faction fight on the Cape Frontier had flared up into a full-scale war – the Ninth – while in the Transvaal the Boers were locked in their fruitless struggle against Sekhukhune. The Basotho were restless and one chief, Moorosi, was already in rebellion. In fact, this was little more than coincidence, a common reaction to years of misfortune and hardship. Reduced by war or treaty to cramped reserves or restricted homelands, southern Africa's disparate black groups were over-crowded and impoverished. Over-grazing had destroyed pasture and soil erosion was rife. In 1875 a drought had begun which ravaged the whole area. Grasses failed to regenerate and in some areas there was a real danger of famine. Even the powerful Zulus were not immune, and it seems likely that Cetshwayo had a very real need for the comparatively empty disputed territory. For most blacks, a lack of alternative solutions manifested itself in an angry attack on an obvious source of tribulation – the white man. In this they were aided by the very capitalism that had contributed to their predicament; they were

able to acquire large numbers of firearms which were readily available in the diamond fields. The result was a series of unco-ordinated flare-ups the length and breadth of the country.

To Frere, however, these outbreaks were anything but coincidental. He was convinced that a guiding hand was behind them and he found one in Cetshwayo. There was of course, a complex network of communication between blacks in southern Africa, and Cetshwayo was remarkably well informed of what was happening elsewhere, but there is no evidence to suggest that he supported the uprisings, let alone organized them. Yet Frere began a propaganda war which painted the Zulu king as an 'irresponsible, bloodthirsty and treacherous despot', the 'head and moving spirit' of the 'native combination'. Quoting Shepstone and the Zululand missionaries, Frere began to prepare both Natal and Britain for the possibility of a Zulu war. Across the Thukela, Cetshwayo was bewildered by this rapid and sinister turn of events. His quarrel with the Transvaal had been a long one, but now it seemed to have provoked the wrath of Britain with whom he had been on good terms. He was

vaguely aware that some other purpose must lie behind Frere's aggressive posturing, but he was at a loss to explain it. A series of messages sent across the border failed to secure enlightening answers.

There were some in Natal, too, who were keen to halt the sudden lurch towards war. The head of the local Colonial administration, the Lieutenant-Governor of Natal, Sir Henry Bulwer, shared neither Frere's view that a Zulu war was politically inevitable, nor Shepstone's that it was economically desirable. He was acutely conscious of the vulnerability of Natal's scattered settler community, and the poisonous effect a war might have on race-relations for generations to come. In December 1877 he intervened to head off the crisis. He offered to set up an impartial commission to arbitrate in the boundary dispute. Cetshwayo accepted with relief.

The Commission met at Rorke's Drift, a mission station overlooking the Mzinyathi River, in March 1878. Among its members was Colonel Anthony Durnford, Royal Engineers, who was widely known in the Colony as the commander of the party that had tried to prevent Langalibalele's escape. Durnford had lost the use of his left arm as the result of a stab wound during the action. For a month the Commission took statements from both Boer and Zulu witnesses, examined documents, and assessed the claims. In June it presented its report to Bulwer, who passed it on to Frere in Cape Town in July,

Frere had high hopes of this report. He was by now convinced that a short, sharp and, above all, successful campaign against the Zulus was the best way to advance the cause of Confederation. If the report upheld the Boer position it would serve as an ideal justification for an ultimatum. He was aghast, therefore, when it found in favour of the Zulus. Although it recommended that several long-established farms west of the Ncome be allowed to remain, it found that the Zulu kings had never given away title to the land and that the Boer claim was based on hearsay and dubious evidence, much of it unsupported, some of it forged. Such a fair and impartial judgement was a set-back to Frere. He had no intention of changing his position, but he would clearly have to rethink his plans. For the time being he suppressed the report's findings, and dispatched the senior British commander in southern Africa, Lieutenant-General the Honourable Sir Frederic Augustus Thesiger, to Pietermaritzburg to prepare a military appraisal of the situation. Thesiger, the son of Lord Chelmsford, was then fifty, a career soldier, who had joined the army in 1844, served in the Indian Mutiny and the Abyssinian campaign of 1868. He had just brought the messy war on the Cape's Eastern Frontier to a successful conclusion, where his handling of his motley army of British regulars, Colonial volunteers and African levies, under trying circumstances in impossible terrain, had earned him

Above left: Sir Henry Bulwer, the Lieutenant-Governor of Natal; a bitter opponent of the war, who continually resisted Chelmsford's attempts to employ Natal troops across the border in Zululand.

Above: Brevet Colonel A. W. Durnford, RE. Durnford was a sympathetic leader of African troops who had lost the use of an arm during an uprising in 1873; placed in command of No. 2 Column, he was killed at Isandlwana.

Right: An NCO of the Durban Mounted Rifles, and his groom, c.1879. The DMRs' uniform consisted of blue jacket with black velvet facings trimmed with red, and blue trousers with a scarlet stripe and black welt down the outer seam. The regiment served with Pearson's column during the First Invasion of Zululand.

Right: Officers of the Victoria Mounted Rifles and Stanger Mounted Rifles in 1879. The influence of the British Rifle Volunteer movement is very clear on the uniforms of these men, who fought at Nyezane.

wide approval. A tall man with the perfect manners of a Victorian gentleman, he struck those who met him as charming, if a little aloof. He brought with him a professional military eye, and rather too little respect for the fighting qualities of African enemies.

Thesiger was not encouraged by the view from Pietermaritzburg. If it came to war he would have to wage an offensive campaign, which meant invading Zululand, a country whose only roads were a few traders' wagon-tracks, and large parts of which were unmapped. The border was more than 200 miles long, and consisted for the most part of rivers running through difficult country. The water-levels were unpredictable at the best of times, and if in flood, they would be impassable to a British army encumbered by baggage wagons, but when low could easily be crossed at dozens of points by the Zulus. There were no border defences, just a handful of African policemen working for district magistrates, who kept an eye on the traffic across the best known drifts. Indeed, Natal did not boast much in the way of defensive arrangements at all. The Colony was divided up into Counties, which were broken down into wards, and the adult white men of each ward could be called out to defend their district, rather like the Boer commando system. Since they were untrained and undisciplined, their military value was limited. Of more worth were a handful of volunteer units which had sprung up from the 1850s, once it had become clear that Natal could not expect a permanent imperial garrison. These men provided

their own uniforms and horses, elected their own officers and were armed by the Government. If they were enthusiastic they trained regularly; they might or might not be good shots, but they were used to the country. Their numbers were small; the Buffalo Border Guard, for example, mustered 31 men, the Newcastle Mounted Rifles 37, the Durban Mounted Rifles 64. Only the quasi-military Natal Mounted Police approached the discipline of regular troops. Although it was official policy to provide *laagers*, protected defensive areas, for the white civilian population, few in fact existed and no provision was made for Natal's blacks, who might reasonably be expected to suffer heavily in the event of a Zulu raid.

In the face of such unpreparedness Thesiger was free to draw up his own plans from scratch. Inevitably he would have to rely most heavily on imperial troops, several battalions of which were already in southern Africa, mopping-up on the Frontier, garrisoning the Colonies, or stationed on the Transvaal border, keeping a wary eye on the sullen Boers and Pedi. Contrary to popular belief, the British army of the 1870s was undergoing a period of increasing professionalism. The much-publicized shambles of the Crimean War had ushered in an era of reform which reached a peak during Edward Cardwell's tenure as Secretary of State for War, from 1868. In the teeth of opposition from the conservative high command, Cardwell had abolished the system whereby officers purchased commissions, and

introduced short-service for the rank and file which meant that a soldier had to spend only six years on active service rather than twelve, with a further six on the Reserve. The result was a gradual change in the composition and outlook of the army. Although many senior officers had purchased their commissions under the old system, and the necessity of a large private income ensured that officers remained a social élite, there was a greater emphasis on training and proficiency of junior officers, who were more likely to achieve promotion through merit. The private soldier, too, was no longer drawn from the opposite social extreme, the dregs of society, and, although 'Jack Frost and unemployment' were still the best recruiting-sergeants, there was a noticeable increase in the literacy and educational standards of the other ranks. New, more fluid, ideas were beginning to influence battlefield theory away from the rigid columns and lines of the Napoleonic era towards more flexible and rapid deployment in open order. And the army had ample opportunity to test its skills in its demanding role as imperial policeman, which pitted it against foes as different as Afghans on the North-West Frontier and Maoris in New Zealand.

Cardwell's reforms had also affected the way the army was organized. From 1871 each infantry regiment was linked to a specified district within the United Kingdom, where it established a depot and concentrated its training and recruitment. The 109 Line regiments retained their old numbers, but many

Above: Part of the tremendous number of transport wagons Chelmsford had to accumulate to launch the invasion; note the soldiers sleeping under the wagons (right).

Left: Mehlokazulu ('eyes of Zulu') kaSihayo, whose raid into Natal precipitated the British Ultimatum, photographed as a prisoner-of-war. A junior officer in the iNgobamakhosi ibutho, he fought at Isandlwana, Khambula and Ulundi.

had a subsidiary county title – the 13th Light infantry, for example, were the 1st Somersetshire, Prince Albert's, while the 3rd Foot were the East Kents, the Buffs. The first twenty-five regiments were made up of two battalions, and the remainder one. In theory, one battalion of each regiment was supposed to remain at depot while the other served abroad, but in practice more were required for overseas duty. It was most unusual for the two battalions of the same regiment to be stationed in the same part of the world, but the 1st and 2nd 24th (2nd Warwickshires) had achieved that distinction, having been dispatched separately to the Cape Frontier. Each imperial battalion consisted of eight lettered companies of roughly one hundred men each, though few were ever up to strength because of

casualties and sickness. South Africa was by no means an unhealthy station, but the heat and rain of the summer months could rapidly undermine sanitary arrangements in camp, with a resulting increase in fevers and stomach disorders.

Despite progress with modernization, the troops still fought wearing uniforms more suited to a European parade-ground than a Colonial war. The mid-1850s had seen a number of experiments in dull and neutral-coloured clothing, but khaki remained in service only in India, and troops in southern Africa went into action wearing scarlet jackets, with distinctive facing colours on the cuff and collar, edged in white braid. Trousers were blue with a red stripe, and headgear consisted of a white 'foreign service'

helmet, with a regimental badge on the front. In practice, the coat was not as conspicuous as it might seem, because once it had faded and weathered it was not totally out of place in the sometimes harsh reds, browns and greens of the African landscape, but the helmet remained dazzling in the sun's glare, an obvious and inviting target. The troops soon learned to remove the badge and dull down the helmet with a variety of improvised dyes ranging from tea or coffee to mud, boiled tree bark or cattle dung. Officers often preferred a comfortable dark-blue patrol jacket to their scarlet tunic. The soldiers' main weapon was the 1871-pattern Martini-Henry rifle, a single-shot breech-loader which fired a heavy .450 calibre lead bullet. It was sighted up to 1,450 yards, although aimed fire was only effective at half that distance; its ideal battle range was between 300 and 450 yards. It had been tested in action both on the Cape Frontier and in Afghanistan, where it was found to have the stopping power necessary to drop a charging warrior in his tracks, often inflicting ghastly wounds. Its chief disadvantage was that it soon became fouled with heavy use, which made it prone to jam and exaggerated the already pronounced recoil, and the barrel tended to overheat. Veterans of the Cape Frontier War countered this by sewing bullock-hide over the barrel and stock. Each private carried a 21.5-inch triangular socket bayonet, nick-named 'the lunger', which, on top of the rifle's length of 4 feet 1.5 inches, gave him a reach of more than six feet. Sergeants carried a sword-bayonet.

Ammunition, a total of seventy rounds per man, was carried in two buff leather pouches on each side of the waist-belt, and in a black leather 'expense pouch' either at the back of the belt or below the right-hand pouch. Other features of the 1871 Valise Pattern Equipment were a haversack, a wooden water-bottle and, when on the march, a mess-tin and greatcoat. Officers were armed with swords and revolvers.

In late 1878 Thesiger had at his disposal two artillery batteries and five infantry battalions: the 2/3rd, 1/13th, 1st and 2nd 24th, and 90th – with one more, the 88th, scattered between Mauritius and the Cape, and another, the 80th, on the Transvaal border. He had no regiments of imperial cavalry, although an experiment to mount selected infantrymen on horses had resulted in two effective squadrons of mounted infantry. Such a force was clearly not up to the task required of it, however, and the General cast about to see what effective use could be made of Natal's manpower. In the meantime he put in a request to the Home Government for reinforcements.

The rub was, however, that the Home Government was not at all prepared to back Frere's war-mongering. Carnarvon, it will be remembered, had accepted that Confederation would mean a confrontation with the Zulus, 'but not just now', and Disraeli's administration was poised on the brink of a far more serious clash with the Russians over the Balkans, and a

Below: *A remarkable photograph of an Imperial infantry battalion lined-up in companies, with the band to one side, in Pietermaritzburg just before the start of the war. Judging from the fact that their helmets are pristine and still have helmet-spikes, the men have probably been ordered to appear smart for the camera. On campaign the troops had a more 'lived-in' look.*

renewed war in Afghanistan. It had no time, troops or money to spare on a little war in Africa. Thesiger was sent only two more infantry battalions – the 2/4th and 99th – and two companies of Royal Engineers, far less than he required. Carnarvon's successor in the Colonial office, Sir Michael Hicks Beach, sent Frere a stern message suggesting that dealings with the Zulus be conducted with 'a spirit of forbearance'. But forbearance was not Frere's intention, and while Thesiger juggled his plans, Frere cast about for a *casus belli*. He found one on the unsettled border, where tension was running high.

The first and most serious of two incidents took place in July 1878. Across the Mzinyathi from Rorke's Drift lived the Qungebe people under their induna, Sihayo kaXongo. Sihayo was an important man. He had been one of Cetshwayo's loyal supporters in 1856 and was something of a favourite despite the fact that he fostered close ties with Natal, often dressed in European clothes, dined with missionaries, and had extensive trade contacts which stretched as far as Portuguese Delagoa Bay. Two of Sihayo's wives had been unfaithful to him, however, and both had become pregnant by other lovers, one, moreover, standing accused of bewitching her husband. These were serious crimes, punishable by death under Zulu law, and once discovered the women fled to Natal. Both rather foolishly settled in the border region,

Left: Men of Hlubi Molife's Tlokwa horsemen, photographed during the Langalibalele Rebellion in 1873. During the rebellion Hlubi's men established a good relationship with Durnford, with whom they later fought at Isandlwana. Their appearance would have been similar in 1879.

Above: The Lower Drift on the River Thukela, photographed from the Zulu side; Fort Pearson was built on the knoll, right.

Left: A group of Levy Leaders on the Mzinyathi border in 1879. From left to right they are (top row): W. C. Warner, H. F. Fynn, Jnr, J. G. Dartnell and N. H. Robinson. Bottom row: H. E. Kirby, T. Wheeler, J. L. Knight, T. H. Reynolds, R. A. Beachcroft and J. Frankish. Like many Colonial officers, their uniforms have an improvised look!

however. Sihayo was away at Ulundi when his sons discovered the women's whereabouts and decided to avenge their family honour. On 28 July, three of Sihayo's sons, Mehlokazulu, Bhekulu and Tshekwana, together with the Chief's brother, Zuluhlenga, crossed the border at the head of about thirty mounted and forty dismounted warriors. They marched several miles into Natal, and found one of the women at the homestead of Border Policeman Mswagele. Despite his protests, they dragged her screaming back into Zululand where they put her to death. A second raid dealt with the other woman in the same way.

White opinion in Natal was appalled, both by the violation of its sovereignty and by the brutality of the deed. While it was still digesting that incident, however, another took place. In mid-September the Zulus across the border organized a ceremonial hunt. A common enough ritual, on this occasion it was intended to alert the spirits to the need for rain, before the crops withered beyond repair. However, the large numbers of warriors involved panicked white farmers in exposed areas, who abandoned their property for the dubious safety of several improvised laagers. Before the scare had died down, a Natal surveyor named David Smith and a trader named W.H.Deighton went down to the Thukela at Middle Drift to examine the state of the road. The water was low and the two men accidentally wandered on to an island considered part of the Zulu bank. Here they were immediately detained by a party of warriors who had been watching the drift for signs of military activity. Smith and Deighton were jostled and abused and accused of being spies – a fair accusation under the circumstances – but finally released unharmed.

These fracas, by no means unique in the Colony's history, played right into Frere's hands. He sent a stiff message to King Cetshwayo demanding that Sihayo's sons be handed over for trial and that a large fine in cattle be paid. Cetshwayo probably realized the gravity

of the situation, but he was in a cleft stick. Sihayo was not unnaturally reluctant to surrender his sons. Although young, Mehlokazulu was a man of some repute, a personal attendant of the king and a company commander in the iNgobamakhosi *ibutho*. His fellow warriors refused to countenance giving him up. Opinion within the army began to run high at this slight to national prestige. Cetshwayo attempted a compromise; he made excuses for the youths and offered to pay a large fine in cattle. Frere refused with calculated indignation, stepping up the diplomatic pressure while Thesiger completed his preparations, knowing that the king was unlikely to comply. In vain did Cetshwayo send a rather poignant message in November 1878 that 'he hereby swears, in the presence of Hamu, Mnyamana, Ntshingwayo, and all the other chiefs, that he has no intention or wish to quarrel with the English'. But the English had every intention of quarrelling with him, and by that time the military preparations were complete.

Thesiger, who had inherited the title Lord Chelmsford on the death of his father in October, had originally intended to invade Zululand with five separate columns from different points along the border. This would spread his troops dangerously thin and risk diluting his greatest asset, his firepower. But Chelmsford had formed a low opinion of the African capabilities of staging massed attacks on the Cape Frontier, and his main concern was to force the Zulus to fight, rather than slip around him and raid across the border. He was determined not to allow the Zulus to outmanoeuvre him, and by advancing from all the main crossing-points he calculated that he had much more chance of bringing the enemy to battle. There were three main routes into Zululand from Natal: at the Lower Drift near the mouth of the Thukela; at the Middle Drift where the road hugged the steep sides of the spectacular Kranskop escarpment; and at Rorke's Drift on the Mzinyathi. In addition, there were a number of entry points along the Ncome river from

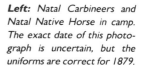

Above: HMS Active's Naval Brigade, lined-up to impress the Zulu delegation at the Lower Drift, 12 December 1878. Note the Royal Marines, centre, and the Gatling, right.

Left: Natal Carbineers and Natal Native Horse in camp. The exact date of this photograph is uncertain, but the uniforms are correct for 1879.

Left: A historic photograph; Frere's representatives read the British Ultimatum to the Zulus, 11 December 1878.

the Transvaal, and a small British force was already in position in the north-west, where it had been engaged in an unsuccessful campaign against the Pedi.

Chelmsford had planned to assemble a column at each of these points, but it soon became clear this would be a logistical impracticality. Each column would require a large baggage train to support it, since it was not possible for a European army to live off the land as a Zulu army could. Each infantry battalion had to carry its own ammunition, tents, entrenching tools, signalling and medical equipment, blankets and rations – meat was usually 'on the hoof', but mealic corn was carried in large sacks, and coarse army biscuits in heavy wooden boxes. These stores alone would require not less than seventeen wagons, excluding the luxuries of the officers' personal luggage, the rum ration, and bottled beer. And since horses used to British grasses would not eat local ones, fodder, too, would have to be transported, as would wood for fuel in areas where there was none. The Commissariat situation in southern Africa was already a mess. Chelmsford's Commissary General, Edward Strickland, had just nineteen officers and twenty-nine men to staff the whole of the Cape, Transvaal and Natal. Several of these were sick, and most of the remainder were fully employed in the aftermath of the Cape Frontier War or the annexation of the Transvaal. A limited number of military transport wagons was available, but, having been designed for narrow European roads, many were proving unsuited to the Colonies' tracks. The obvious solution was to augment them with civilian wagons which mostly consisted of large, heavy vehicles requiring fourteen to eighteen oxen apiece to pull them. If the oxen were to remain healthy they needed sixteen hours each day for rest and grazing, which reduced their potential progress to about ten miles a day. On bad tracks bisected by dongas, broken with boulders or turned into a quagmire by sudden rain, it would be much less. Bulwer refused to smooth Chelmsford's path by

allowing him to declare martial law and thus requisition the transport he needed. In any case, Natal's transport system was grinding to a halt under the effects of the drought which had devastated wayside pasture. Chelmsford could do little more than allocate Strickland a handful of unattached officers – all untrained, and with little idea of the skills that would be required of them – and scour Natal and the Transvaal for transport which, for the most part, was hired at exorbitant rates. Unscrupulous contractors took every opportunity to cheat the unsuspecting Transport Officers.

Even so, by the time hostilities began Chelmsford had amassed 977 wagons, 56 carts, 10,023 oxen, 803 horses and 398 mules. The Colonial economy was further paralyzed as many colonists, both black and white, abandoned their regular employment for the rich pickings to be had as transport riders and drivers for the army. The protection of the long columns and the chain of supply which would follow them as they advanced deeper and deeper into enemy territory, would tie down a huge number of troops for patrolling, escort duties, and manning forts and depots. Although Chelmsford was considering ways to ease his manpower shortage there would still not be enough. Reluctantly he reduced his strike force to three columns, deciding their routes according to his ability to mass supplies at their starting-points. He would advance across the Thukela at the Lower Drift, across the Mzinyathi at Rorke's Drift, and from a hill known as Bemba's Kop on the Ncome. The columns at the Middle Drift and on the northern Transvaal border would be reduced and given a purely defensive role.

To solve his manpower problems Chelmsford had looked to the Native Locations, the home of a large African population, generally hostile to the Zulus. A section of the settler community was opposed to arming Natal blacks for fear of a possible uprising, and Sir Henry Bulwer was unwilling to see Natal's blacks turned against the Zulus at the risk of damaging future relations. Despite these objections, however, Chelmsford insisted, and raised the three regiments of the Natal Native Contingent. The 1st Regiment had three battalions and the rest two each. Each battalion consisted of ten companies of nine European NCOs and one hundred levies. Some attempts were made to maintain clan ties within companies – supporters of the exiled Zulu Princes Mkhungo and Sikhota made up several companies of the 3rd NNC, for example – but for the most part the force was organized on European lines. Officers were usually seconded from imperial regiments, where possible from those who could speak Zulu or had at least some experience leading levies. The white NCOs, however, were generally of poor calibre, being drawn from the dregs of Colonial society, since most of the better volunteers had already joined the more prestigious mounted Corps. Many NNC NCOs were European immigrants who spoke minimal English, let alone Zulu, and treated their men with contempt. Early plans to dress the NNC in scarlet tunics were abandoned, and the

chief mark of distinction became a red rag tied around the head, although some wore items of European cast-off clothing. Arming them proved scarcely less difficult, and only one in ten were issued with firearms. These were often of obsolete pattern and ammunition was limited to a few rounds per man to prevent wastage. The remainder were armed with their own shields and spears.

Rather more successful were five troops of about fifty mounted men apiece known as the Natal Native Horse. Three of these were troops drawn from the amaNgwane tribe who lived in the Drakensberg foothills, traditional enemies of the Zulus since the days of the *mfecane*, when Shaka had driven out their Chief Matiwane. They were known to the British as the Sikhali Horse, after their present Chief, Zikhali. A fourth troop was composed of Christian converts from the Edendale mission, and the fifth of Tlokwa Basotho led by Hlubi Molife. Hlubi's men had served with Colonel Durnford during the ill-fated Langalibalele expedition, and had distinguished themselves in the skirmish at Bushman's Pass. All the NNH wore European clothing and were armed with carbines.

In addition to these permanent levy groups, under his direct command, Chelmsford made provision for the raising of local units to protect the border. The existing uniformed black Border Police, responsible to local magistrates and Border Agents, were increased although their numbers remained small. There were also Border Guards, raised from clans living along the Thukela and Mzinyathi, and placed under the command of white levy-leaders. These were to be posted in detachments of a hundred, with two hundred more living nearby and ready to rotate duty, at points overlooking the minor drifts. Finally, there was a Border Levy, to be drawn again from local clans, but only in time of emergency. A number of stone-walled or earthwork laagers was hastily erected to protect the white population. Since the white Volunteer Corps were only required to serve in defence of Natal, it was necessary that they should formally volunteer to serve across the border. When they were canvassed, most said they would. On 26 November Bulwer bowed to Chelmsford's pressure, and the Volunteer Corps were mobilized.

All that was needed now was to start the war. Chelmsford had views on the timing of this, too. If the war went ahead in the southern African winter – June, July and August – the weather might be ideal, with warm days and little rain to swell the rivers or ruin the roads. But the grass would be dry, with little grazing value, and there was a terrible risk of the Zulus lighting grass-fires. Summer held the danger of heavy rain and uncomfortable heat, but the grass would be fresh, healthy and wet. If Chelmsford were lucky, the drought might hold, and not only would he be spared the worst of the rain, but the Zulus might be distracted by a delayed harvest. A January start to the campaign was therefore ideal. Frere, who by now had manipulated the political crisis to breaking point, concurred. A message was sent to King Cetshwayo, instructing him to send his representatives to a

Above: *The three senior Zulu representatives who received the British Ultimatum; on the left is Vumandaba, an attendant of the late king Mpande, and a commander of the Khande-mpemvu ibutho.*

meeting on 11 December at the Lower Drift on the Thukela, ostensibly to receive the decision of the Boundary Commission.

The Lower Drift was already the scene of some military activity. A Naval Brigade from HMS *Active*, (a small party of sailors and Marines landed to support Chelmsford's army) had already built an earthwork redoubt on a knoll overlooking the Drift, naming it Fort Pearson after the Colonel of the Buffs who were also camped nearby. The meeting took place on the Natal bank beneath a wild fig-tree across which a wagon-awning had been stretched to keep off the sun. Three senior Zulu *izinduna* supported by a large number of attendants squatted in the shade, while Frere's representatives sat at a table. The Naval Brigade lined up near-by, with a 12-pounder gun and a Gatling, a hand-cranked, ten-barrelled machine-gun, yet to be tested on active service by British troops, prominently displayed. The *izinduna* listened patiently while the award of the Boundary Commission was read out to them. Then, to their surprise, they found conditions had been added to the award. The king, they were told, had broken the promises he had made to Shepstone at his coronation. He had allowed certain wrongs to go unpunished. He would now have to surrender Sihayo's sons and the marauder Mbilini for trial, and pay substantial compensation for their depredations. The *amabutho* system would have to be abolished, the king would have to relinquish control over his young men, and allow the *amabutho* to marry at will. Arbitrary killings

must cease and the missionaries, all of whom had fled Zululand several months before, be allowed to return. If Cetshwayo were not inclined to comply within thirty days, he would find himself at war.

The demands were cynical and brutal, and the Zulus were astonished, 'You mean you are going to destroy Zululand for the sake of two foolish children?' one asked. They were fully aware of the impossibility of accepting the British demands. The wanted men might be turned over, but the economic and political structure of the kingdom could not withstand the sudden overthrow of the *amabutho*. If they were to comply, these conditions, they said, would 'lower the country to the debased level of the amaKhafula (Natal Africans) . . . therefore we will fight rather than give in on those points'. That was precisely what Frere had intended.

The *izinduna* departed mournfully to take the ultimatum to Cetshwayo. Frere chose to inform his own superiors in London only when he knew the dispatch would arrive too late for them to countermand his actions.

When the news reached Ulundi Cetshwayo summoned his *ibandla*. Several of the most senior *izikhulu* including Mnyamana Buthelezi, the Prime Minister, Hamu kaNzibe and Zibhebhu of the Mandlakazi were vehemently opposed to a war. They urged that it could only bring defeat and disaster, and that the British should be placated whatever the cost. But the mood in the country was against them. The army was outraged by the British arrogance and clamoured to fight. Anti-white feeling was running high and even John Dunn was accused of being a spy. Dunn's position was unenviable; he had lived for many years as a chief and was an important *isikhulu* as well as a confidant of the king's. He had adopted Zulu custom and had a large number of Zulu wives, and his followers numbered thousands. Cetshwayo's suggestion that he should 'stand on one side' and be neutral if the worst came to the worst was unlikely to be practicable. Like everyone else he awaited the king's decision; but in fact there was little for the king to decide. He sent men to arrest Sihayo's sons who had fled to northern Zululand and were in hiding, he began to collect cattle to pay the fines, and he sent a stream of messengers to Natal to ask for more time. He could not disband the regiments.

Chelmsford's plans, meanwhile, inexorably pressed on. Huge supply depots sprang up at appointed places behind the designated border crossings. The hills behind Fort Pearson were covered with tents. The two lonely huts which comprised the hamlet of Helpmekaar on the windy well-watered plateau above Rorke's Drift were swamped by three giant sheds of corrugated iron, erected to protect rations, and the sprawling tents which surrounded them. Convoys of wagons began to ferry equipment through the villages of Newcastle and Dundee to Balte Spruit, in readiness for the advance on Bemba's Kop, and Chelmsford appointed his column commanders. No. 1 Column, at the Lower Drift, was to be commanded by Colonel Charles Knight Pearson of the Buffs, a steady and methodical veteran of the Crimea; No.2 Column, a small force of African levies to remain on the defensive at Middle Drift, was given to Colonel Durnford who was a sympathetic leader of black troops, though considered a little reckless after the Langalibalele débâcle; No.3 Column at Rorke's Drift was commanded by Colonel Richard Glyn of the 24th, a veteran of the Cape Frontier War; and No.4 Column, advancing from the Transvaal, was to be led by Colonel Evelyn Wood whose colourful career had taken him from a Midshipman in the Navy to a Victoria Cross in the Indian Mutiny. The last column, No.5, was also to remain on the defensive in the north, under its present commander, Colonel Hugh Rowlands, VC. By late December most of the troops had arrived at their advanced depots and early in January they began to move forward to the border. On 30 December Dunn made up his mind; he brought 2,000 of his followers and 3,000 of his cattle across the Thukela. The Natal authorities settled them in a temporary location. Dunn himself made one last effort to persuade Chelmsford to call off the war, and then, having been rebuffed, sat back to watch the calamity unfold. On 6 January a heavy pont was assembled at the Lower Drift, and hawsers were attached to both banks of the river. On 10 January the troops waited anxiously to see if any word arrived from Cetshwayo accepting the British demands. None did.

On 11 January 1879 the Anglo-Zulu War began.

Below: *The Naval Brigade pont at the Lower Thukela Drift. Its hawsers are fastened to the so-called 'Ultimatum Tree', beneath which the events of 12 December had taken place.*

Below right: *Zulu warriors in action, 1879. This picture gives a very good impression of the appearance of the warriors in battle — note number of firearms.*

THUNDERCLAP

*The Zulu response to the Ultimatum, and the **mobilization** of the Zulu Army. Lord Chelmsford's Centre Column crosses into Zululand. The attack on Sihayo's homestead, and the camp-site at Mount Isandlwana. The reconnaissance of 21 January 1879, and Chelmsford's advance. The movements of Durnford, and the discovery of the Zulu impi. The **Battle of Isandlwana**. The advance of the Zulu reserves on the supply depot at Rorke's Drift. Preparations for defence; The Battle of **Rorke's Drift**. Chelmsford's return to Isandlwana, and the relief of Rorke's Drift. Panic in Natal at the fear of a Zulu invasion.*

'Dead was the horse, dead too, the mule, dead was the dog, dead was the monkey, dead were the wagons, dead were the tents, dead were the boxes, dead was everything, even to the very metals.'
Muziwento, a Zulu boy.

During the last few weeks before the invasion Natal's Border Agents were able to glean something of King Cetshwayo's preparations from the movements of the Zulus across the Thukela and Mzinyathi rivers. As early as October 1878 small parties of warriors from Sihayo's Qungebe people, who lived along the projected advance of the centre column, were slipping across the Mzinyathi to plunder deserted farms and homesteads. By December large numbers of warriors had gathered

in the vicinity of Sihayo's *umuzi*, Sogekle, and the women and children were being sent into hiding in the caves and forests of the nation's strongholds. Opposite the Middle Drift, too, sharp- eyed border police noticed temporary huts being built in the hills overlooking the Zulu bank, while reports suggested that Mabedla, the *induna* whose men had detained Smith and Deighton, returned from a visit to Ulundi with orders to guard the crossing. Then, on 8 January, the young men disappeared all along the border as the

king called up his army.

After the alarms of the previous months it came as a relief to many warriors that the waiting was over and the fighting was to begin. Chelmsford's hopes that the harvest would distract the Zulus from the muster were to prove unfounded; the imminence of the harvest meant in fact that Cetshwayo had already called up many of the *amabutho* ready for the *umKhosi*, the First Fruits ceremonies. According to a careful count made by Chelmsford's Intelligence Department, the king had a total of thirty-three *amabutho* of various sizes available to him, although seven of these were composed of men in their sixties, whose military value was negligible. The remainder amounted to more than 40,000 warriors, the majority young unmarried men in their twenties and thirties, reflecting the success of Cetshwayo's attempts to revive the regimental system. As the regiments assembled at Ulundi they paraded before the king, who ordered them to display their firearms. Those with only a few were hastily issued more, scraped together from around the country. By the time the army was fully mustered in mid-January most warriors had access to some sort of firearm, though most were obsolete flint-lock or percussion patterns, and ammunition and powder were poor. In addition to their firearms each warrior carried the traditional shield and spears.

Despite its technological inferiority the Zulu army was still an impressive fighting machine. Each *ibutho* was commanded by a senior *induna* and broken down into two wings, each under a subordinate commander. It was further sub-divided into *amaViyo*, companies of between fifty and seventy men, often drawn from the same part of the country and led by a warrior chosen from their own ranks. Morale was exceedingly high as the *amabutho* underwent the rituals necessary to prepare them for the coming campaign. Warriors from the youngest regiment were chosen to kill a wild black bull with their bare hands and the bull's flesh was roasted, sprinkled with magic potions and distributed among the army to bind it together and endow it with the beast's strength and ferocity. Younger regiments were called out in pairs, challenging one another to perform the bravest deeds in the coming fight. Perhaps their greatest chance of success would have been to take to the hills and wage a guerrilla war against Chelmsford's unwieldy columns, but there would be no question of that; since the time of Shaka the Zulus had waged aggressive wars in which everything depended upon the outcome of pitched battles fought in the open. The army clamoured to be allowed to 'eat up' the invading columns.

Yet Cetshwayo hesitated to unleash them until the last moment. Even as the British columns were crossing the borders he dispatched messengers begging for more time to consider the ultimatum. His importuning was ignored, however, and reluctantly he and the *ibandla* planned their strategy. The Centre Column was correctly identified as the most powerful threat, and against this the main striking force of the army, more than 20,000 strong, would be directed. It

was placed under the command of Chief Ntshingwayo kaMahole Khoza and accompanied by Mnyamana kaNgqengelele. The abaQulusi, who lived in northern Zululand, would be ordered to oppose Wood's column while a small holding force, consisting mostly of men from the local area, would be sent to try to halt Pearson's advance. By the third week in January it was clear that the king could wait no longer; it was common knowledge that the British Invasion had begun, that homesteads were being burnt and skirmishing was taking place. On the 17th the army was paraded in the vast central enclosure at Ulundi and the king appeared before them. He told the warriors that he was sending them against the abeLungu; that they should march slowly and not tire themselves, avoid attacking entrenched positions and drive the enemy back across the border. On no account, however, were they to cross into the Colony itself; it was to be a purely defensive war. In private Cetshwayo told his generals to make one last attempt to open negotiations with the British. Beyond that he had no specific orders and they were to use their discretion in the field and act as they saw fit. The great army marched off, a host of thousands which blackened the hills. To many present it seemed nothing could stop them.

Their enemy, too, was supremely confident about the coming fray. Chelmsford's No. 3 Column had moved down from the Helpmekaar heights in the first week of January, and by the 9th was encamped between the two thatched buildings which comprised the Swedish mission at Rorke's Drift, and the Mzinyathi. The buildings themselves had been requisitioned and turned into a supply depot and a base hospital. It looked as if it would be a wet crossing for, curiously, the long and damaging drought had at last broken. The weather in January in Zululand can be unpredictable at the best of times, alternating between bakingly hot sunshine and torrential, chilling downpours. As the invasion force completed its preparations the clouds closed in and the rain fell in heavy showers. The level of the Mzinyathi rose and it soon became apparent that the Drift would be impracticable for regular troops. Preparations began to span the river with hawsers and build ponts to ferry them across.

Chelmsford himself had decided to accompany the Column which was both his strongest and most experienced. It comprised both battalions of the 24th who had seen active service on the Cape Frontier. The 1/24th had been abroad for a number of years, and nearly half its men and a majority of its NCOs were long-service men. It had been in South Africa since 1875 and had taken part in the battle of Centane in February 1878, when it had broken a massed Xhosa attack with steady volley-fire. Although natural wastage had reduced its battalion strength to fewer than 700 men, these were perfectly acclimatized, experienced veterans, whose officers were accustomed to working together under campaign conditions. The 2/24th consisted of short-service men, many from Wales where the depot had been established at Brecon

Right: The camp at Rorke's Drift, with the Mzinyathi in the background. This picture was probably taken later in the war, but the site would have looked much the same in January.

Right: Officers of the 1/24th, photographed in King Wiliam's Town in 1878. They are (standing, left to right): Captain W. T. Much, Captain T. Rainforth, Paymaster F. F. White, Captain Hillier (Staff), Captain H. H. Parr (Staff), QM J. Pullen, Lieutenant F. P. Porteous, Major H. B. Pulleine, Lieutenant G. F. J. Hodson, Lieutenant-Colonel F. W. Walker (Staff), Mr Silverwright, Lieutenant C. J. Atkinson, Captain G. V. Wardell. Sitting, left to right: Lieutenant J. P. Daly, Hon. C. P. Brownlee, Sir Bartle Frere, Lieutenant-General Sir Arthur Cunynghame, Colonel R. T. Glyn, Hon. John X. Merriman. Front: Lieutenant N. J. A. Coghill (Staff), Hon. W. Littleton. Most of these officers were killed at Isandlwana.

in 1873. It had arrived in Africa in early 1878 and had been employed mopping-up Xhosa resistance in the tough hill-country on the Frontier. The two battalions were delighted to be working together, and officers and men alike were confident that they would be more than a match for the Zulus. In addition Chelmsford had at his disposal 'N' Battery, 5 Brigade, Royal Artillery, consisting of six 7-pounder muzzle-loading guns, a squadron of mounted infantry, detachments of the Natal Mounted Police, Natal Carbineers, Newcastle Mounted Rifles and Buffalo Border Guard, both battalions of the 3rd NNC, and a company of uniformed Native Pioneers. Chelmsford fully expected that this force would bear the brunt of the fighting against the Zulus, and had high hopes of the concentrated firepower of the two regular battalions. His main concern was that he might have difficulties pinning the Zulus down and making them fight.

The troops were roused before dawn on 11 January and the invasion began at about 4.30. It was cold, wet, misty and miserable. The RA guns covered the crossing from the Natal bank while the ponts began to ferry the infantry across. The NNC crossed at the Drift itself, a few hundred yards downstream, wading through fast-flowing muddy water up to their waists. The crossing was unopposed but not without casualties, several of the NNC being swept away in the river and drowned. The mounted volunteers pushed ahead to a slight rise on the Zulu bank, but as the mist lifted it became clear that no Zulus were in sight. The troops set up a temporary camp, and the remainder of the day passed in patrolling while the wagons and supplies were laboriously ferried across.

The track to Ulundi cut across the valley of the Batshe, a small stream which flowed into the

Above: The Centre Column's dawn crossing at Rorke's Drift, 11 January 1879. The ponts are in the centre of the picture, while the NNC cross downstream, right. The peak of Isandlwana looms ominously on the horizon.

Left: Private John Power, 1/24th. Power served with the Mounted Infantry, and distinguished himself on the Cape Frontier. He survived Isandlwana and was later among Russell's troops who stopped to help Buller's descent at Hlobane, for which action he was awarded the DCM.

Right: An unspecified artillery train on the march in Zululand; it suggests something of the difficulties experienced by the Centre Column.

Mzinyathi. The Batshe was Sihayo's territory, and his *umuzi*, Sogekle, nestled at the foot of a line of cliffs which marked the eastern edge of the valley. For the most part the Qungebe homesteads appeared deserted, but Chelmsford could hardly ignore a potentially hostile force along his line of advance; and, of course, it had been Sihayo's sons who had provoked the British ultimatum. On 12 January Chelmsford took the bulk of his force across the Batshe and advanced along the base of the cliffs. A Zulu war chant betrayed the presence of an *impi* hidden amongst a jumble of boulders, fallen rock and caves in a fold in the cliffs. This was Sihayo's son Mkhumbikazulu who had been left to guard the valley with a small force of warriors while his father, brothers and the rest of the fighting men had gone to Ulundi. As the British troops advanced the Zulus opened an ill-directed fire and shouted their defiance. Chelmsford split his troops into three sections, the NNC making a frontal assault into the shallow gorge while Volunteers and redcoats climbed the hills on each side to surround the Zulu position. There was a brief flurry of hand-to-hand fighting among the rocks, but the struggle was uneven. The Zulus broke and fled leaving behind a number of dead including Mkhumbikazulu. The troops then pushed further up the Batshe to Sogekle. This had apparently been prepared for defence, with loop-holes built into the stone cattle enclosure, but it had been abandoned. The troops set fire to it and returned to camp with about four hundred captured cattle and a number of guns, in good spirits despite a sudden downpour.

With Sihayo's people dispatched to his satisfaction, Chelmsford turned his attention to his advance. Although the track through the Batshe valley was fairly level, it crossed several boulder-strewn slopes, and where it was low-lying the rain had turned it into a morass. Accordingly, Chelmsford moved the camp inland from the Drift, siting it beneath a low ridge on the western side of the Batshe, known to the Zulus to this day as Masotsheni, 'the place of soldiers'. From here his Engineers laboured to prepare the track for the heavy wagon convoy. Chelmsford's scouts indicated that a few miles further on the road emerged from the Batshe valley and skirted a distinctive mountain known as Isandlwana. On the 20th Chelmsford decided to move forward and establish his next camp beneath Mount Isandlwana.

In the light of subsequent events, the choice of the Isandlwana site was much criticized, but in truth it was as good as any. The hill itself, whose name meant 'something like a small hut', the designation given by the Zulus, obsessed as ever with cattle, to part of a cow's stomach which they fancied it resembled, was a detached spur of the Nquthu hills. Shaped curiously like a sphinx – the Regimental badge of the 24th – it lay on a north-south axis, connected by a spur or rising ground to the Nquthu upland which ran for several miles at right-angles to it in the north. To the south, a saddle, or *nek* in local parlance, joined Isandlwana to a low rocky kopje. The track from Rorke's Drift ran through a valley behind the mountain, then crested the *nek* and traversed the plain in front of Isandlwana, running parallel to the Nquthu escarpment on its left for a mile or so before shifting south-east on the winding road to Ulundi. Visibility extended for several miles across the plain, which was broken only by a solitary conical kopje, and several dongas draining the Nquthu hills. Provided that the Nquthu heights were properly patrolled enemy movements should have been easily detectable. Those other camp essentials, wood and water, were readily available.

As the column crossed over the *nek* it spread out and a camp was formed along the front of the mountain where the ground sloped down to the plain. The NNC tents were at the northern end of a line which continued south with the 2/24th camp, the artillery, then the mounted troops and finally, at the foot of the kopje, the 1/24th camp. The wagons were parked on the saddle itself and Chelmsford established his headquarters above the centre of the line. The General's own regulations for the Field Force required all camps to be either laagered in the Boer fashion or partially entrenched, but when the Column Commander, Colonel Glyn, pointed this out Chelmsford himself decided against it. The ground was too rocky to facilitate entrenchment, some of the wagons would be needed to ferry up supplies from Rorke's Drift, and in any case the camp was intended to be purely temporary. Chelmsford expected to advance within a day or two. No attempt was made to form even a barricade of thorn-bush and one or two officers of the 24th expressed misgivings that there was nothing to prevent the Zulus from charging home except the fire from the troops.

But Chelmsford was already looking to his advance. The country to the south and east of Isandlwana was hilly and extended to the spectacular Mangeni gorge and Isiphezi mountain, both of which commanded the track to Ulundi. The Mangeni was the stronghold of Chief Matshana kaMondise, whose powerful Sithole clan might reasonably be expected to oppose Chelmsford's advance. Accordingly, Chelmsford dispatched sixteen companies of Commandant Rupert Lonsdale's 3rd NNC, and a mounted detachment comprising most of the Natal Mounted Police and about half the Volunteers, all under the command of Major Dartnell, to sweep the hills and reconnoitre as far as Mangeni, some ten or twelve miles distant.

The NNC accomplished their task without too much trouble, occasionally destroying homesteads, rounding up cattle and exchanging long-range shots with small parties of Zulus. For the most part, however, the country was free of large bodies of the enemy. Until, that is, Dartnell's advance party reached the point where the hills drop down to the Mangeni. Here they spotted a party of more than a thousand warriors apparently blocking the track as it crossed the head of the gorge. The NNC were brought up and Dartnell sent a small mounted patrol down from the hills to probe the Zulu intentions. Instantly and with perfect precision the warriors threw out horns and took up a battle formation. Dartnell called his men back. It was now late evening. There was no telling how many Zulus might be in the area. Despite having no tents, Dartnell decided to bivouac where he was for the night, and sent a message back to Isandlwana asking Chelmsford to reinforce him.

Chelmsford received the message at about 2 a.m. on the 22nd. It put him in something of a quandary. He had not expected Dartnell's men to remain out overnight or indeed engage the enemy. However, they had apparently encountered a sizeable Zulu force and Chelmsford had been expecting just such an encounter for several days, since his intelligence system had picked up rumours of the Zulu advance. He decided to support Dartnell first thing in the morning, and gave orders that six companies of the 2/24th, four of the guns, a detachment of Mounted Infantry and the Natal Native Pioneers should be ready to march out at dawn. The men fell in at about 4 a.m. with seventy rounds of ammunition and a day's rations. The wagons and supplies would remain in the camp. Colonel Glyn would accompany the General and the camp would be left in charge of Lieutenant-Colonel Henry Pulleine, commander of the 1/24th. Chelmsford's orders to Pulleine were vague, but he was instructed to 'defend the camp'. As an afterthought Chelmsford sent a note to Colonel Durnford at Rorke's Drift, and asked him to move up to Isandlwana.

Durnford's column had originally been No. 2 in Chelmsford's strategic plan, commanding the central Thukela at Middle Drift. Chelmsford had found Durnford rather too independent-minded for his liking, however, and had decided to bring him up to Rorke's Drift where he might co-operate with Glyn's column. Durnford had arrived there on the 17th, but had found no further specific orders. His command amounted to about five hundred men, about half of whom were cavalry of the Natal Native Horse and all of whom were black apart from a small Rocket Battery commanded by Major Russell, RA. This consisted of three troughs firing 9-pounder rockets which, while generally inaccurate, were held to be of tremendous psychological advantage against an unsophisticated enemy because of the terrifying noise, smoke and sparks they gave off in their erratic flight.

After the General's departure work in the camp proceeded as normal. Pulleine still had a substantial force at his disposal: five companies of the 1/24th, one

Above: *An unusual, if poor quality, view of Isandlwana showing the camp spread out at the foot of the mountain, before the attack.*

Right: *A modern (1989) panorama of Isandlwana, taken from the Itusi lip on the Nquthu escarpment. The mountain is centre, with the saddle connecting it to the Stoney Koppie; the Conical Koppie is on the left. The Rocket Battery came to grief amidst the dongas in the foreground.*

company of the 2/24th, two of N/5's guns, four companies of the 3rd NNC, and about a hundred mounted men, detachments of the Natal Carbineers. Natal Mounted Police, Buffalo Border Guard, and Newcastle Mounted Rifles. In addition there were probably more than a hundred white soldiers from the various units out with Chelmsford, left in camp with a variety of duties. The total came to 67 officers and 1,707 men of whom 800 were white and 907 black. Pulleine placed his usual pickets and sat back to await Durnford's arrival. About mid-morning heavy firing could be heard from the direction of Chelmsford's advance, and the officers in the camp speculated that the General had found the main Zulu *impi* and the battle he was looking for. Reports also came in that small parties of Zulus were moving about on the Nquthu hills to the left front. Pulleine was wondering what to do about these when Durnford rode into the camp at about 10.30 a.m.

Chelmsford's orders to Durnford had been vague and resulted in a slight awkwardness. It had not been specified what Durnford was supposed to do at the camp, and Durnford clearly considered that he was there to support the General's advance, rather than reinforce Pulleine. In any case he was senior in rank to Pulleine so there was no question of his subordinating his command. When he and Pulleine discussed the reports of Zulus on the hills, Durnford expressed concern that it might be part of a flanking movement designed to cut off the General from the camp. He proposed to take his own column out to investigate the Zulu movements and to prevent them encircling Chelmsford. He asked Pulleine for several of his infantry companies, but Pulleine, remembering his orders to defend the camp, demurred. Durnford accepted the decision amicably enough, but departed with the comment that he would expect support if he got into difficulties. Before he left, Pulleine sent a company of the 1/24th under Lieutenant Cavaye up on to the hills to the north, where a spur runs down to the tail of Mount Isandlwana. They were to picket the hills.

Durnford rode out of the camp at about 11.30, moving east and keeping the Nquthu escarpment on his left. He rounded the Conical Kop, then veered slightly north, following the line of hills, on a course that would have brought him out several miles north of Mangeni. He also sent small parties of the NNH and NNC up into the hills to probe the Zulu movements. Although the undulating surface of the Nquthu range is not visible from the plain in front of Isandlwana – or, indeed, from the top of the mountain itself – the view is reasonably uninterrupted across the top. Durnford's patrols could see over several miles of rolling grassland where small parties of Zulus were roaming about, some apparently driving cattle. A party of amaNgwane led by Lieutenant Raw set off after a small herd whose escort frantically tried to escape. Pursuers and pursued were more than four miles north-east of the camp when the cattle herders suddenly disappeared into a fold in the ground. Cantering up behind them, Raw's

Left: Colonel Richard Glyn, the commander of Chelmsford's centre column. Glyn drew attention to the un-laagered state of the camp, but was overruled by Chelmsford.

Left: Brevet Lieutenant-Colonel Henry Pulleine whom Chelmsford left in charge of the Isandlwana camp.

Above: A trooper of the Natal Native Horse, sketched by Lieutenant W. Fairlie, who served with Shepstone's Horse.

Right: Brevet Major Stuart Smith, RA, who commanded the two 7pdrs of N-5 Battery throughout the battle and was killed in the Mzinyathi valley.

Far right: Lieutenant Charles Pope, who commanded the only company of the 2/24th at Isandlwana.

patrol reigned in short. In front of them was a steep slope dropping into a narrow valley studded with trees and boulders, through which flowed a stream known as the Ngwebeni. In the bottom of the valley, squatting in serried ranks, were more than 20,000 Zulu warriors. It was the main Zulu army.

After leaving Ulundi the *impi* had marched westwards at a leisurely pace and by the night of the 20th had reached Isiphezi where it bivouacked. The next morning it had moved into the Nquthu hills, sending out patrols to liaise with Matshana's fighting men. This was the manoeuvre which Dartnell's men had spotted. Although its movements were screened by a large number of scouts, and its foraging parties were scouring the countryside for miles around, its presence had gone completely undetected until the morning of the 22nd. At one point the sound of firing from Mangeni had brought two or three regiments out on to the hills in the belief that they had been discovered, but when it proved to be a false alarm they returned to the valley unnoticed. They had lit no fires and were waiting in silence for the day to pass since that night, the 22nd, would see a new moon, an inauspicious time to attack. They were no doubt expecting to attack on the 23rd, 'in the horns of the morning', that time in the grey light of dawn when cattle could first be discerned against the sky. Now, there could be no more waiting. For a few electric moments the amaNgwane stared straight into the faces of the Khandempemvu (umCijo) *ibutho*, and then the regiment sprang up and began scrambling up the slope towards them. Within minutes the whole army was on the move. The *izinduna* frantically tried to impose some order but only the uNdi corps led by Prince Dabulamanzi kaMpande could be held back and formed into the traditional circle to receive last-minute instructions. Raw's men, hopelessly outnumbered, began to fall back, firing as they went. As they emerged from the ravine the warriors instinctively jostled into the 'beast's horns' formation. The uDududu, imBube, isAngqu and uNokhenke regiments formed the right horn, the Khandempemvu and uMxhapho the chest, with the uMbonambi, iNgobamakhosi and uVe on the left. The 'loins', the uNdi regiments comprising the uThulwana, iNdluyengwe, iNdlondlo and uDloko *amabutho*, followed at the right rear. By the time they had crossed the Nquthu plateau their deployment was complete.

The discovery of the *impi* was not apparent on the plain, either to Durnford or Pulleine, and the NNH sent riders to warn both of their approach. The news was received coolly by both commanders who still believed that the real danger lay twelve miles away, with Chelmsford. Durnford was the first to realize something of the truth when advanced parties of the left horn crested the escarpment to his left. He halted his troops, delivered a volley, and then began to retire the way he had come. While doing so, he sent a message to Major Russell, commanding the rocket battery and its NNC infantry escort which, not being mounted, had lagged behind. Russell had just passed

Left: *Lieutenant George Hodson, 1-24th, one of the officers killed at Isandlwana. In this formal portrait he is wearing the full-dress tunic and carrying his shako.*

Right: *Lieutenant Edgar Anstey, whose body was found among those who had made a 'last stand' near the banks of the Manzimnyana stream behind Isandlwana.*

Far right: *Lieutenant and Adjutant Teignmouth Melvill, 1/24th who attempted to escape with the Queen's Colour of his battalion.*

Right: *Lieutenant Nevill Coghill, 24th who tried to save Lieutenant Melvill.*

the Conical Kop when news of the Zulu presence on the hills reached him. He was not far from the escarpment and he turned to his left to ascend it, aiming to the left of a high knoll above the slope, known as Itusi. He had just reached the foot of the slope when the first Zulus spilled over the crest a few hundred yards ahead of him. Russell hastily set up his rocket troughs and unleashed a salvo which burst near the Zulus without apparent physical or moral effect. The Zulus began to stream down the escarpment under cover of some dongas and opened up with a volley which so startled Russell's NNC escort that they dropped their weapons and ran. With just the few men of his battery, Russell was easily overrun. The Zulus had scored their first success of the day.

In the camp Pulleine was still unaware of the extent of the danger. Cavaye's company on the spur had

advanced beyond the sky-line and so was out of sight, though the sound of firing indicated that they were engaged. Durnford's men were probably just visible retreating fast across the plain. Pulleine formed his men up in front of the camp site, then dispatched another company under Captain Mostyn to support Cavaye. Mostyn's men advanced rapidly up the spur and were met with a disconcerting sight. Cavaye's company was deployed on the slope of a shallow valley with a small detachment some way to the left. They were firing at a huge column of warriors, the Zulu right horn, which was moving from right to left across their front on the slope opposite. The 24th were firing steady, well-aimed shots, but they were slowing the Zulu advance not one jot. Mostyn's men spread out and joined them.

By this stage the Zulus were beginning to appear along the Nquthu crest at several points above the slope. The main threat was clearly from this direction and Pulleine made his dispositions accordingly. The land in front of Isandlwana is more or less flat for several hundred yards and then begins to drop gently down to two dongas which bisect the plain. To the north there is no cover, but as it curves to the south and east the lip of this drop is marked by boulders and at one point, directly east of the NNC camp and about six hundred yards from the base of the mountain, was a low rocky knoll. Here the two guns under Major Stuart Smith, RA took up a position and began shelling the concentrations of warriors moving down

from the heights. 'A' Company, 1/24th under Lieutenant Porteous and 'H' Company under Captain Wardell fell in on either side of them. The solitary company of the 2/24th under Lieutenant Charles Pope had been on picket duty that morning, and was on the plain halfway towards the Conical Kop where there remained a picket of the Natal Carbineers. Pope's company also deployed facing north. Where possible the 24th crouched down to take what cover they could behind the boulders.

As more and more Zulus came over the hills it became apparent to Pulleine that he had a major battle on his hands, and that he could not leave Mostyn and Cavaye exposed up on the spur. He sent his last 24th company under Captain Younghusband to cover their retreat, then ordered them to fall back. They began to retire steadily down the slope with the Zulus following them up. As to the NNC, Pulleine does not seem to have been unduly concerned. The parties of retiring NNH had fallen into the line next to the 24th, and Captain Krohn's No.6 Company, 3rd NNC was drawn up in front of its camp, but no-one seemed too sure where the remaining three companies were. They were apparently somewhere out on the right.

By this time Durnford's mounted men had continued their retreat followed by a great wave of Zulus (the left horn) which had swept down the Nquthu slope behind them. When they reached a large donga at a point where it was crossed by the track, still nearly a mile from the camp, Durnford's men dismounted and turned to make a stand. Here they were joined by the Carbineer picket from the Conical Kop and the rest of the Volunteers. The donga was deep enough to shelter the horses completely, and the men hugged the eastern bank and opened a heavy fire on the Zulus who had to advance down a slope towards them. The firing was most galling, and the iNgobamakhosi regiment suffered so many casualties that it was forced to go to ground, the warriors alternately rushing forward then throwing themselves down into the grass.

The advance of the left horn and Durnford's stand at the donga required Pulleine to change his front slightly. Pope's men were brought back to fall in on Wardell's right, with the NNC apparently between them and Durnford, so that the whole British line was in a curve facing north-east, stretching from Younghusband on the left to Durnford on the right. This position was far too extended for the six hundred riflemen of the 24th to cover effectively, but Pulleine had had little option given the way the attack had developed, and his requirement to support Durnford.

Above: A detail from a contemporary engraving that depicts the height of the battle. In fact, the 24th did not take up such tight formations until they retreated to the camp, by which time it was too late.

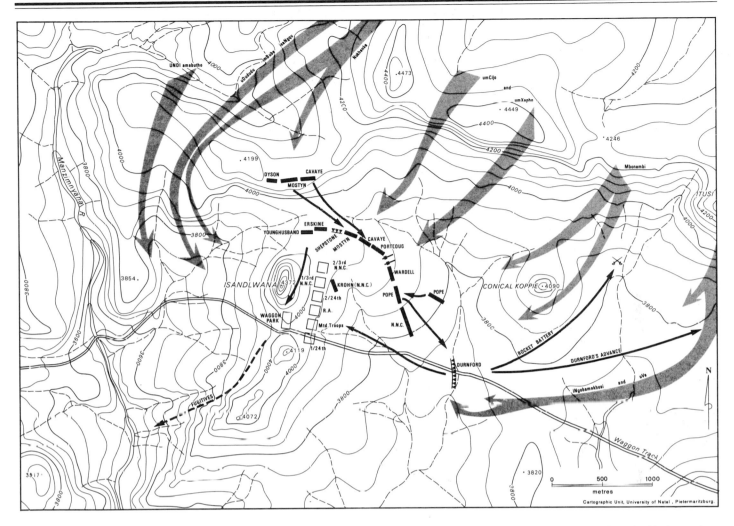

Above: The Battle of Isandlwana, 22 January 1879. The map shows the climax of the battle and movements between about 12.15 p.m. and 1.15 p.m.

Overleaf: "At Bay": although couched in the typically heroic images the Victorian public liked to see of their army, this dramatic engraving does capture something of the horror of the 24th's last moments at Isandlwana.

In any case the Zulus seemed to be suffering heavily. The 24th were in good spirits, placing their shots carefully and steadily, and the Zulu advance had stalled under their fire. About three hundred yards from the slight rise held by the soldiers, was a ring of dead ground, marshy hollows where water ran off the Nquthu escarpment and into the dongas. Here the warriors massed. At that range the Martini-Henry was at its most deadly, and to get up and run forward invited certain death. On the Zulu right the uNokhenke, pushing down the spur, was caught against the skyline and forced to retire out of sight. All along the line the Zulus were pinned down, humming like a swarm of angry bees.

But the stalemate could not last indefinitely. On Pulleine's right the iNgobamakhosi and uVe began to extend, trying to cross the donga further downstream and outflank Durnford's men. Recognizing the danger, Pulleine ordered one of Smith's guns out of position to shell the warriors massing at an *umuzi* in front of Durnford. The gunners lobbed several well-placed shells into the huts and broke up the concentration before returning to the knoll. Pulleine then asked Pope's men to try to extend to cover the gap between them and Durnford, only protected by the NNC whose firepower was negligible and erratic. At

this very point, however, Durnford decided to retire.

The truth was that Durnford's position had become untenable. His men were beginning to run out of ammunition, and riders he had sent back to camp to secure supplies had been unable to find their own ammunition wagon and had been turned away by the infantry quartermasters. Now he was in danger of being outflanked too. Durnford ordered his men to mount up and fell back on the camp.

Pulleine must have watched the movement with dismay. However legitimate Durnford's reasons, it left his own flank high and dry. Pope, in particular, was left over-extended and exposed, and it was probably at about this time that the NNC on the right threw down their weapons and ran to the rear. Pulleine seems to have decided that the safest course of action was to fall back on the tents and present a solid formation in front of the mountain. The bugles sang out the recall and the 24th ceased firing and stood up to retreat.

It was the turning-point of the battle. Until now the Zulu centre had been in such dire straits that a senior *induna*, Mkhosana kaMvundlana, had run down from the Nquthu escarpment where the commanders were watching the battle, and called on the Khandempemvu in the name of Cetshwayo to advance. Mkhosana was killed, shot through the head, as he ran forward, but

the Khandempemvu rose up after him. All along the line *izinduna* taunted their own regiments with the Khandempemvu's example and the Zulus surged forward.

For the most part the soldiers managed to retreat to the tents in good order. The guns remained in action until the last minute, firing canister at point-blank range until the Zulus were almost on top of them before limbering up. One gunner was stabbed to death as he climbed on to the axle-tree. A small party of the 24th under Colour-Sergeant Wolfe was cut off and wiped out near the firing line, but most of the infantry maintained formation – probably rallying squares – until they reached the camp where the Zulus overtook them. After the battle, there was considerable discussion among the *amabutho* as to which could claim the honour of being the first into the tents; it was eventually decided that the uMbonambi had swept in round the collapsed British right. There was no longer any question of forming a solid position beneath the mountain; the scattered groups made what stands they could. Durnford excused the men of the NNH, who had fought well, and they began to retreat over the *nek*, on the road to Rorke's Drift. The Natal Volunteers, who still had ammunition left, formed a line across the road and tried to keep back the left horn. It was too late. By now the fight was raging among the tents and the troops and warriors were intermingled. Small groups of soldiers standing back to back or grouped around a wagon or tree kept firing while their ammunition lasted, then had recourse to the bayonet. Zulus who rushed in were quickly spitted, and the warriors soon learned to stand off and shoot the soldiers or kill them with flung spears. A few incidents surface from the horror of the camp's last moments. A Zulu named Khumbeka Gwabe of the Khandempemvu remembered killing an officer who had been firing about him with his revolver; Khumbeka stabbed him in the right arm-pit, the blade coming out between his ribs on the left side. Two officers with eyeglasses stood side by side until one was shot and the other stabbed by an *induna*. Another officer was killed while writing in his tent when a warrior burst in and stabbed him. Generally, it is not possible to identify these officers and their deaths are as anonymous as those of the ordinary privates. One tall man took up a position in a wagon bed and killed every warrior who approached, until someone shot him. A sailor, the servant of a naval officer on Chelmsford's staff, stood with his back to a wagon cutting down warriors with his cutlass, until someone crawled under the wagon and stabbed him from between the spokes. A few men, presumably Colonials, called out in Zulu, begging to be spared. The Zulus replied, 'How can we give you mercy when you have come to us, and want to take away our country and eat us up?' and killed them. For the most part the men stood, angry and indignant, until they were overcome. Some hid in tents and were

Below: *The valley of the Manzimnyana with Isandlwana in the distance; part of the 'Fugitives' Trail'. The cairns in the foreground mark some of the graves.*

speared through the canvas: others covered their faces with their hands, 'not wishing to see death'.

The fate of a few individuals and companies is known. Durnford was seen on the *nek* surrounded by a group of Volunteers and 24th, cheering his men on until they ran out of ammunition and were overrun. Captain Younghusband managed to extricate most of his company from the chaos of the camp and climb a shoulder of Isandlwana itself. They held out for some time until they had no bullets left, then charged down into the mêlée and died. One of them, perhaps cut off from the rest, retreated up the shoulder to the cliff which rings the summit of Isandlwana. Here he found a shallow cave and, crouching behind a boulder at the entrance, defended it 'until the shadows were long on the hills', when Zulus with rifles fired a volley and killed him. Much of the fighting took place over the *nek* and down the track on the Rorke's Drift side. Months later the bodies were found in ones and twos, like a string with knots in it, where they were clustered together in a stand. The body of Lieutenant Anstey was found surrounded by a large group on the banks of the Manzimnyana, a stream which runs several hundred yards behind the mountain.

But there was no escape. The first trickle of fleeing NNC slipped away while the firing line was still intact, but their numbers multiplied as the camp collapsed, and as the last stands were slowly eliminated it became a question of every man for himself. Yet only the first

lucky few were able to escape by way of Rorke's Drift, because the Zulu right horn, the uDududu, imBube and isAngqu *amabutho*, had cut the track. It was they who had passed across the front of Mostyn and Cavaye early in the fight, and they had descended into the valley behind Isandlwana to the west of the spur. They had advanced cautiously, taking cover amidst the long grass and boulders, and they reached the *nek* even before the soldiers were driven over it. Their presence forced the fugitives further south, hoping to cross the Manzimnyana further down stream, but the country was rugged and seamed with dongas, and soon the iNgobamakhosi came over the ridge below the stony kopje and the horns of the buffalo closed in. It was impossible now to make it to Rorke's Drift; instead, a wild jumble of men and horses followed those NNC who knew the way across country to a ford several miles downriver of Rorke's Drift. It was a nightmare journey of about four miles, across the Manzimnyana up a hill known as Mpete, across a marshy hollow which the rain had turned into a bog, and down into the steep Mzinyathi valley. At each obstacle the survivors slowed or bunched and the pursuing Zulus closed in. Stuart Smith's guns made it through the camp and along the start of the trail, but came to grief at a deep gully running down to the stream. A gun overturned and the horses were speared in their traces, their bodies dangling over the edge of the chasm. Smith himself managed to ride as far as the bank of the

Below: The nek (saddle) area at Isandlwana photographed in June 1879; the skeletons of animals and men are still strewn across the battlefield.

Mzinyathi before he was killed. Surgeon Major Shepherd, the Column's chief medical officer, stopped to help a wounded man and both were speared to death. When the exhausted fugitives reached the river they found it a raging brown torrent, surging and foaming over its rocky bed. For some the sight was too much; one man was seen calmly emptying the water from his boots and waiting for the Zulus to find him.

A number of mounted men did make it to the river, among them Lieutenants Melvill and Coghill of the 24th. Melvill was the 1/24th's Adjutant, and when the camp collapsed the battalion's Queen's Colour was entrusted to his care. Each imperial battalion had two Colours: the Queen's (the Union flag bearing the regiment's numeral) and the Regimental (bearing the regiment's battle honours). The Colours were a great source of regimental pride, and honour dictated that they be saved at all costs. The 2/24th's Colours had been in the guard tent in their camp and were never seen again. The 1/24th's Regimental Colour was with an outpost in Natal. Melvill's Queen's Colour was furled and sheathed in a heavy black leather case and he rode out of the camp clutching it across his saddle. Somewhere on the trail he came across Lieutenant Coghill and the two men reached the river.

Coghill spurred his horse into the torrent and got to the opposite bank. Melvill, unbalanced by the weight of the Colour, came off his horse in midstream. He clung to a boulder until the Colour was swept from his grasp by the current. Seeing his predicament Coghill

swam his horse back to rescue him. Bullets from the Zulus splashed around them and Coghill's horse was killed. They swam to the steep Natal bank and clambered across the boulders until they could go no further. Finding a large rock, they turned with their backs to it and faced their pursuers.

A few men did manage to make it across the river and ride to the safety of Helpmekaar, but the disaster was stunningly comprehensive. The official returns listed 52 officers and 806 white NCOs and men killed and nearly five hundred blacks. Of the six companies of the 24th who had been in the firing line, not one man survived. Of the 1,700 men whom Chelmsford had left in the camp at Isandlwana on the morning of 22 January, less than sixty whites and four hundred blacks were alive at sunset.

Organized resistance was over by about 2 p.m., though some groups held out until late afternoon. After the fighting had stopped, the Zulus, overwrought with the tension of battle, vented their fury on the camp. Zulu custom dictated that every warrior who had killed a man in battle should slit his victim's stomach to allow the spirit to escape to the after-life, and then wear the victim's clothes until certain purification rituals had been undertaken. Accordingly, every European body in the camp was stripped and disembowelled, and many were stabbed again and again by passing warriors, a custom observed in lion hunts. In some cases, maddened warriors took a terrible toll of the corpses, slashing,

Above: A recent photograph of the Mzinyathi gorge, just downstream of Fugitives' Drift. The Fugitives' descended the hill left; in 1879 all the rocks in the foreground were under a torrent of water.

hacking, mutilating and dismembering. Apart from some of the transport oxen, which were driven off, everything in the camp was killed – horses, mules, even regimental pets. Tents were burnt and slashed and every box and crate broken open. Sacks of meal and tins of meat were ripped open and their contents scattered about. The beer ration was consumed and the bottles smashed. Warriors desperate for drink gulped down medicines from the hospital tents and several were poisoned. The Martini-Henry rifles of the dead were eagerly seized and the ammunition crates broken open. Those who had not managed to loot a breech-loader tore the bullets from the cartridges with their teeth and took the powder for their muzzle-loaders. Within an hour or two the camp at Isandlwana became a scene of utter devastation. Then, slowly, the great army began to drift away and for the first time the terrible cost of the victory became clear. Friends and relatives tried to take away the bodies of the fallen, but there were far too many. They were buried in grain-pits of nearby homesteads, piled into dongas, or simply covered over with shields. More than a thousand warriors had been killed and hundreds more carried terrible wounds from heavy-calibre bullets and bayonets that were beyond the skills of the *izinyanga*, traditional herbal doctors, to cure.

Generally, the Zulu attack was spent by the time it reached the Mzinyathi, and the warriors were mindful of Cetshwayo's order not to cross into Natal. One body, however, had not taken an active part in the

Above: *Although rather dramatic, this sketch of Melvill's escape from Isandlwana is more accurate than most in that it shows him carrying the cased Colour.*

Right: *C. E. Fripp's painting of Coghill standing over the body of Melvill, awaiting death at the hands of the Zulus. Although the terrain features are not quite right – the pair stood with their backs to a large rock – this picture is probably the best representation of the scene.*

battle, and that was the uNdi Corps, comprising the senior uThulwana regiment, the inDlondlo, the iNdluyengwe and uDloko *amabutho*. The iNdluyengwe were young men in their early thirties and still unmarried, but the others were a decade older and headringed, and they were commanded by the king's brother, the headstrong and aggressive Prince Dabulamanzi kaMpande. They had been held in reserve earlier in the day and had swung round to descend the Nquthu hills to the west of the right horn. They had moved down the valley behind Isandlwana, and a few companies of the iNdluyengwe had been involved in the pursuit. They had crossed the Mzinyathi upstream of the fugitives and had paused to take snuff and perhaps narcotics. Apparently prompted by a desire to gain the glory they had been cheated of, they began to advance upstream towards Rorke's Drift.

Life at Rorke's Drift had been quiet since Chelmsford had crossed the border eleven days before. The post itself consisted of two low, thatched bungalows facing the river, beneath the shadow of a hill known to the Zulus as Shiyane, 'the eyebrow', and to the missionaries as Oskarberg. They had been built by a trader named James Rorke. The current occupant, the Swedish missionary Otto Witt, used one building as his house and the other as a church. Their presence so near the border crossing was a boon to Chelmsford, who had requisitioned the buildings as the column's main advanced supply depot. The army had turned Witt's chapel into a store, where Commissariat staff – Assistant Commissary Walter Dunn, Acting Assistant Commissary James Dalton, and Storekeeper Louis Byrne – supervised the

Above: *Prince Dabulamanzi kaMpande, the headstrong commander who led the uNdi reserve in the attack on Rorke's Drift. Photograph c. 1882.*

Left: *John Chard – promoted Major after the battle – wearing his VC, with fellow Royal Engineer officers later in the war.*

Above: Lieutenant Gonville Bromhead, 'B' Company's commander. The badge on the forage cap suggests that this photograph was taken c.1873.

mountain of mealie sacks and biscuit boxes which were due to be shipped forward to the column. Witt's house had been turned into a makeshift hospital where Surgeon Reynolds and three men of the Army Hospital Corps tended thirty-five sick including a couple of wounded from the attack on Sihayo's homestead. The post was guarded by Lieutenant Gonville Bromhead and the 80 men of 'B' Company, 2/24th. Down by the river a subaltern of the Royal Engineers, Lieutenant John Chard, was working to keep the ponts in repair. Rorke's Drift was under the command of Major Spalding, the column's chief supply officer, but during the morning Spalding rode back to Helpmekaar to find out why a company of the 24th, ordered down to reinforce the post sometime before, had not arrived. Before he left he checked his Army List and found that Chard was the senior officer remaining; he rode off with the casual comment, 'I see you are senior, so you will be in charge, although, of course, nothing will happen and I shall be back again this evening early.'

The 22nd had passed peacefully enough at the post although some thought they heard the sound of distant firing late in the morning. Chard had ridden up from the ponts to confer with Bromhead, and had just returned to his job when two breathless riders, officers

of the NNC, crossed the drift. They were from Isandlwana and they brought the astonishing news; the camp had been attacked, and every defender wiped out. Furthermore, a Zulu force was even then on its way to attack Rorke's Drift. Chard rode back up to the post, where another survivor had already given the news to Bromhead, and found it in turmoil. The men were excitedly leading up two transport wagons in preparation for defence or flight. Surgeon Reynolds, together with the Centre Column's chaplain, George Smith, had set out to climb Shiyane. From the top they would be able to make out some of the fighting on the banks of the Manzimnyana. Chard held a hurried consultation with Bromhead and Dalton, an ex-Quartermaster Sergeant whose experience ensured that his views were respected. Dalton pointed out that flight was suicide, since the Zulus could easily overtake a column hampered with sick and wagons. He urged Chard to utilize the huge store of mealie sacks and biscuit boxes to barricade the post. The two officers agreed and 'B' Company and the NNC men were set to work dragging out the supplies.

The post was not a bad defensive position considering the sort of attack it could expect. The two buildings backed on to the Oskarberg, with the hospital on the right and the storehouse on the left. About four hundred yards away a seam of exposed strata ran around the base of the hill. This jumble of shallow caves and sandstone boulders formed a terrace overlooking the post. Another ledge ran across the front of both buildings; opposite the hospital this ledge was little more than a gentle slope, but in places between the buildings it was four feet high. On the left front corner of the storehouse was a well-built stone cattle kraal with an interior partition; below the ledge was a rougher stone enclosure. The two wagons were run in between the rear corners of the buildings and a barricade of biscuit boxes and mealie bags linked them together. Another barricade was run along the front of the post, above the ledge, and across the slope in front of the hospital veranda. There were several small outbuildings behind the post and a stone wall and garden in front of the hospital. There was no time to demolish these, but the post was reasonably secure. The barricades were nearly complete when a party of NNH under a white officer rode in from the direction of Fugitive's Drift and asked Chard for orders. Chard gratefully spread them out in a screen on the southern flank of the Oskarberg. About this time Smith and Reynolds returned with the news that large bodies of Zulus were moving behind Isandlwana and in the Mzinyathi valley.

At about 4.30 pm there was a crackle of shots from the south, and the NNH streamed past in retreat. Their officer shouted that his men – who had, after all, already acquitted themselves well at Isandlwana – had had enough, before he too rode off. The sight was too much for the nerves of Stephenson's NNC who promptly vaulted the barricades and fled after them. The infuriated 24th fired a smattering of shots after them. In an instant Chard's position had drastically

deteriorated. He had counted on three hundred men to guard his perimeter; now he had less than half that number and they were spread dangerously thin. He decided to bisect his position with a line of biscuit boxes connecting the front left of the storehouse with the barricade above the ledge. He had no sooner set men to work when a look-out came in with the shout, 'Here they come, black as hell and thick as grass!'

The *impi* swung into view around the flank of the Oskarberg, screened by a swarm of skirmishers. Chard estimated its strength at about four thousand warriors; odds of nearly forty to one. The regiments came on with precision in close formation, aiming straight for the back walls of the post. Bromhead's men opened fire at 450 yards, noting with satisfaction that their well-placed shots were sending warriors somersaulting back into their ranks. The back of the post was most secure, however, because the buildings had been loopholed and the wagons provided a stout barricade. The Zulu charge pressed forward to within fifty or sixty yards then faltered, caught in a heavy cross-fire between the buildings which prevented them closing. Some warriors threw themselves down behind the deserted cook-house and a drainage ditch, but the rest veered slightly to their left where their momentum carried them round to the front of the hospital. They poured *en masse* into the gardens and bush and began a heavy fire on the defenders.

The hospital was the post's danger-point. It had not been possible to evacuate the sick, so parties of 'B'

Company had been told off to defend the claustrophobic rooms inside, and those patients well enough to use them had been given rifles. Because of the nature of the slope it had not been possible to build a very secure barricade along the front. In several short, violent rushes the Zulus drove the defenders back from the front of the hospital and, despite the efforts of Lieutenant Bromhead who led a bayonet charge to keep them back, took possession of the veranda and began hammering on the doors to break in.

Meanwhile another party of warriors had moved up to occupy the Oskarberg terraces whence they opened a heavy fire, mostly with old muzzle-loading rifles. The men facing them, on the back wall, were safe enough as only their helmets showed above the barricade, but those on the front wall beyond had their backs to the fire and no protection. A fire-fight developed in which the 24th had the upper hand. Although the Zulus were well hidden they were within the Martini-Henry's most effective range and the defenders on the back wall included several excellent shots. Conversely, the range tested the Zulus' antiquated guns to the limit. Nevertheless, the sheer volume of fire had its effect. Private Hitch was struck in the shoulder by a bullet which shattered his shoulder-blade. Corporal Allen was hit in the arm. Storekeeper Byrne was stooping to give a drink to a wounded NNC NCO when a bullet struck him in the head. Dalton was walking around the post, exhorting

Left: The post at Rorke's Drift, c.1882. The mission station is just visible centre left, beneath the Shiyane hill; the Zulus approached down the valley to the right of the picture.

Right: Lady Butler's famous painting of the yard at Rorke's Drift at the height of the battle. Lieutenant Chard and Bromhead confer in the centre of the picture, while Corporal Schiess leaps on to a barricade and Chaplain Smith hands out ammunition behind them. Storekeeper Byrne falls shot through the head as he hands water to a wounded man, while right, Private Hitch carries ammunition despite being wounded.

Left: A well-known photograph of the storehouse building at Rorke's Drift, probably taken in June 1879, when the post had been turned into a secure fort by the addition of loop-holed stone walls.

Left: Rorke's Drift, 1989. This building stands on the foundations of the original hospital and, apart from the thatched roof, much resembles it; this is the view the attacking Zulus would have had as they rushed at the back of the post.

Right: The Battle of Rorke's Drift, 22/23 January 1879. The map shows the positions at the start of the fight (aprox. 4.30 p.m. on the 22nd), as well as Chard's final defences around the storehouse (right).

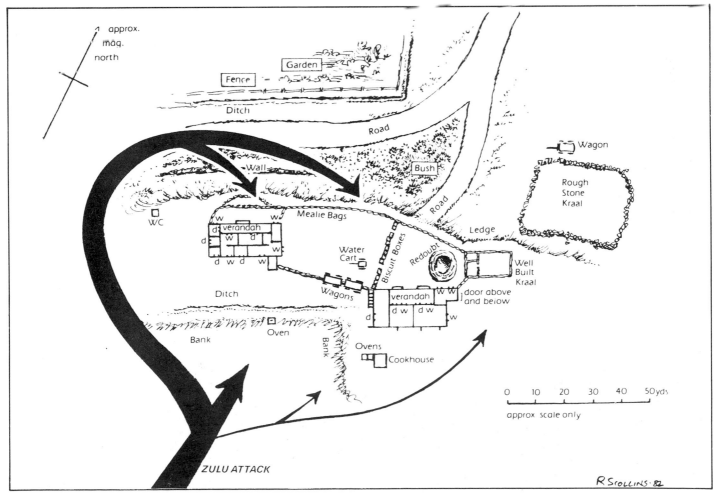

approx. mag. north

Garden

Fence

Ditch

Road

Wall

Bush

Road

Wagon

Rough Stone Kraal

WC

Mealie Bags

verandah

Water Cart

Biscuit Boxes

Redoubt

Ledge

Well Built Kraal

Ditch

Wagons

verandah

door above and below

Bank

Oven

Bank

Ovens

Cookhouse

0   10   20   30   40   50 yds
approx scale only

ZULU ATTACK

R Scollins·82

the men and firing over the barricade. A warrior leapt on to the mealie bags next to him; Dalton called out 'Pot that fellow!' The warrior had just dropped when Dalton was shot through the body. He coolly handed his rifle to Chard beside him, and walked to the storehouse veranda where Surgeon Reynolds had set up a makeshift field hospital.

In the hospital itself the fight was most desperate. The Zulus had at last burst in, killing several of the defenders in the front rooms. There was no interconnecting passage between the rooms, however, and to get from one to the next the warriors had to take each room separately. These were little more than cramped cubby-holes in which the defenders, men like Privates Henry Hook, John Williams, Robert Jones and William Jones, had loopholed and barricaded as best they could. Once the Zulus had entered the building the defenders used pickaxes and bayonets to knock holes through the interior partitions, working towards the eastern end of the building and the defended enclosure outside. One man would hold the Zulus at bay, defending a doorway or the hole through which they had just come, while another passed through the patients into the next room. Finally they reached the outside wall where a window opened into the yard.

By this time it was nearly dark and the fire from the terraces had forced Chard to abandon his original line and fall back to the more secure position in front of the storehouse. The Zulus had succeeded in setting fire to the thatch of the hospital and a pall of heavy smoke drifted across the battlefield. The defenders of the hospital hefted their patients out through the window where Corporal Allen and Private Hitch, both wounded, helped them down and rushed them across to the line of biscuit boxes. The yard itself was now a no man's land, exposed to Zulu fire and the occasional brave warrior who dashed across it. Most of these were easily shot, but one succeeded in spearing a patient, Trooper Hunter of the Natal Mounted Police, before he was hit.

As soon as it was dark the Zulus encircled the post completely, directing their attention to the cattle kraal at the eastern end of the storehouse. Once the deserted hospital really began to blaze it illuminated the western end of the post so that the Zulu charges were just as exposed as ever, but the far side of the storehouse was in shadow, and a number of charges heaved up out of the darkness, heralded by the great war-cry, 'uSuthu!' The defenders were driven slowly back towards the interior wall. Two great piles of mealie bags still lay in front of the storehouse and Chard directed that they be formed into a redoubt. Assistant Commissary Dunne, a tall man, clambered up and, although very exposed to Zulu fire, dragged them together and scooped out the top to provide sanctuary for the critically wounded and a few riflemen. Chard's men were now concentrated on a very small front and their firepower and bayonets kept the Zulus back. The rushes lasted well into the night, but gradually lost momentum. About an hour before

dawn the Zulu fire spluttered out and the warriors faded into the darkness.

Daylight brought no sign of the Zulus, but a scene of desolation. The hospital was gutted and a curtain of smoke lay over the field, carrying with it the stench of those who had died and been cremated within its walls. The dead lay everywhere; here and there a soldier who had died along the abandoned perimeter, but mostly Zulus, piled up in some places to the top of the barricade. One man lay with his heels on the parapet and his head on the ground, supported by the bodies of his comrades. Curiously a number were drawn up in the same posture, crouched forward on their knees with their faces on the ground. Chard noted some of the awful wounds. One warrior's head had been split in two as if with an axe; another's face was perfect except for a small bullet hole between his eyes, but the back of his head was blown away. Hundreds of empty paper ammunition packets and thousands of cartridges littered the site, together with shields, spears, broken

Above: The fight for the hospital. One man defends the door against the Zulus while another helps the patients escape. This picture exaggerates the size of the holes made between rooms, but suggests the claustrophobic nature of the struggle.

Top: The defenders of Rorke's Drift; 'B' Company, 2/24th. Lieutenant Bromhead is standing on the left. This photograph was probably taken at Pinetown, Natal, after the war.

Above: The post at Rorke's Drift. This picture clearly shows the Oskarberg terrace which overlooked the mission station. The sunken area to the right of the road may be a mass Zulu grave. Photographed late 1879.

guns and discarded and torn equipment. Fifteen of Chard's men were dead and two more dying; many of the remainder were wounded and all were exhausted.

Chard sent out patrols to collect Zulu weapons. It was dangerous work; Private Hook was wandering near a donga down by the river when an apparently dead Zulu sprang up at him. Hook had an armful of spears and only just managed to drop them and grab his rifle in time. Then Chard recalled his patrols; the Zulus had returned.

They came round the slope of Shiyane, keeping out of rifle range and squatted down on a hill opposite, taking snuff. Chard's men watched them tensely, but at last they rose and trotted back the way they had come. Why did they go? They had been on the move since the NNH had discovered them the morning before in the Ngwebeni valley. They had covered more than fifteen miles of rugged country, most of it at a run, and had fought a battle in the teeth of a ferocious fire for a further twelve hours. They had lost heavily,

they were hungry and, worse, their enemy were still apparently as entrenched as ever. And from their position they saw what Chard could not; redcoats were approaching the Drift from the direction of Isandlwana.

Lord Chelmsford had not had a good day on 22 January. He had ridden out of the camp ahead of his column, but by the time he had reached the Mangeni there was no sign of the Zulu concentration reported by Dartnell. The hills around the river were alive with small parties of warriors, however, and Chelmsford ordered the Volunteers out in pursuit. A desultory and inconclusive skirmishing lasted all morning. The General dispersed his troops throughout the hills, but there was no sign of the main *impi*. By late mid-morning he was convinced the alarm had been a false one and turned his attention towards the question of a new camp site. He decided to establish it at the head of the Mangeni gorge, and a message was sent back to Pulleine ordering him to advance the wagons to the

Left: Lieutenant-Colonel E. W. Bray, 4th Foot, who was commanding a convoy on the road to Helpmekaar when news of Isandlwana reached him.

Left: British soldiers building gravestones in the vicinity of Rorke's Drift. The monument appears to be that of Lt. R. W. Franklin of the 24th, who died of disease at Helpmekaar on 20th February.

Right: The fortified post at Helpmekaar; an earthwork thrown up around the original store sheds.

Right: Major Bengough's NNC battalion lined-up outside Fort Bengough. The main stone bastion is on the top of the rise, with huts for the men just visible on the right.

new camp. It arrived at Isandlwana just as the Zulu attack was developing and Chelmsford received the curious reply that Pulleine could not comply immediately because there was 'heavy firing on left of camp'. Chelmsford and his staff rode on to some high ground, but Isandlwana, partly obscured by mist or haze, seemed perfectly normal. Throughout the morning, however, a number of reports came in which suggested something serious was happening at the camp. At one point the dull and distant thud or the two 7-pounder guns firing could be heard. Chelmsford ordered the 1/3rd NNC back to camp. They had marched several miles across the plain when a large body of Zulus – presumably the Zulu left horn – swept across their front some way off. The camp area was clearly visible and there appeared to be fighting among the tents. The NNC fell back to a more secure position and their Commandant sent a terse message to Chelmsford; 'For God's sake come back, the camp is surrounded and things, I fear, are going badly.'

At first Chelmsford could not believe it. Even if a Zulu force had eluded his probe, he had left more than enough men in the camp to defend it. He began a leisurely retreat, convinced that there could be no cause for alarm. He was a few miles from the camp when he was disabused. Here he met Commandant Lonsdale, commander of the 3rd NNC. Lonsdale had ridden alone into the camp to arrange for supplies for his men. He had recently suffered from sunstroke and a fall from his horse and was still a little dazed, and was

only a few hundred yards from the tents when he realized that they were occupied by Zulus finishing off the survivors. He had just managed to turn his horse and escape as the warriors saw him and began firing after him.

News broke among the troops like a thunderclap. By now it was mid-afternoon and there seemed to be little chance of reaching the camp in time to save it. But Chelmsford could hardly stay where he was. Wearily and weighed down with foreboding his men marched back across the plain. By the time they reached the Conical Kop it was dark; just beyond, they drew up in formation. The guns unlimbered and fired several rounds into the camp in case the Zulus were waiting in ambush. There was no reply. Some companies of the 24th fixed bayonets and marched off to storm the stony kopje on the southern end of the *nek*; there was no opposition, though Zulu signal fires were thick on the surrounding hills. At last Chelmsford advanced and took possession of the camp. The night masked the worst of the horrors, but as the line picked its way forward over the broken ground, the men stumbled on bodies and the carcasses of slaughtered animals. Cold and exhausted, without blankets, they lay down to sleep on the *nek*. Out in the darkness a solitary drunken Zulu could be heard shouting. The aura of death and ruin hung over everything. Several times during the night the NNC panicked and crowded in upon the 24th. There was little sleep. Before dawn a few officers rose and rummaged through the chaos, looking for friends and possessions. Too often they found colleagues or servants dead, stripped and mutilated, their horses and even their pets killed, and everything smashed or burnt. Rumours of Zulu savagery passed through the ranks like a grass-fire; of drummer boys, hung up on a wagon and gutted like sheep, and of a circle of severed heads found neatly placed around a broken wheel.

Before first light, Chelmsford fell the men in and they began to march down the road to Rorke's Drift. They encountered a few Zulu stragglers, and the Volunteers, in no mood to be merciful, finished them off. Somewhere near the Batshe they passed an *impi* moving in the opposite direction, part of the force retiring from Rorke's Drift; both sides were too tired to fight and they passed out of rifle range in silence. At the Drift itself the General was relieved to find the ponts still intact and he began to ferry his men across. The Mounted Infantry rode ahead to scout and there was a tense moment as the column waited to hear whether the post had fallen. Then there was a distant cheer and with relief Chelmsford marched up and relieved the mission station.

The General himself interviewed those individuals who had distinguished themselves in the defence – Private Hook was in his shirt-sleeves when summoned, and gave his report in an agony of embarrassment – while his men spread out examining evidence of the fight. The NNC fanned out over the surrounding countryside killing the Zulu wounded. More than 370 Zulu dead were found near the post, many of them around the hospital, where the fight had been thickest, and their bodies turned up behind

boulders or in the long grass for weeks afterwards. The burial details dumped them in grain pits or mass graves, or burnt them, a grim but necessary task, since the column intended to remain encamped at Rorke's Drift. The British dead were buried in a neat walled cemetery behind the post.

Chelmsford's original invasion plan lay in ruins. He gave orders to consolidate the position at Rorke's Drift, then rode on to Pietermaritzburg. Glyn was to remain at the Drift for several weeks, in cramped conditions which soon became unsanitary because of the nightly downpours. The white troops camped in an improved fort built around the storehouse, but the NNC were left in the open on the Oskarberg terraces. It soon became clear that the strain of Isandlwana had so severely undermined their morale that they were no longer an effective force. On 24 January they were disbanded.

News of the disaster had preceded Chelmsford, carried by both black and white survivors. On the evening of 22 January two companies of the 24th were marching down from Helpmekaar to Rorke's Drift – as a result of Major Spalding's chivvying – when survivors met them and told them of Isandlwana. Ahead of them the hospital at the Drift appeared to be in flames and the post seemed to have fallen. They marched back to Helpmekaar, where the garrison was hastily throwing up defences around the stores. Survivors came into the camp throughout the night and nerves were stretched to breaking-point in hourly expectation of attack. Further back along the road, Colonel Bray of the 4th Foot had been escorting a convoy of wagons when a crowd of fleeing NNC

Left: Lord Chelmsford's retreat from the devastated camp on the morning of 23 January.

Right: In the aftermath of Isandlwana, fear in Natal of a Zulu invasion was very great; this picture shows an 'anti-invasion barrier' built across the docks at Durban.

Right: Manning the defences at Greytown in expectation of the Zulu attack, 23 January 1879.

Right: Reading the list of missing Volunteers, Pieter-maritzburg, 24 January.

passed him on the track. Bray made for the nearest European building – the magistracy at Msinga – knocked loopholes through the walls and settled down to wait for the Zulus. All along the border white and black Natalians fled as soon as they heard the news. So great was the panic that many abandoned their livestock. Some whites crossed north into the Transvaal, many flocked to the border laagers, and some did not stop till they reached Durban, and a ship to take them away from the Colony altogether. Pietermaritzburg had awoken to the news on the 24th, to find that many of the town's black servants had heard already and left in the night. Anxious Colonists crowded round survivors seeking news of friends and relatives who had been with Chelmsford. When the lists of killed and missing Volunteers were posted the effect on the close-knit settler community was devastating. When Chelmsford arrived his first concern was to arrange for an organized border defence. The laagers in Pietermaritzburg were reinforced and orders were sent to entrench Helpmekaar. Major Bengough's battalion, 2/1st NNC, who were camped near Msinga, built a stone redoubt, Fort Bengough, on a knoll by the side of the road.

Yet once the initial panic subsided it became clear that there was no major Zulu incursion. When the black Border Police returned to their posts at the end of January they found nothing more than small parties of warriors crossing the Mzinyathi to loot and burn deserted homesteads. It had never been King Cetshwayo's intention to take the war into Natal and in truth he probably could not have done so had he wanted. No sooner had the fighting stopped than the great *impi* had dispersed, the men returning to their homesteads to carry out purification rituals and recover. Even on the morning of the 23rd Chelmsford's men had noticed *imizi* that had been deserted on the advance were now full of men quietly watching the troops pass by. When the king heard this he was angry and demanded to know why the army had not returned to him; when told of the Zulu losses he was appalled. 'A spear has been thrust into the belly of the nation,' he said. 'There are not enough tears to mourn for the dead.' Dabulamanzi, who had disobeyed his instructions and had nothing but casualties to show for it, left Ulundi in disgrace.

In not following up his victory Cetshwayo let his one great chance of success slip through his fingers. He gave Chelmsford time to regroup, and British opinion both in Natal and at home clamoured for revenge. In his moderation he handed Chelmsford a propaganda victory; the heroic defence of Rorke's Drift was presented to a grateful public as a major strategic success, the action which snatched victory from the jaws of defeat and saved Natal from the barbarism of the Zulu onslaught. No less than eleven of the defenders of the mission station were subsequently given the highest award for bravery in action, the Victoria Cross. Lieutenants Chard and Bromhead, Surgeon Reynolds, Acting Assistant Commissary

Dalton, Corporal Allen, Privates Hitch, Hook, Robert Jones, William Jones and John Williams of the 24th, and Frederick Schiess, a Corporal of the NNC who, although a patient in the hospital, continued to serve with reckless bravery throughout the fight. The day's tally of VCs was completed by the award to Private Wassall of the 80th, serving with the Mounted Infantry, who rescued a wounded comrade under fire at Fugitive's Drift. There was no provision for the posthumous award of the VC in 1879, but it was noted that Melvill and Coghill would have been awarded one for their efforts to save the Queen's Colour 'had they lived'; years later, the first two posthumous VCs awarded were sent to their families.

Above: Corporal William Allen – promoted Sergeant, and wearing his VC – one of the heroes of Rorke's Drift.

BESIEGED

The advance of the Right Flank Column; crossing the Thukela. The Battle of Nyezane, 22 January 1879. The advance to the mission station at Eshowe. Pearson receives news of Isandlwana, and digs in. Life at Eshowe during the siege; skirmishing with Zulu forces. The arrival of Zulu peace envoys. Chelmsford is reinforced; preparations for a relief column. The advance and the Battle of Gingindlovu. Eshowe is relieved; Chelmsford abandons the post and withdraws to Natal.

'We had fearful hard times of it in Eshowe.' Corporal F.W.Licence, RE.

Right: Colonel Charles Knight Pearson of the Buffs, the commander of the Right Flank Column.

Reveille sounded at 3.30 am in the camp of HMS *Active's* Naval Brigade near Fort Pearson on the morning of Sunday, 12 January, for the sailors and Marines had been allocated the task of ferrying Colonel Pearson's No.1 (Right Flank) Column across the Lower Thukela. Although it was known that Lord Chelmsford expected the brunt of the fighting to fall on the centre column, each part of the invasion force had to be strong enough to withstand a possible Zulu attack, and Pearson's command was not insubstantial. As well as the Naval Brigade – roughly two hundred men, with two 7-pounder guns, two heavy 24-pound rocket tubes, and one Gatling gun – his force consisted of two imperial infantry battalions, the 2/3rd (Buffs) and 99th, one section of 11/7 Battery RA, with two 7-pounder guns and one rocket trough, a company of Royal Engineers, a troop of Mounted Infantry, five troops of Natal Volunteers (from the Natal Hussars, Durban, Alexandra, Stanger and Victoria Mounted Rifles), the two battalions of the 2nd NNC, and a company of Natal Native Pioneers – a total of nearly 5,000 men, with a supply train of more than 380 wagons and 600 drivers. Transporting such an accumulation of men and baggage across the river was a time-consuming task. The Thukela flows into the sea not far below the lower drift, and the river is wide, with large sandbanks between the channels when the water is running low. But the same rains which had swollen the Mzinyathi up-country had made the Thukela rise, and the ponts had to ferry the troops piecemeal across a wide, brown expanse of fast-flowing water. The landing was unopposed, however, and Pearson established a camp on the Zulu side, and a site for a new fort, Fort Tenedos, was marked out.

Once the crossing was secure several days were spent ferrying over the convoy. Pearson's first strategic objective was to advance to a range of heights thirty-seven miles away, a spot the Zulus called *Eshowe* after a distinctive shrub which characterized the area. In 1860 the Norwegian mission had built a station there, known as KwaMondi, after the Christian name of the missionary, Ommund Oftebro. It had been deserted when the missionaries fled the country before the war, but Chelmsford intended to use the buildings as an advanced supply depot, from which Pearson's movements could be more easily co-ordinated with his own. Pearson's advance would take him across sub-tropical country, carpeted with tall green grass and exotic bush, including wild banana palms, skirting some of the largest ridge-top forests in the country. He could look forward to stiflingly hot days, with thunderstorms in the evening and heavy rain throughout the night which would be sure to make the rivers that bisected his path difficult, and reduce the roads to a quagmire under the wheels of his

Left: A group of Buffs officers in South Africa, c.1878. Colonel Pearson seated left; most of the men are wearing either blue patrol jackets or the officers' 'undress frock', a loose scarlet working jacket, more comfortable than the formal tunic.

Left: The stores of Pearson's Medical Department – just part of the huge amount of stores which had to be ferried across the Thukela.

Right: A company of the 99th Regiment about to be ferried across the river to join Pearson's advance.

wagons. The road itself ran flat for several miles, but then began to climb in a series of steps which led up to Eshowe itself.

Leaving some of his men behind to man the forts and guard the supply lines, Pearson began to move forward on 18 January, advancing in two manageable sections a few miles apart. The first division, commanded by Pearson himself, consisted of five companies of the Buffs, the Naval Brigade and Royal Artillery, the Royal Engineers, about 150 mounted troops, and one battalion of the NNC, with about 50 wagons. The second division was commanded by Colonel Welman of the 99th, with four companies of his regiment, three of the Buffs, the other battalion of the 2nd NNC, and the remainder of the cavalry. Welman's division escorted about 80 wagons, and it was intended that the remainder should be ferried up in due course. By the 20th both sections were nearing the Amatikulu, a narrow but deep river, one of the more serious obstacles on the march. It proved fordable, but it took most of the 21st before the wagons could be dragged through the steep muddy banks. That night was spent a few miles from the River Nyezane. Communications with the other columns were minimal and Pearson's men had no idea that that same night, across country, Dartnell was bivouacking opposite the Zulu force at Mangeni.

At about 5 am on the 22nd – not long after Chelmsford had marched out of Isandlwana – Pearson's division moved forward to the Nyezane. The river was not wide, but it was full and the banks were overgrown with a tangle of grass and bush. Beyond the river the track cut across a small flat area before climbing a range of hills. The track ran up a sloping spur, flanked on each side by two higher hills running parallel to it, and separated from them by narrow, bush-choked gullies. The position was shaped roughly like a letter 'E', with the road on the centre stroke, and the ridges on each side. The higher hill, on the right of the track, was known to the Zulus as Wombane.

Pearson's patrols suggested that the far bank of the Nyezane was clear of Zulus and he decided to halt the column on the flats for breakfast before climbing the hills. The head of the column – the Naval Brigade, Artillery and two companies of the Buffs – crossed the river and advanced to the foot of the spur and fell out on the right-hand side of the road. The Engineers were still working at the ford and the wagons crossing the river were moving to the parking area, when small parties of Zulus appeared on the crest of the hills. Pearson sent a company of the NNC to chase them off, but the Zulus disappeared into the bush of the gully on the right of the road before re-emerging on the slope of Wombane. The NNC enthusiastically went in after them, but became disordered in the bush and had to pause to reform on the far side of the gully. While they were doing so a long column of warriors burst over the skyline, and streamed rapidly down the flank of Wombane towards them. Most of the NNC warriors turned and fled back the way they had come, but their

officers and NCOs rallied and made a stand. The Zulus fired a heavy volley at close range and then overran them. One NNC officer, three white NCOs, and three men were killed.

Pearson's men had walked into a carefully prepared trap. The Zulus were the men ordered by King Cetshwayo to defend the coastal strip. The uDlambedlu, izinGulube and uMxapho *amabutho* were present in strength and there were elements from other regiments who lived locally. There were between 4,000 and 6,000 warriors in all, commanded by the elderly Godide kaNdlela, Chief of the Ntuli clan, supported by the *izinduna* Mbilwane kaMahlanganisa, Masegwane kaSopigwasi, and Matshiya. Several of these officers were attached to Gingindlovu, a local *ikhanda* which Pearson had passed and destroyed the day before, and which had perhaps served the *impi* as a base until it had retired behind Wombane to lie in wait for the column as it crossed the drift. Now it deployed in the classic 'horns' formation, the left horn pursuing the fleeing NNC, the chest advancing down the road, taking possession of a small homestead at the top of the spur, and the right horn moving behind the hill on Pearson's left.

Pearson was, indeed, in a difficult position. His wagons were still sprawled across the drift and he would have to leave a large proportion of his force to guard them. An attack on a column on the move in difficult circumstances was the event every commander dreaded most; the convoy was inevitably extended and exposed, and it was difficult to form a compact firing line. As soon as the attack developed,

Pearson pushed his advanced party up the spur and formed them up on a knoll by the side of the road. From here they opened a heavy fire across the gully at the warriors moving down Wombane. The Zulus were advancing steadily with precision at great speed, but the heavy fire supported by the rockets and guns began to take effect and they were forced to slow down, taking whatever advantage could be had from the long grass and bush. Nevertheless, they came right down Wombane and began to sweep round towards the column at the drift. Pearson sent a hurried message to two companies of the Buffs who formed up on the right of the road and began to advance in skirmishing order, firing as they did so. The heavy and accurate fire was too much for the Zulus whose own rifles were far less effective at the same range, and the tip of the left horn began to retire. Once the wagons were safely across, Captain Wynne's Royal Engineer company grabbed their rifles and joined the firing line, and the Natal Volunteers fell in to the right of them. They swept slowly out to the right, driving the Zulus back up Wombane where they came under fire again from the knoll.

Meanwhile the Zulu centre had been steadily massing at the homestead further up the spur and was seriously threatening Pearson's position on the knoll. A rocket from the Naval Brigade went clean through one of the huts, setting it on fire and driving the warriors out. Commander Campbell of the *Active* asked Pearson's permission to storm the *umuzi* and Pearson assented. The blue-jackets, supported by officers and NCOs of the NNC, pushed up the slope.

Above: *A column crossing the River Amatikulu. This is probably a Second Invasion photograph but it does suggest something of the transport difficulties; the banks have had to be flattened to allow the wagons to cross.*

Right: *The height of the Battle of Nyezane; the Zulu left horn streams down Wombane, opposite Pearson's position on the knoll. Notice the men opening ammunition boxes in the foreground. Sketch by Lieutenant Evelyn of the Buffs, who was present at the action.*

Right: The battlefield of Nyezane, 1989, photographed downstream of Pearson's crossing point. Most of the column was parked on the flat ground centre right, when its advanced parties, ascending the hills on the skyline, encountered the Zulus. The large hill, centre, is Wombane.

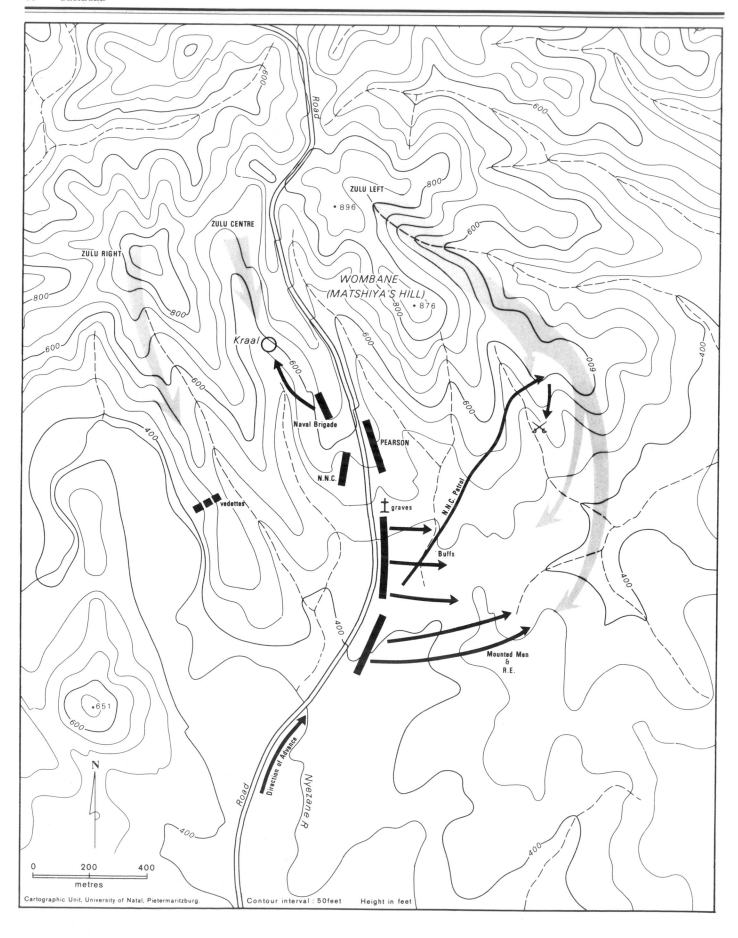

ZULU LEFT
• 896

ZULU CENTRE

ZULU RIGHT

WOMBANE
(MATSHIYA'S HILL)
• 876

Kraal

Naval Brigade

PEARSON

N.N.C.

vedettes

✝ graves

N.N.C. Patrol

Buffs

Mounted Men
&
R.E.

•651

Road

Direction of Advance

Nyezane R.

N

0   200   400
metres

Cartographic Unit, University of Natal, Pietermaritzburg.   Contour interval : 50feet   Height in feet

By now, the Brigade's Gatling gun, which had been in the rear, had been manhandled up the spur, beyond the knoll, where it took up a position facing the Zulu concentrations near the top of Wombane. This was to be the Gatling's baptism of fire for the British Army; it was crude and cumbersome, its ten barrels rotating by means of a hand crank, and it was prone to jamming when the heat of the barrels softened the thin brass cartridges, but it fired the same heavy bullet as the Martini-Henry, and when it opened fire with a noisy clatter it ripped great holes in the Zulu ranks. The knots of warriors began to fall back behind the crest of Wombane as Campbell's men doubled up towards the homestead. There was a brief flurry of hand-to-hand fighting and the Zulus were driven out.

Throughout the battle the Zulu right horn made little attempt to close. The warriors pushed forward some way beyond the crest of the ridge on the left of the road, but found their way contested by a small picket of Mounted Volunteers. Seeing that they stood no chance of achieving surprise, they too began to retire. All along the front, therefore, the Zulus were falling back and Pearson ordered the troops on the knoll to advance, led by Colonel Parnell of the Buffs, and clear the crest of the ridge. The Gatling was brought up and, with a clearer field of fire, scythed down the Zulus wavering behind Wombane. As they began to turn and flee Parnell's men followed them up and cleared the heights.

The battle had begun just after 8 am, and the last shots were fired at about 9.30. The Zulu fire had been

heavy throughout but inaccurate, and none of the charges had hit home. Pearson's casualties were ten whites and four blacks killed, and both he and Parnell had horses killed under them. Nevertheless, it had been a close-run thing. Officers and men alike were impressed by the Zulu determination and discipline, and had the odds been greater – Godide had an uncharacteristically low superiority of 2:1 – and the Zulu attacks better co-ordinated, the result might have been different. Only the left horn deployed fully, suggesting the attack had been sparked off prematurely. Yet none of this was apparent to the Zulus who left more than 400 dead scattered across the field, and carried off many more dreadfully wounded, a shocking price paid when their own fire had apparently caused so little damage. The Zulus had fought a fair fight in the open and their defeat was a severe blow to their morale.

The day was suffocatingly hot and the column was exhausted by the fight. The dead were buried under a shady tree by the side of the road, and Pearson advanced a few miles to get away from the battlefield. There his forces camped. On the morning of the 23rd they advanced to Eshowe.

The KwaMondi mission consisted of a church and three small stores and houses. It was not ideally sited from a tactical point of view, nestling in a range of hills, the peak of one of which overlooked it only a few hundred yards away. But a nearby stream provided water, and there was plenty of firewood available. Best of all, the buildings themselves would be invaluable as

The Buffs & Naval Brigade
Turning the right flank of the ~
at Inyezane
Jan 22

Left: Officers of HMS Active's Naval Brigade. Midshipman Coker, who manned the Gatling at Nyezane and later died at Eshowe, is sitting second from the left in the front row.

Below left: Lieutenant Evelyn's sketch of the end of the battle of Nyezane; the Zulus are driven out of the burning homestead (left) and beyond the crest of Wombane (right).

Right: The graves of those killed at Nyezane. The wooden cross was made by the garrison during the siege of Eshowe and erected as the column marched back past the battlefield in April.

Below: An overview of the Fort at Eshowe, showing the rampart built around the mission station.

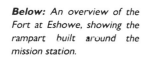

a permanent advanced depot. The church was requisitioned as a hospital and Pearson's men began unloading their stores and stacking them in the huts. The Royal Engineers marked out a line of fortifications around the post and, with some reluctance, working parties began cutting down a small orchard of fruit trees outside. So far Pearson had every reason to be satisfied with his progress. He had advanced according to his orders and occupied his first objective, and he was quite unaware of events in the rest of the country. Then, on the 25th, only two days after his arrival, the first rumours began to circulate of Chelmsford's disaster. Consternation turned to alarm on the 28th when a runner arrived with a detailed dispatch; Pearson was told that his column was unsupported, that he might expect an attack by the entire Zulu army, and that he should retreat or dig-in as he saw fit. After a hurried consultation with his officers it was decided to stay put, but that, to reduce the burden on the rations and camp, the Natal Volunteers and Native Contingent should be sent back to the Thukela. It was a trying day; as the little column marched off the garrison threw themselves into building the fort with a will. Large parties of Zulus were reported lurking in the hills and an attack was expected hourly. Officers stripped off their jackets and sweated digging trenches with the men. Every available bag was filled with clay and heaped into barricades. At night the troops remained at the ready until the early hours. Pearson ordered that there would be no more sleeping in tents – the men would have to sleep fully accoutred under wagons, ready to turn out at a moment's notice.

And yet the expected attack did not materialize. The Volunteers and NNC reached the Thukela in safety. The local Zulus had not yet regrouped after the defeat at Nyezane, and the king and *ibandla* were still digesting the implications of Isandlwana. Small Zulu patrols kept watch on the fort and when, on the 29th, Pearson tried to send back part of his huge,

Ekowe. Church, Head Quarter Tents, Ammunition + Quarter Masters Stores, The bell is the one now in the me...

unmanageable herd of transport oxen, the Zulus swept down, drove off the guard and seized more than 900 head. They did not attempt to close in, however, and Pearson was able to finish the fortifications without interruption. And a very impressive bastion it proved, surrounded by a deep ditch, reinforced with stakes, with a high rampart and firing steps on the inside. A ring of wagons ran round the interior and the column's guns and Gatling were raised on platforms and carefully enplaced. Gradually range markers were added near conspicuous objects and wire entanglements and broken bottles were strewn in the grass to impede a Zulu advance.

The first few weeks at Eshowe were uncomfortable, made trying by constant false alarms and the difficulties of sleeping out in such a confined space. But if, with a force of 1,339 whites and 355 blacks, Fort Eshowe was overcrowded, it was at least strong enough to defend itself and Pearson had enough supplies to last three months, and plenty of ammunition. At first runners were easily able to elude the Zulu patrols and keep Pearson in touch with Chelmsford. The General was desperately trying to restore his forces to order and his advice to Pearson was to hang on. Boredom was a major problem for the troops, but their officers found plenty of work for them to do, scouting the surrounding hills, escorting those cattle which remained and which needed to be driven to graze further and further from the camp as they exhausted the grass, or adding new refinements to the Fort. The adjutant of the 99th, Lieutenant Davison, found time between his duties to go for walks, to lie reading on the hill overlooking the post, and to indulge his botanical interests by planting eucalyptus cuttings and collecting mossy ferns. The bands of the Buffs and 99th played regularly to keep the spirits up, there was a Church service every Sunday and the Reverend Robertson, a missionary who had accompanied the column, gave lectures on Zulu life.

Such comforts could not last indefinitely, however, and towards the middle of February the Zulu net tightened. King Cetshwayo was incensed that Pearson should apparently settle in so calmly as if the country were already pacified, and ordered his coastal army to lay siege to the post. Reports of Zulu concentrations along the Nyezane became more numerous and runners were unable to get through. Rather than risk the enormous casualties which would inevitably result from a frontal attack on the fort, the Zulus preferred to isolate it and wait to attack any relieving column which might approach in the open. Large numbers of warriors built temporary camps just beyond the reach of the garrison, and stepped-up attacks on Pearson's patrols. Others collected in the regional *amakhanda* waiting their chance to strike. Inside the fort, a change in the weather was making life unpleasant. The first few weeks of the siege had been hot and sunny, but now the rain came in steady downpours every night, making sleep in the open difficult. The first of a steady trickle of men to succumb to dysentery was buried on the slope below the fort, his grave framed with staves from a wooden barrel and marked with a simple cross. On 11 February a runner got through the Zulu gauntlet with news that Chelmsford was planning a relief column, but that it would be unable to advance for a number of weeks.

Perhaps to boost his men's flagging morale, Pearson decided to go on to the offensive. Before dawn on 1 March a small force set out to attack a large *umuzi* some seven miles away from the fort. The movement caught the Zulus by surprise and not until the troops were deploying overlooking the homestead – believed to have been one of Prince Dabulamanzi's – were they spotted. The Naval Brigade 7-pounder lobbed shells into the *umuzi*, setting it alight, and a long-range fire-fight developed as the enraged warriors streamed out. Having achieved its objective the column began a hasty retreat with the Zulus following close behind. At one point the Marines who made up the rearguard turned to disperse the warriors only to find themselves the subject of a heavy volley from dense bush not 300 yards off. But despite steady skirmishing which continued to within a mile or two of the fort, the column suffered no casualties.

The next day the garrison noticed a faltering light flickering from the direction of the distant Thukela. It turned out to be a heliograph and, although it was difficult to make out the message, spirits rose at being in contact with the outside world again. The signalling clearly suggested relief and Pearson set his Engineers to work surveying a new road towards the Thukela. Near the fort a route was found that cut several miles off the distance, and working parties were sent out daily to prepare a track. They were subject to constant harassment by the Zulus. On one occasion the guns in the fort had to open fire to disperse parties of warriors seen creeping through the bush, and on another an officer of the Buffs was slightly wounded in the head by sniper fire. The Engineers took to leaving booby traps by their works when they returned to the fort each night. Attacks on the vedettes stepped-up, too; on 7 March Private Carson of the 99th was fired on by a group of warriors who ambushed him in long grass – he was wounded four times, in the back, thigh, wrist, and hand, losing two fingers, but he managed to escape, and was later promoted Sergeant for his gallantry. Private Kent was not so lucky; a few days

Left: To discourage the Zulus from interfering with their work, Pearson's Engineers left booby traps; here unsuspecting warriors set off a 'torpedo'.

Left: A romanticised view of the attempts by Lord Chelmsford's men, on the Thukela River, to open communications with Eshowe. In fact, no heliographs were available until the end of the war.

Right: A veteran of the Army Service Corps, dispatched as part of Chelmsford's reinforcement. He appears to be wearing his 'campaign kit' (apart from the white foreign service helmet) although this pattern of tunic was not officially adopted until after the Zulu War.

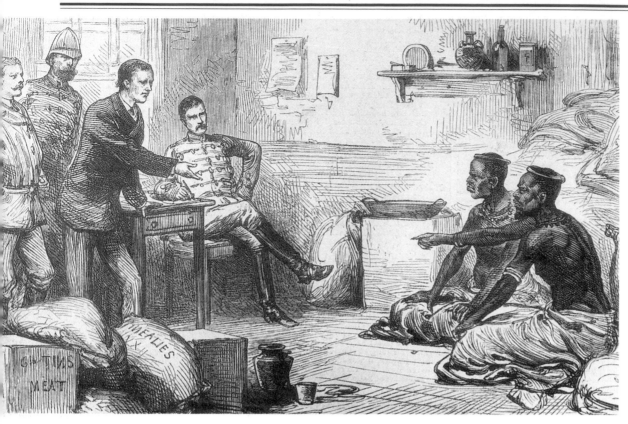

Left: *The Zulu envoys led by Mfunzi are interrogated at Fort Cherry on the Middle Drift, March 1879.*

Below, left and right: *Members of the Army Service Corps, part of the reinforcements, in the field.*

Right: *Light relief on board a troopship on the long and tedious journey round the Cape to Natal.*

Light relief on board a troopship on the long and tedious journey round the Cape to Natal.

later he was pounced upon and stabbed eighteen times before his colleagues could drive the Zulus off.

Despite the promise offered by the heliograph, March dragged by. Pearson had no signalling equipment in Eshowe and various methods were tried to establish a means of reply, ranging from large bonfires to huge screens on the hillside and a paper hot-air balloon. At last someone managed to improvise a heliograph using a mirror reflected through a piece of lead pipe found in the church. But the renewed communication only heightened the sense of frustration as the garrison learned of the delays and changes of plan which prevented the relief column from starting out. There was one moment of light relief, however, when one of the wagons was found to contain supplies left behind by the Natal Volunteers, far in excess of their baggage allowances. A variety of choice morsels were put up for auction, and fetched many times their value in the outside world. A box of sardines worth sixpence at home went for 27 shillings, a small tin of preserved herrings for 13 shillings, a pot of jam for 24 shillings, and a 12lb ham the princely sum of £6 5s.0d. Tobacco, by now a rare and much prized luxury, was snapped up, six cigars fetching 9 shillings. There were other distractions too; on the 23rd two Zulus arrived outside the fort carrying a white flag. They were blindfolded and brought in under guard and were found to be envoys from the Zulu Royal House. They brought a message from the King suggesting that if Pearson evacuated Eshowe he would be given safe passage to the Thukela. The general opinion within the garrison was that this was a trick and the men spies, and they were promptly clapped in irons.

Yet the offer was probably genuine, for all its true significance was lost in Eshowe. In fact it was clear to both sides that the war was about to enter a new phase and King Cetshwayo was desperate to seize the diplomatic initiative. These envoys, so roughly treated, were not the first he had sent. On 1 March two messengers had crossed the Middle Drift near Kranskop and made their way to Bishop Schreuder's nearby kwaNtunjambili mission station. Schreuder had maintained a friendship with Cetshwayo despite missionary involvement in the 'cold war' of 1878 and was presumably chosen as the nearest sympathetic white man. The messengers asked that the British troops withdraw from Zululand and begin talks on a peace settlement. They were told that the British would only accept Cetshwayo's unconditional surrender to the terms of the Ultimatum. Three weeks later the messengers returned bringing with them a presentation copy of the 'laws' promulgated by Shepstone at Cetshwayo's 'coronation'. They demanded to know which laws the king had broken and why he was being punished; the Bishop was unable to enlighten them. A week later a weightier deputation including the king's most trusted ambassador, Mfunzi Mpungose, appeared on the Zulu bank at Middle Drift. They were fired upon, but improvised a white flag and were allowed to cross.

They were bound and taken to Fort Cherry, a large earthwork built to guard the crossing, and interrogated. Once more Cetshwayo asked that the fighting should cease and that a place be appointed for a peace conference. They received the same cool treatment meted out to the others, for the brutal truth was that Cetshwayo had missed his chance.

In the first fortnight after Isandlwana he was master of the field and Natal lay quaking in its bed at the nightly prospect of a Zulu raid. But by the middle of February it was clear that there was to be no large-scale Zulu incursion. The British put this down to the flooded state of the Thukela and Mzinyathi, but in fact the Zulu army had been as shocked by Isandlwana as the British. By his inability to keep his troops in the field and by his unwillingness to cross into Natal, Cetshwayo had proved incapable of exploiting his position of strength. Early in March the king had summoned his *izikhulu*, and they had decided on a renewed joint diplomatic and military offensive. The warriors had licked their wounds and the *amabutho* were again mustering at the *amakhanda* on Mahlabathini plain. But their threat was greatly diminished since Chelmsford, too, had regrouped. Heavily reinforced and supported by Frere, whose reputation had been severely embarrassed by the defeat at Isandlwana, Chelmsford was not prepared to negotiate until he was master of the field. The British terms were simple; Cetshwayo must accept the conditions outlined in the Ultimatum. If he did not he would be made to do so by force. Already the new phase of fighting was under way; on the same day as Mfunzi's party arrived at Middle Drift, a battle was taking place in the north, and within a week two more battles would swing the war decisively in Britain's favour.

That first fortnight after Isandlwana must have been a nightmare for Chelmsford. Apart from the remains of the Centre Column, nervously shut up in the cramped and unsanitary new fort at Rorke's Drift, the border was wide open between Fort Pearson and Wood's column in the north. There was nothing to stop a Zulu invasion except a few border police, a handful of forts, and the scattered civilian laagers. The General's master plan had been smashed and there was little he could do except tell his remaining columns they were on their own, and try to recoup his losses from somewhere. From Durban he had sent a terse message informing the Home Government of the news, and asking for reinforcements. There was no telegraphic link between South Africa and London and it was 11 February before the dispatch reached Disraeli's cabinet. When it did so, it caused uproar. Disraeli, deeply involved with the Afghan War and the prospect of conflict with Russia, had left the Zulu crisis to Hicks Beach in the Colonial Office. Now came news that Frere, acting on his own initiative, had not only provoked an unwanted war, but, with scarcely a pause, had handed Britain one of its worst military disasters in years. The story of Isandlwana, suitably dramatized, was served up in the newspapers and the

Below: A very unusual photograph of the Border Guard at Thring's Post – lined-up by companies, with skirmishers to the front. Note the fort on the horizon, typical of the Natal border posts.

great British middle classes were very nearly put off their breakfast. Disraeli, although suffering from gout, was seen to run from Downing Street to Horse Guards to escape reporters, and Sir Stafford Northcote was beset by a mob clamoring for news. Later the cabinet would have its revenge and Frere would be censured and his policies renounced, but in the meantime there was no question of accepting defeat. The barbarous and savage Zulus depicted in the Press would have to be put in their place and Britain's honour restored. Chelmsford would be sent an embarrassment of military riches. No less than four Major-Generals were dispatched to fill places on his staff, together with five infantry battalions from Britain and one from Ceylon, two regiments of regular cavalry, two batteries of artillery, detachments from the Engineers, Army Service Corps, Commissariat and Transport Department, medical facilities, and even nine veterinary surgeons. From late February a stream of laden transports set sail from Victoria Docks, Woolwich, Portsmouth and Southampton. The first to arrive in Durban was HMS *Shah* on 6 March. *Shah* had been in port at St. Helena when the news reached there, and the garrison on the island, a company of the 88th Regiment and 8/7 Battery, RA was promptly taken aboard for the front. *Shah* also landed 400 of its own ship's complement as a Naval Brigade. In all, by the time the last ships had arrived in mid-April, Chelmsford would have received 418 officers, 9,996 men, 1,868 horses and 238 wagons as reinforcements.

In the meantime, while he waited for them to arrive he made what he could of the troops to hand. The old 3rd Regiment, NNC had been disbanded and Chelmsford drafted its European NCOs into a mounted unit. The five battalions of the 1st and 2nd NNC were reorganized into independent battalions and given a higher percentage of fire arms. Scraping the barrel of Colonial manpower, Chelmsford mustered a further black unit from southern Natal and began to put pressure on John Dunn. Dunn, it will be remembered, had moved out of his territory in southern Zululand with his followers on the eve of the invasion. He had been allocated a reserve in Natal and was keen to remain neutral. But when Chelmsford was finally able to mount his relief column to extricate Pearson, he would have to march through Dunn's territory, and Dunn's services would be invaluable. Dunn's position was impossible in any case, since he was already compromised in the eyes of the Zulus, and Colonial society would never forgive him for having adopted the lifestyle of an *isikhulu*. Since it seemed inevitable that the British would win the war eventually, Dunn's best chance of returning to his old position was to side with his countrymen: when at last Chelmsford crossed the Thukela on his way to Eshowe, he would take with him 'Dunn's Scouts', the white Chief himself and 240 of his followers, mostly armed with rifles. At the same time Chelmsford began an acrimonious correspondence with the Lieutenant-Governor, Sir Henry Bulwer. Chelmsford wanted the existing Border Guards and Levies to be more firmly under his control and to cross into Zululand, if necessary, like the NNC. But the terms under which the levies and many of the Volunteers had been raised, specified that they were to be used in defence of Natal soil only. Bulwer was firmly opposed to their joining any invasion, just as he was opposed to raids across the border. Chelmsford was quite prepared to use

Left: Major Black returns the lost Queen's Colour of the 1/24th to Colonel Glyn at Helpmekaar.

Below: Mule-drawn ammunition wagons at Fort Pearson, part of the build-up for the Eshowe Relief Column.

duplicity to achieve his ends, apparently submitting to Bulwer's protestations while secretly ordering the small garrisons along the border to make diversionary demonstrations as he prepared to go on to the offensive again. Bulwer was not told of these plans until it was too late to stop them; when he found out, his rift with Chelmsford was complete.

Minor incidents along the border were nothing new. Although there had been no major invasion, the first fortnight after Isandlwana had seen a number of minor incursions. Small parties of Zulus, back in their homesteads following the dispersal of the army, crossed the rivers and raided African homes on the Natal bank. Typical of this skirmishing was a raid early in March, when seven warriors, wearing greatcoats taken at Isandlwana, slipped across the Mzinyathi downstream from Fugitive's Drift, and captured several women and cattle, shooting in the thigh one man who tried to stop them. They had retired back across the river before the Border Guard could catch them. The British had attempted to counter these raids by forward patrolling of their own. The garrison cooped-up at Rorke's Drift sent out several patrols which burnt Zulu *imizi* and, on one occasion, shot two *izangoma* who had been attempting to bring down the wrath of the spirits from the opposite bank. Occasionally these patrols had a significant success; as early as 4 February Major Black of the 24th led a patrol to the Fugitive's Drift. The area was still littered with debris and the bodies of the dead.

Melvill and Coghill were found by the track where they had turned to stand, and stones were piled over them in an improvised burial. The level of the Mzinyathi had dropped and one of the patrol noticed among the wreckage beached in the shallows a wooden pole sticking upright. Wading out to investigate he pulled out the Queen's Colour of the 1/24th which had been washed downstream after it had slipped from Melvill's grasp, and had caught in the rocks. It was largely intact and the patrol carried it back in triumph to Helpmekaar where it was presented to Colonel Glyn in an emotional ceremony watched by the troops. On 14 March the indefatigable Black led a further patrol, this time across Rorke's Drift and into Zululand. His intention was to visit the field of Isandlwana, to discover the state of the dead and whether anything could be salvaged from the camp. Many of the wagons were still in place, but the guns had been dragged away, and the battlefield reeked with the overpowering stench of decomposition. On their way back to the Drift via the Batshe the patrol was fired upon by local Zulus who had hastily mustered to harass it. Black informed Chelmsford that a major expedition to bury the dead was inadvisable for the time being.

Throughout March Chelmsford collected his reinforcements at Fort Pearson, in readiness for an attempt to relieve Eshowe. It proved a troublesome business; the first invasion had stretched his transport facilities to the full and it was difficult to accumulate

new wagons. The weather was unpredictable, bright sunshine alternating with the usual rain. The river rose and fell, and the tracks turned to mud. On one occasion the hawser connecting the pont to the Zulu bank snapped. The delays were as frustrating to Chelmsford as they were to Pearson. By late March, however, there were sufficient reinforcements in place to begin the advance. Chelmsford sent orders to his border commanders to make incursions in force. On the 25th Major Twentyman, 4th Foot, in command of the Middle Drift sector, moved his Guards and levies down from Fort Cherry to the drift where they built a raft. The fluctuating level of the river frustrated their plans for a few days, but on 2 April a small party crossed into Zululand and destroyed several homesteads. At the lower Drift Captain Lucas also marched his Guard down to the drift, intimidating the Zulus opposite who fled into the hills. At Rorke's Drift Black led an extended patrol past Isandlwana and back via Fugitive's Drift. In the north Colonel Wood mounted the most serious expedition, an attack on the abaQulusi stronghold of Hlobane, which was to have serious consequences.

In heavy rain on the 27th Chelmsford ferried his troops across to Fort Tenedos and on the morning of the 28th he began his advance. His force consisted of

the 57th and 91st Regiments, six companies of the 3/60th Rifles, five companies of the 99th, two companies of the Buffs and a Naval Brigade contingent which included two heavy 24-pounder rocket tubes, two 9-pounder guns and the two Gatlings. In addition there were two NNC battalions – the newly designated 4th and 5th – and a force of Natal Volunteers and Mounted Infantry; a total of 3,390 whites and 2,280 blacks. Ammunition and supplies were carried in 122 wagons and carts, but no tents were taken and the troops faced uncomfortable nights sleeping in the mud. The column moved off in two divisions, taking a different route from Pearson's to avoid the more dangerous

hills. After his experience at Isandlwana Chelmsford was taking no chances; each night the wagons were drawn into a square laager and a deep shelter trench was dug around them with the earth piled up inside to form a parapet. Progress was slow; the streams and rivers were full and the roads were soon ruined by the traffic. However, on the night of 1 April the column selected a position on a low ridge near the ruins of the Gingindlovu *ikhanda*, which Pearson's men had burnt exactly ten weeks earlier. At Chelmsford's request Dunn rode out to scout and returned with the information that there appeared to be Zulu concentrations some miles distant. The camp was entrenched in the usual way, and that night a heavy thunderstorm flooded the trench. The troops spent a tense and miserable night huddled under the wagons.

The next morning, 2 April broke fine and clear, though a mist hung in the valley of the River Nyezane, more than a thousand yards away. The area round the laager was largely free of significant terrain features. A low hill, Umisi, was a mile off to the left and there were a few shallow dongas running down to the river, but for the most part the country was gently undulating and covered in tall, wet, green grass. The British troops stood-to, lining the parapet in the gap between it and the wagons. The perimeter was manned by the regular infantry, while the Naval Brigade, with their guns and Gatlings, held the corners. The NNC were posted out of harm's way in the centre of the square. As the mist lifted, two long columns of Zulus could be seen moving down towards the Nyezane.

It will be remembered that the Zulu strategy had been to invest Eshowe and prepare to attack the relief column in the open. The Zulu force, commanded by Somopho kaZikhala, had heard of Chelmsford's approach and moved forward to the Nyezane hills the day before. It was about 12,000 strong and comprised local sections of the uThulwana, uMbonambi, Khandempemvu,uVe and iNgobamakhosi amabutho.

Many of these men had fought at Isandlwana, including Prince Dabulamanzi kaMpande who led the right wing, and Sigcewelegcwele kaMhlekehleke who led the iNgobamakhosi. When these men had reported for duty at the muster a couple of weeks before, they had been told to stay in their home areas and defend them. They had been living in the local amakhanda and that morning had been joined by the warriors in the temporary camps about Eshowe. Their attack was not well co-ordinated, however, because their scouts had had no time to assess the British strength. The Zulus simply crossed the river in two long columns, then deployed to skirmishing order and converged on the square.

The British troops, watching their approach, were impressed by the order and precision of their attack, as the horns swept past the sides of the laager and headed for the rear face. At about a thousand yards Chelmsford gave permission for one of the Gatlings to open up and a short burst chopped straight through the Zulu line. The warriors dived into the long grass and opened a heavy fire. At 400 yards the troops replied with crashing volleys, rippling down the line by sections to prevent the smoke obscuring the view. As the Zulu advance pressed forward, the warriors bobbing up and down as they ran through the grass,

Below: The Battle of Gingindlovu, 6.00 a.m. to 7.30 a.m., 2 April 1879. The exact dispositions of the Zulu regiments are not known.

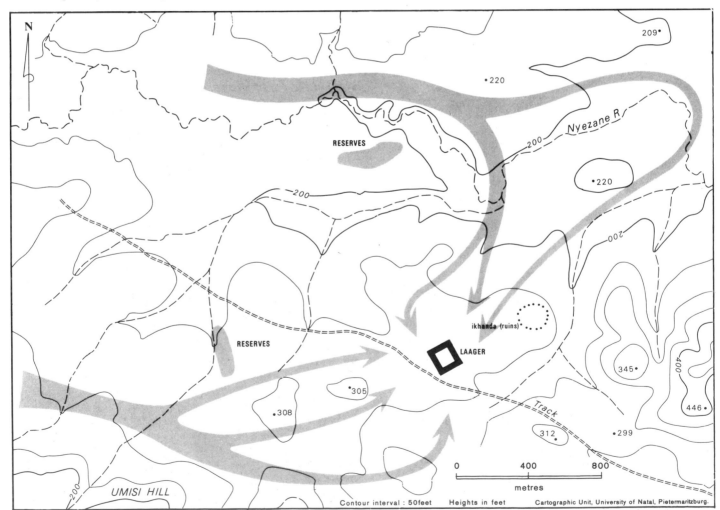

Right: Commodore Richards who commanded HMS Boadicea's Naval Brigade at Gingindlovu.

Far right: Chief Somopho kaZikhala, the Zulu commander-in-chief at Gingindlovu.

Below left: Lieutenant-Colonel Francis Northey, 60th Rifles, killed at Gingindlovu.

Below right: Major Percy Barrow, 19th Hussars, commanded Pearson's mounted troops during the advance on Eshowe, and subsequently during the relief expedition and at Gingindlovu. He later took part in the hunt for the king.

the firing became general around the laager. John Dunn, standing on a wagon and carefully picking off his targets, noticed that many of the volleys were striking the ground way beyond their targets, since the men still had their long-range sights up. He told Chelmsford, and the men immediately adjusted them. Generally, Dunn, the great hunter and professional marksman, was not impressed with the soldiers' shooting. These were not the 'old steady shots' of the 24th, but inexperienced men fresh out from Britain. Now and then a man would lose his composure and fire off shots wildly until a smart rap from his officer's stick pulled him together. Yet the average expenditure of shots was still surprisingly low – one officer of the 60th, who held the front of the square, commented that his men fired about seven rounds apiece – but its effect was deadly. In one or two places the Zulus ran to within twenty yards of the square, but their rushes were all cut down. For the most part their charges petered out on the edge of the cover where they opened up a heavy fire. Lieutenant-Colonel Northey, commanding the 60th, was standing near a Gatling shouting commands when a bullet struck him in the shoulder. He was helped to the hospital wagon where his wound was dressed, but returned to the fight; a few moments later he collapsed and died shortly after.

Left: Members of HMS Boadicea's Naval Brigade, with a Gatling gun.

Below: The height of the battle of Gingindlovu, with the 91st Highlanders manning the south face of the laager (right). Note the wagon-drivers firing from their wagons over the heads of the troops.

Above: The mounted pursuit after Gingindlovu. The Mounted Infantry who, unlike the Volunteers, were armed with sabres, cut down fleeing Zulus.

As soon as the Zulu attacks faltered Chelmsford ordered out the cavalry. Led by Major Percy Barrow, who had commanded them under Pearson until they were sent back to the Thukela, the Mounted Infantry and Volunteers streamed out, riding down the warriors who were beginning to retreat towards the Nyezane. The British pursuit was ruthless, the mounted men sabreing or shooting any exhausted warriors who crossed their path. Now and then one would turn and stand and a brief mêlée ensued, but their height gave the cavalry an advantage, and the Zulus were invariably killed. At the river, the high water slowed the warriors and the mounted men cut them down wherever they bunched. The NNC were ordered out and followed in the cavalry's wake, flushing out any warriors hiding in the grass or lying wounded along the banks of the streams and dongas which they had been unable to cross. After Isandlwana, there was no hope of mercy.

The attack had lasted about an hour and a half and ended in a complete Zulu rout. About five hundred dead warriors were counted in front of the square, and hundreds more were along the line of retreat. In all, their losses totalled about 1,100 men. Chelmsford's losses were 2 officers and 11 men killed, and 4 officers and 44 men wounded. The garrison at Eshowe, fifteen miles away, had watched the fight through field glasses, and signalled their congratulations. Chelmsford, the spectre of Isandlwana partially erased, was content to spend the day mopping-up and tending his wounded. The Zulu bodies were left to rot where they lay.

Right: Zulu skeletons on the field of Gingindlovu. Both shields visible are black with white spots, suggesting the dead are from one of the younger amabutho.

Overleaf: The success of Zulu battlefield tactics depended on their ability to come to close quarters with their enemy; the laager, or barricaded circle of wagons, was a very effective countermeasure perfected by the Boers, and used successfully by the British at Khambula and Gingindlovu.

Left: Zulu prisoners, apparently taken after Gingindlovu, guarded by troops, probably the Buffs.

Left: The site of Chelmsford's temporary earthwork at Gingindlovu did not long survive, but the trench is just visible on this photograph taken in late 1879; the white cross is Northey's grave.

Left: Battlefield debris from Gingindlovu; Martini-Henry bullets (top right) and cartridge cases, a Snider bullet, and musket and shrapnel balls. Digging for relics on Zulu War battle sites is now strictly illegal.

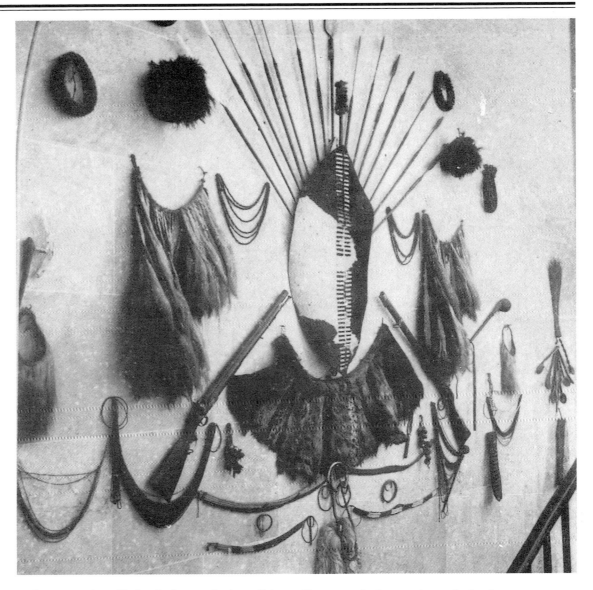

Next morning Chelmsford organized a flying column and pushed on to Eshowe. Pearson rode out to meet him and the column, led by the pipes of the 91st Highlanders, marched past the small cemetery where the victims of disease lay buried and, to the cheers of the garrison, entered the fort. That night the price of tobacco dropped to rock bottom, as the relievers made free with their supplies. The men wandered the Fort, swapping stories. The column had brought a wagonload of mail and the garrison caught up with their accumulated letters from home.

Chelmsford had decided not to defend Eshowe and the next morning he began to evacuate it, ferrying the garrison back down to Fort Pearson. By the 6th the post, which had been so crowded for nearly three months, was empty, apart from the 28 dead in the little cemetery. As a final gesture, Chelmsford mounted a raid early on the morning of the 4th, which destroyed *Ezulweni*, 'The Heavens', the principal homestead of Prince Dabulamanzi, about eight miles from Eshowe. Following their defeat at Gingindlovu, the Zulus were in no mood to close when the Volunteers and Native Horse put the huts to the torch, but kept up an angry fire from the crest of an overlooking hill. No sooner had the last of the troops gone than the Zulus vented their frustration on the fort, and burnt KwaMondi to the ground.

Only one incident marred Chelmsford's retreat to the Thukela. After a stiflingly hot day on the 4th, when the troops suffered heavily from exhaustion and lack of water, a false alarm took place at one of the bivouacs. At about 3 am a picket of the 91st fired a warning shot at what he thought was a party of Zulus. The camp stood to and the 60th, manning one side of the square, saw figures rushing towards them. They opened fire with a volley at close range which bowled several men over. They turned out to be members of the 60th's own advanced picket and several of Dunn's Scouts who, alarmed by the first shot, had been running back to the safety of the laager. Three men were killed and eleven wounded. It was to be the first of many such alarms and a sharp reminder that, despite their recent defeat, the Zulus were still held in marked dread by their opponents.

Above: Relief at last; Chelmsford's flying column marches past the graveyard and into Eshowe.

Left: The ruins of Eshowe, destroyed by the Zulus after the British evacuation; photograph probably taken during the Second Invasion.

Above: *Chelmsford's last act of defiance at Eshowe; burning Prince Dabulamanzi's homestead. Note the NNH troopers, centre.*

Right: *Mr McKenzie, the Special Correspondent of The Standard, one of a host of war correspondents sent out with the reinforcements. McKenzie was present at Gingindlovu, and apparently took part in the pursuit.*

TURNING-POINT

The movements of the Left Flank Column. The nature of Zulu opposition, and early skirmishes. Wood establishes his base at Khambula. Raids by Mbilini and the abaQulusi. The defection of Prince Hamu; the attack on the 80th convoy at **Ntombe River***. Woods resolves to attack the Zulu strongholds; The Battle of* **Hlobane***. The main Zulu* impi *attacks* **Khambula** *and is severely defeated. The death of Mbilini.*

Of Chelmsford's original three columns, it was acknowledged from the first that No. 4, Colonel Evelyn Wood's Left Column, would have to act on its own initiative to a greater degree than the others. It would be advancing through the heart of the disputed territory, a long way from the central control of either Natal, the Transvaal or Zululand, and the local inhabitants, both black and white, were notorious for their independent and self-serving attitude. Wood's column was by no means a weak one, consisting as it did of two infantry battalions – the 1/13th and 90th Light Infantry – an artillery battery (11/7 RA, less one section; four 7-pounder guns and two rocket troughs), six troops of mounted volunteers, and two battalions of locally recruited Zulus, known as Wood's Irregulars. Wood himself was a thorough and energetic officer whose slightly vain personality and reputation for being accident-prone – he was once trampled on by a giraffe – concealed a rare flair for Colonial warfare. His cavalry were under the command of Lieutenant-Colonel Redvers Buller, a veteran of China and Asante, who had worked with irregular troops on the Cape Frontier and against Sekhukhune and who, unlike most regular officers, was quick to appreciate the value of local men fighting in their own environment. Buller was tough, indefatigable and possessed of the sort of bulldog courage that earned the devotion of his men. The irregulars themselves – the Frontier Light Horse and Baker's Horse – were not part of the Natal Volunteer system, but had been raised for the war against the Xhosa on the Cape Frontier. The FLH had started out in neat buff cord uniforms with a black trim and, apparently, black dress uniforms, but their well-deserved reputation for hard riding had taken its toll and most of the men were reduced to wearing civilian clothes with a red rag twisted around their wide-brimmed hats. Considerable efforts had been made to persuade local Boers to turn out to support the British, but most of the border farmers were die-hard

Left: Brevet Colonel Henry Evelyn Wood, VC, commander of the Left Flank Column, in the uniform he wore throughout the war.

Right: Commandant Piet Uys (centre) and his sons. Uys was the only Boer of note to join the British forces, and was killed at Hlobane.

Below: Lieutenant-Colonel Redvers Buller, Wood's dynamic commander of cavalry.

republicans who relished the prospect of their two worst enemies, the British and the Zulus, fighting it out. Only one Boer leader of note, Piet Uys, took to the field with his sons and supporters. Uys's family were noted Zulu-fighters – they had been among the Trekker groups fighting Dingane in 1838 – and Uys's farm lay in the disputed territory.

Although Wood was expected to advance towards Ulundi in support of Chelmsford's centre column, it was recognized that he would have to expend considerable energy pacifying the country as he did so. The border town of Utrecht, which served as his base depot, would need to be protected as would the vulnerable hamlet of German Lutheran settlers at Luneburg, thirty miles away to the north-west. During the boundary dispute, Cetshwayo had repeatedly stated his claim to the Luneburg area and it was an obvious target for loyalist Zulu raiders. Beyond Luneburg, at Derby in the Transvaal, Colonel Hugh Rowland's column was stationed. Rowlands's forces consisted of the 80th Regiment, seven small corps of mounted volunteers raised in the Cape or Transvaal, and a force of Swazi levies, traditional rivals of the Zulu in that area. At Wood's instruction, Rowlands had sent a detachment of his troops to Luneburg to build and garrison a fort there.

The reason for Luneburg's vulnerability was that it lay close to the confluence of the Phongolo and Ntombe Rivers, both strongholds of predatory local chiefs, and only fifty miles north of the Hlobane complex, the refuge of the abaQulusi. The Ntombe valley, particularly, was scarred with dongas and the hills on each side were pitted with shallow caves, and it was the retreat of two noted marauders. Manyanyoba kaMaqondo held authority in the name of Cetshwayo over the descendants of various tribes broken by Shaka and resettled in the area. He lived near the Ntombe headwaters and regularly raided both Boers and Swazi alike for their cattle. Further down the valley in caves along the Tafelberg mountain, overlooking Myer's Drift on the Ntombe, lived the famous Mbilini kaMswati, whose depredations had been one of the causes of the war. Mbilini had close links with the abaQulusi, the local royal section who had been ordered by the king to harass Wood's advance and, indeed, had built another homestead on the inaccessible terraces on the southern slopes of the abaQulusi stronghold, Hlobane.

When in early January 1879, therefore, Wood moved forward from Utrecht to Bemba's Kop, the Zulu boundary on the Ntombe River, he expected considerable difficulty from Manyanyoba, Mbilini, and the abaQulusi. He was not to be disappointed. No sooner had he crossed into Zululand than he became involved in a series of skirmishes with the abaQulusi. For the most part these amounted to little more than cattle raids, but on the night of 21 January while Wood was establishing his first camp in Zululand, Fort Thinta, Buller's patrols ran into large Zulu concentrations on the Zungwini mountain. Zungwini was the western anchor of a chain of flat-topped mountain strongholds, linked by interconnecting *neks*, which extended eastwards for twenty miles. Beyond Zungwini lay Ntendeka, a triangular plateau attached at its tip to the famous Hlobane mountain, and behind Hlobane, Ityenka. In times of stress it was the

Left: This rare photograph is thought to show an NCO of the Frontier Light Horse, in their original braided uniform. Photograph taken at King William's Town, Cape Frontier, c.1877.

Below: The exterior of the military laager at Utrecht, Wood's main supply depot.

Above: A camp scene in Wood's Column: the Commissariat wagons of the 90th Light Infantry.

abaQulusi habit to drive their cattle on to the summits of these mountains and block the access paths with stone defences. Hlobane, some 3.5 miles long and 1.5 miles wide, the windy heights protected by an almost unbroken line of cliffs, was most ideally suited to the purpose.

When Wood heard that the abaQulusi were massing on Zungwini he decided to attack them at once. He divided his force into three sections which marched out to surround Zungwini during the night. Shortly after dawn on the 22nd they ascended the mountain unopposed. The attack seems to have taken the Zulus by surprise since they abandoned a herd of cattle on the summit with a minimum of skirmishing. Once up on the mountain, however, Wood was treated to the rather more sinister spectacle of about 4,000 abaQulusi drilling in perfect order on the opposite crest of Hlobane. Wood brought his men safely down Zungwini and the following day was spent resting, but on the 24th he advanced towards Hlobane. There was a sharp skirmish to the north of the mountain during the course of which a messenger arrived with a dispatch from Lord Chelmsford. It contained the stunning news of Isandlwana and offered the same comforting advice that had been sent to Pearson; Wood was unsupported, could expect a major attack at any time and should act as he saw fit. Wood broke of the engagement and retired to Fort Thinta to consider his position.

Under the changed circumstances the camp at Fort Thinta was rather too exposed. It was too close to the Hlobane complex and it left an easy route open for a counter-strike at Utrecht. Wood therefore cast about for a more suitable site and found one at Khambula hill, a narrow ridge extending south-east from a hill known as Ngaba kaHawane, 'Hawane's stronghold', a place of refuge during Shaka's wars. Khambula was a few miles north of Fort Thinta and stood squarely between Hlobane and Utrecht. It was also closer to Rowlands's outpost at Luneburg and the dangerous Ntombe valley. By the end of the month Wood had built himself a secure new camp on the crest of the ridge, a combined redoubt and wagon-laager. Thus secure, there was little more he could do than aggressively raid the Qulusi in an attempt to convince them that the British were by no means disheartened by Isandlwana. On 1 February Buller and his men pushed out as far as the ebaQulusini *ikhanda* itself near Hlobane. Most of the abaQulusi lived in family homesteads across the region, but the *ikhanda*, consisting of about 250 huts, still served as a centre of royal authority and was a rallying point. Buller burnt it without any opposition.

In the Ntombe valley, meanwhile, there had been a number of skirmishes between Manyanyoba and the Luneburg garrison. Most of these had been minor, but early in February Manyanyoba called upon Mbilini to support him in a major raid. No doubt encouraged by news of Isandlwana and angered by the destruction of ebaQulusini, the two chiefs mustered a force of 1,500 men from among their own supporters and the abaQulusi. On the night of 10/11 February they slipped into the Ntombe valley and silently moved on the white farms in the area. For the most part the farmers themselves were in the Luneburg laager or elsewhere, but their black farmworkers, many of them *kholwa*, or Christian Africans, were still on the premises. The Zulus went from farm to farm killing six men, twenty-eight women, and twenty-five children, setting fire to farm buildings and rounding-up cattle. Personal scores were being paid off, since Boer farmers friendly to the raiders were left

Left: Camp scenes in Wood's Column: above, the field bakery, below, the field butchery.

Right: 'Lizzie', the pet zebra of the 1/13th Light Infantry.

untouched, while the *kholwa* were particularly despised by the Zulus for their support of white land-claims around Luneburg. As soon as the Luneburg garrison heard of the raid patrols were sent out to intercept the Zulus and a party of 300 warriors was caught trying to cross the Ntombe. Fifteen were killed, but the rest made good their escape to their caves. Wood immediately planned a retaliatory raid and on 15 February Buller led an attack on Manyanyoba's stronghold. The forces at his disposal were small – just one gun, fifty-four white volunteers and 500 blacks – but they succeeded in shelling the Chief's personal homestead, burning several others and capturing a herd of cattle. As soon as they realized they were under attack, however, the Zulus fled up to the caves at the base of the hills and it proved impossible to dislodge them. Colonel Rowlands, meanwhile, had experienced the same sense of frustration. On the 15th he had attacked a Qulusi stronghold at Talaku mountain and succeeded in destroying a number of homesteads, but not in ejecting the defenders. On the 20th he attacked Makateeskop, a cattle-outpost guarded by a company of the iNgobamakhosi. Rowlands drove the warriors off with the loss of a quarter of their men killed, but no sooner had he retired than the Qulusi re-occupied the hill.

Against this background of constant skirmishing Wood scored a notable diplomatic success. The British were well aware of the divisions within the Zulu kingdom, and from the first it had been Chelmsford's intention to precipitate the break up of the state by persuading important *izikhulu* to surrender. Wild reports that the Chiefs were just waiting for their chance to throw off Cetshwayo's despotism and return to their pre-Shakan independence proved unfounded, but as early as November 1878 Prince Hamu kaNzibe had sent secret messages to Wood to assure him of his friendly disposition. Hamu was ripe for defection. He had never fully accepted Cetshwayo's right to the throne, and he ruled his territory, to the east of Wood's advance, with a considerable degree of autonomy. He was heavily involved in private trading with whites and was addicted to European liquor. The king had recognized his dubious loyalty and when Hamu, already under a cloud since the incident at the First Fruits ceremony the year before, attended the meeting of the *ibandla* to consider the Ultimatum, Cetshwayo had him detained. He still managed to send secret messages to the British, however, and as he advanced through Zulu territory Wood received the surrender of a number of lesser *izinduna*. The invasion had scarcely begun when Bemba, an *induna* of the important Mdlalose clan, defected with 80 of his followers, and on 20 January Thinta, also a senior member of the Mdlalose, surrendered. Wood had high hopes that he might persuade the whole clan to come over, but attacks by Mdlalose royalists supported by abaQulusi intimidated the waverers. Nevertheless, in the middle of February Hamu himself slipped away from Ulundi and fled to Swaziland where he begged Wood to offer him asylum. On 10 March he was brought into

Khambula and his adherents followed him during the next few days, until 1,300 of them surrendered in all. The fighting men, some of them members of the uThulwana *ibutho*, were drafted into Wood's Irregulars. Chelmsford must have been greatly heartened by this *coup*, offering as it did the prospect of a Zulu collapse. Wood was even able to report that the aggressive Manyanyoba was sending out feelers for peace. Yet any hopes of a large-scale surrender were dashed almost immediately. Manyanyoba was playing a double game, hedging his bets against the changing fortunes of war; on 12 March the Ntombe valley witnessed the most serious British reverse in the area to date.

Wood's column had benefited from the organizational changes following on from Isandlwana. He had been allocated a squadron of Mounted Infantry under Lieutenant-Colonel Russell, the Edendale Contingent of the NNH and two volunteer units from the Transvaal, Raaf's Transvaal Rangers and the Border Horse. The British defeat had raised republican sentiment in Pretoria and Rowlands was dispatched to keep an eye on the situation. His column was placed under Wood's command, who brought the 80th down to his camp at Khambula, leaving a detachment under Major Charles Tucker to garrison Luneburg. This garrison was provisioned by convoys setting out periodically from Rowlands's old base at Derby. One such column set out in the first week of March and experienced appalling difficulties. The weather was at its worst and the teeming rain caused most of the rivers to burst their banks and the tracks to turn to mud. Tucker, anxious for its safety, ordered it to reach Luneburg by the 6th, but to his surprise the escort misinterpreted his orders and marched in having abandoned the wagons on the road. The next morning Tucker sent out a company of the 80th under Captain

Left: A sketch by W. Fairlie of Redvers Buller in the practical civilian dress he wore as Wood's commander of Volunteer cavalry.

Right: Farriers shoeing horses for Buller's cavalry. This picture gives a good impression of the appearance of his men in the field.

Below: A water-colour by Orlando Norie of the 1/13th on the march, flanked by scouts from the Natal Native Horse.

Below right: Prince Hamu kaNzibe on his way to Utrecht after his surrender to Colonel Wood. The artist had drawn him holding a gin bottle, reflecting his addiction to European liquor.

Above: *A group of Swazi warriors and their officer. The Swazis were traditional enemies of the Zulu and numbers fought with Wood's Column during the later stages of the war. They seem to have worn their full regalia into battle.*

Left: *Commandant Raaf (centre), one of the Volunteer officers who fought with Wood's Column. The man standing left appears to be an officer of the Frontier Light Horse. Volunteer units raised along the Transvaal border had a decidedly piratical look.*

Above: A convoy of the 80th Regiment on the Zulu border.

David Moriarty with equipment to make a raft. Moriarty found the convoy spread over several miles of road. By the 9th he had managed to gather it together and had reached the northern bank of the Ntombe at Myer's Drift, but the swollen state of the river made it impossible to get more than a couple of wagons across. Tucker rode the six miles from Luneburg and expressed his concern at the weakness of the laager. Moriarty protested that it was impossible to build a better one. On the north side of the river the wagons were arranged in an inverted 'V' with the legs resting on the bank. The wagons were not run closely together, however, and there was a gap between each one. At one point the river had risen and flooded half of the laager; it had then dropped leaving the ends of the laager several yards from the bank. Tucker urged Moriarty to cross the river as soon as possible and rode back to Luneburg. The plight of the escort was miserable as they had been unable to dry their clothes for several days and the laager was a sea of mud. Perhaps this, or concern from problems of crossing the river, made Moriarty neglect his security.

He seemed unconcerned about defensive arrangements, despite the fact that Mbilini's stronghold, the Tafelberg, overlooked the drift only a few miles away, and someone claimed to have recognized the Chief himself among a group of peaceful Zulus who visited the laager on the 11th. That

night saw Moriarty – his tent pitched at the apex of the 'V', outside the laager – and 71 men on the north bank, and Lieutenant H.H.Harward, Sergeant Anthony Booth and 34 men on the south bank.

At about 3.30 on the morning of the 12th, as it was beginning to rain and a mist was rising from the river, a shot rang out on the north bank. Harward, across the river, heard it, stood his men to and sent a messenger to ask Moriarty for instructions. Moriarty assured him it was a false alarm and went back to sleep. At about 5 am, just as it was getting light, the sentry on the south bank saw a body of warriors advancing towards the laager on the other side. He fired a warning shot and the troops began to tumble out of their tents, to be greeted by a volley at close range from the Zulus who then threw down their rifles and rushed in with their spears. The *impi* was about 800 strong and led by Mbilini in person, together with a number of Manyanyoba's sons. Some of the soldiers had left their accoutrements on after the first alarm, but many were half-dressed, and some naked. When they rushed out of the tents they found the Zulus right in among them. Moriarty had just come out of his tent when a warrior stabbed him in the back. He shot several warriors with his revolver and turned to climb over the disselboom of a wagon and into the laager. He was shot in the chest and fell to the ground shouting, 'I am done. Fire away boys!'

On the south bank Harward's party, who had remained alert, had a few moments' grace and the men were out of their tents before a party of about 200 warriors plunged into the river and began to cross. Sergeant Booth was standing by a wagon firing his rifle when he heard Harward order the men to fire away; when he looked again Harward had mounted his horse and was riding off. Booth managed to collect Lance-Corporal Burgess and seven men and formed a tiny rallying-square. With them he tried to cover the retreat of the rest of Harward's party who had disappeared after their officer and those few who had managed to cross from the north bank. Keeping up a steady fire, Booth retreated to a deserted farm house about three miles away towards Luneburg. At that point the Zulus gave up the pursuit and returned to the drift to flush out survivors and plunder the wagons of ammunition, flour and mealies.

Harward reached Luneburg at about 6.30 and immediately roused out Tucker. The Major gathered 150 mounted men and rode at once for the drift, passing Booth along the way. By the time he arrived the Zulus were retreating once more to the Ntombe caves. One soldier of the 80th and an African wagon-driver were found sheltering beneath the river banks, but of the original escort of 106 men, 62 were dead, together with 17 civilian drivers. Their bodies lay stripped and disembowelled in the mud amidst the debris of the camp – shredded tents, smashed and looted boxes, scattered mealies and flour, and dead pets. Tucker collected the dead and buried them in a mass grave nearby. The wagons were brought in to Luneburg at last. Only about thirty Zulu bodies were

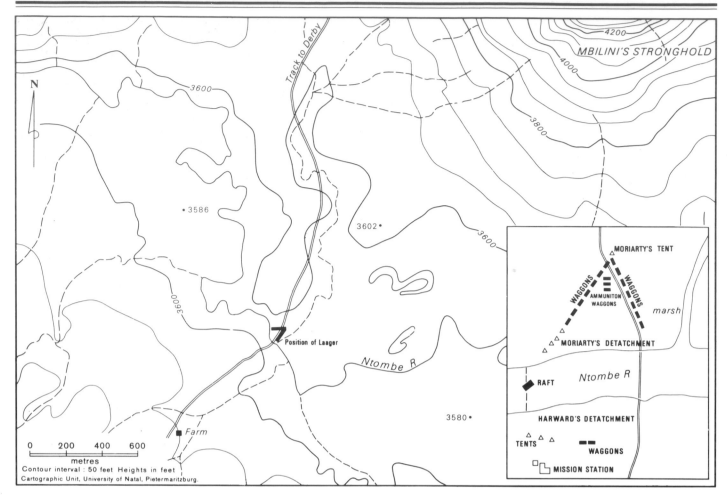

Map labels:
Track to Derby
MBILINI'S STRONGHOLD
4200
4000
3800
3600
3586
3602
3600
Position of Laager
Ntombe R
Farm
3580

0 200 400 600
metres
Contour interval : 50 feet   Heights in feet
Cartographic Unit, University of Natal, Pietermaritzburg.

Inset labels:
MORIARTY'S TENT
WAGGONS
AMMUNITON WAGGONS
WAGGONS
marsh
MORIARTY'S DETATCHMENT
RAFT
Ntombe R
HARWARD'S DETATCHMENT
TENTS
WAGGONS
MISSION STATION

Above: The attack on the 80th convoy at Ntombe River, dawn, 12 March 1879. The main map shows the position of the laager relative to the river and Mbilini's stronghold; the inset shows the respective positions of the Moriarty and Harward detachments.

Far left: Captain David Moriarty, 80th Regiment, the senior officer killed at Ntombe.

Left: Lieutenant H. H. Harward, the surviving officer of the 80th at Ntombe.

Above: Colour-Sergeant A. Booth who won the Victoria Cross for rallying survivors of the Ntombe disaster.

Left: The attack on the convoy at Ntombe. This sketch suggests something of the ferocity of the action, although the topographical detail is inexact; the river was wider.

Below: The Ntombe battlefield, 1987, photographed from Harward's position, with the Drift centre. The laager was on the flat ground opposite. The stones, right, mark the mass grave of the British dead, whilst Mbilini's stronghold was on the Tafelberg, just visible right skyline. In March 1879 the Ntombe had burst its banks and much of the foreground would have been under water.

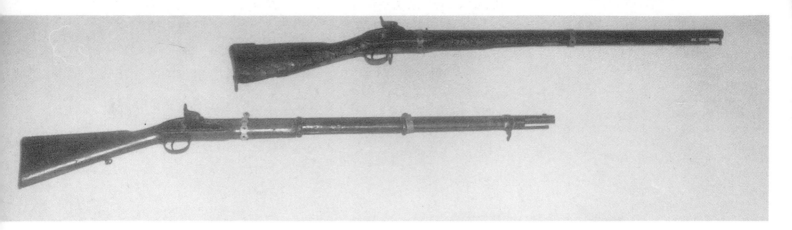

found nearby and, although more had probably been carried off together with the wounded, their losses were disproportionately light considering the extent of their victory.

In due course Booth was awarded the VC, and promoted to Colour-Sergeant. Harward was court-martialled for deserting his men in the face of the enemy. His defence pointed out that he had taken what precautions he could to alert his men during the night, and had been the only man on the south bank with a horse and thus able to raise the alarm. He was found not guilty, but the verdict was greeted with astonishment by the military hierarchy, and comments condemning his conduct were ordered to be read at the head of every regiment in the army.

The immediate effect of the Ntombe disaster was to throw the inhabitants of Luneburg into a state of panic. To restore flagging morale Buller raided the Ntombe valley a week later, but, although he destroyed a large number of homesteads, there was little fighting. In fact, Mbilini had fled the area with many of his adherents after the attack and returned to his residence at Hlobane. It was becoming increasingly clear to Wood that if he was to make an effective reply to the constant Zulu raids he would have to deprive them of their Hlobane retreat. He was given the ideal opportunity to do so by Chelmsford's message towards the end of March, asking his commanders to make diversionary attacks in support of the Eshowe relief expedition. Despite rumours from his intelligence services to the effect that the main Zulu army had once again mustered at Ulundi and that it would be sent to support Mbilini, Wood resolved to attack Hlobane.

It would not be an easy task. The smaller plateau, Ntendeka, rose about four hundred feet from the surrounding plain and, while it was steep, it was accessible, but it was connected with the main mountain, Hlobane, at only one point. The main plateau, Hlobane itself, was two hundred feet higher and ringed all round by cliffs. The summit was uninhabited, but Mbilini and the abaQulusi had a number of homesteads on inaccessible ledges on the southern side, and in times of danger would drive their cattle up through breaks in the cliff wall to graze on the table-top. As far as Wood's scouts had been able to determine there were only two practicable points of access for European troops: via Ntendeka and the

steep pass connecting it with Hlobane at the western end, and by a re-entrant at the eastern end overlooking Ityenka *nek*. Wood decided to assault the stronghold with a pincer movement, as he had done successfully at Zungwini back in January. Leaving his infantry and guns at Khambula, he set out during the night of 27 March with two parties, each composed of mounted troops and levies. One section, under the command of Buller, consisted of half a rocket battery from 11/7 RA, the Frontier Light Horse, The Transvaal Rangers, the Border Horse, Baker's Horse and Piet Uys's Boers, together with the 2nd Battalion of Wood's Irregulars. The other section under Lieutenant-Colonel Russell included the remaining rockets, the Mounted Infantry, the Kaffrarian Rifles, Natal Native Horse, 1st Battalion, Wood's Irregulars and a number of Hamu's men. Buller's column was the stronger of the two and it was intended that he should bear the brunt of the fighting, ascending by the further eastern route and driving across the summit. Russell's column was to occupy Ntendeka and, if possible, climb up to Hlobane to support Buller. Any Zulus on the summit would therefore be caught between two fires. That night Russell's force bivouacked near Zungwini while Buller advanced to the far end of the mountain. With characteristic thoroughness his men lit camp fires to fool Zulu scouts, then moved much closer to the mountain and spent the night in dark silence.

The attack began before dawn. Buller's men began to climb the steep upper slopes leading to their pass, a narrow gap between the lines of cliffs. It was almost an impossible ascent; there was no path, just a jumble of boulders often six or seven feet high, many of them loose and overgrown with grass above head height. Near the summit a line of stones placed by the Zulus to block off the pass could just be seen. As the men struggled up, their horses stumbling and slipping, a sudden thunderstorm broke over their heads. In the darkness and confusion, broken only by the sudden lightning flashes, the Border Horse somehow lost their way and became detached from Buller's party. Just as the rest reached the summit the Zulus discovered them and a smatter of shots burst from the boulders at close range. Two officers and one man of the FLH were shot dead and a number of horses were killed. It was too late to turn back, however, and with a shout Buller's men at last burst over the rocky crest of the pass and on

Above: Two percussion rifles found in Mbilini's caves. Almost certainly used at Ntombe, these are typical of the sort of firearms carried by the Zulus.

Top right: J. N. Crealock's sketch of the Hlobane complex, from Zungwini. Ntendeka, the lower plateau right, with the Devil's Pass marked 'Buller's retreat', centre.

Right: A recent (1987) photograph of Buller's ascent route at Hlobane – a notch between the cliffs on the eastern side of the mountain.

Inhlobane Mountain

Buller's ascent

Buller's retreat

(blue)

(red)

Russell's ascent

the Tonquin ...t Mountain
(or Zenguin)

Page No I.

aeria

to the summit, driving the small band of Zulus before them.

Meanwhile Russell's men had climbed Ntendeka unopposed, but on close examination Russell decided that the pass up to Hlobane was impracticable for mounted men. It was no more than a steep staircase of boulders, twenty or thirty yards wide, falling away to cliffs on each side. It would be a difficult scramble for men on foot, but it would be impossible to get any sort of mounted force up. Russell accordingly halted his force at the foot of the pass and sent Lieutenant Browne with twenty men of the Mounted Infantry up the pass on foot to see if they could find Buller and acquaint him with the situation.

Colonel Wood himself had spent the night with Russell and in the morning set off along the southern slopes of the mountain intending to follow Buller. With him were his personal staff – Mr. Lloyd, his political agent, Captain the Hon. Ronald Campbell, his staff officer and Lieutenant Lysons, his orderly – an escort of eight men from the Mounted Infantry, all 90th LI, and several Zulus accompanied by none other than Prince Mtonga kaMpande, one of Cetshwayo's lesser refugee rivals. Wood had almost reached the eastern end of the mountain and had turned towards it, trying to find Buller's track, when he met the Border Horse and their commander Colonel Weatherley. Weatherley was an ex-army officer and something of an adventurer, but his experience of losing Buller in the ascent seems to have shaken him and his men. As the small party neared the jumble of fallen boulders which marked the base of the cliffs a ragged volley broke out from a group of Zulus sheltering in the caves and crevices formed by the gaps between the boulders. Mr. Lloyd was hit and Wood's horse was killed under him. The Border Horse dived for cover and Wood ordered them to clear the caves. They refused point-blank to advance. Campbell, disgusted offered to go himself and Wood sent him forward with his escort. Most of the shots seemed to be coming from one particular cave and Campbell rushed straight into the entrance followed by Lysons and Private Fowler of the 90th. As he did so a bullet struck Campbell in the head and he died instantly. Lysons and Fowler killed his assailant and drove out a couple of other Zulus who scrambled back into the crevices and away.

Lysons and the men of the 90th brought Campbell's body back to Wood. By this time Lloyd too had died and Wood was greatly affected by the loss of two of his staff to whom he was personally close. Rather than abandon the bodies to the Zulus he decided to retire a few hundred yards down the mountain and bury them despite the fact that he was now under fire from groups of Qulusi collecting all along the cliffs. While he was doing so Weatherley finally managed to prod his men into action and they started off in search of Buller's track. Mtonga's men scraped out a shallow grave with their spears and Wood was preparing to read a burial service when he realized that the small bible which he habitually carried was in the saddle-bag of his horse which had been killed further back up the hill. His

bugler, Walkinshaw of the 90th, volunteered to retrieve it and calmly walked back and searched through the saddle-bags, with Zulu bullets striking the boulders all around him. Wood read a short service over the bodies and the grave was filled in. Deciding that it was now too late to catch up with Buller, he decided to move westward and see how Russell was faring.

Buller was, indeed, safely up on the top of Hlobane by this time, and moving westwards, rounding up scattered herds of Qulusi cattle as he did so. The summit of Hlobane is gently undulating, a crazy-paving of boulders worn almost flat and smooth. In places low-lying hollows were waterlogged and marshy, and a couple of clear, shallow streams ran across the surface, cutting notches in the cliffs where they emptied over the side of the plateau. The area was grassy, but visibility was generally good and the small parties of warriors guarding the cattle were easily

Left: Buller's orderly, Trooper Brown, DCM of the Frontier Light Horse. The FLH's black uniform seems to have been favoured by NCOs, or perhaps as a dress uniform.

Top left: Captain the Hon. Ronald Campbell, Coldstream Guards, Wood's Staff Officer, killed at Hlobane.

Centre Left: Wood's orderly, Lieutenant H. Lysons, who won the VC at Hlobane.

Top right: Wood's bugler, Private Walkinshaw, 90th Light Infantry, who received the DCM for his actions at Hlobane. He is wearing his post-1881 uniform.

Right: Wood's own sketch shows him coolly reading the burial service over the bodies of Campbell and Lloyd, despite the skirmishing behind him.

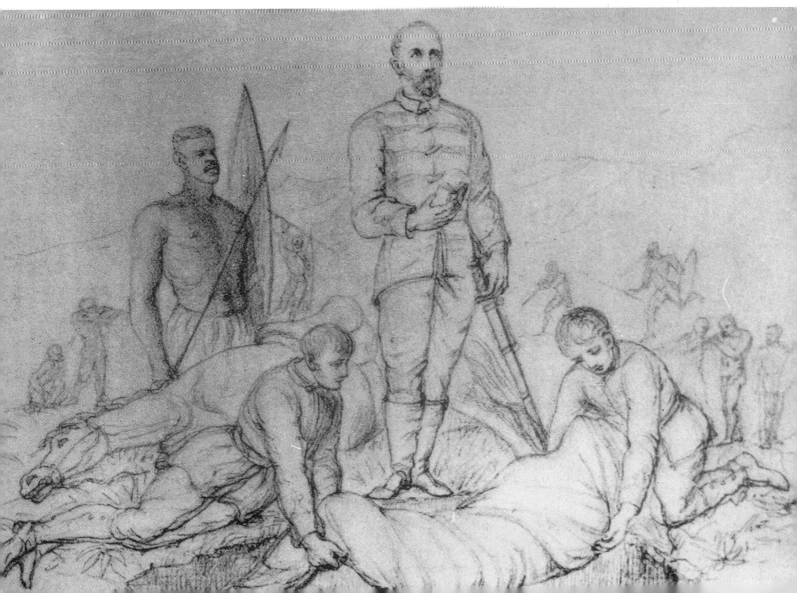

Left: Campbell and Lloyd's grave, 1989, and behind it the cliffs where they were killed.

dispersed. About midway along the mountain at its narrowest point, was a very low rise whose boulders afforded some slight cover, and here Buller detached a squadron of the FLH to act as a rearguard. The Qulusi were beginning to gather on the eastern end of the mountain and had already repossessed the pass by which Buller had ascended. As he rode west along the southern edge of the mountain, however, Buller was in for a shock. Looking to his left, out over the valley south of Hlobane, he saw five long columns of warriors advancing rapidly towards the southern slopes of the mountain. It was the main Zulu army from Ulundi, more than 20,000 strong.

Its appearance at that particular moment was pure coincidence and the worst possible luck for the scattered British groups on Hlobane. When Cetshwayo had mustered his army in early March, he and the *ibandla* had been faced with the problem of deciding a new strategy. It was clear that far from discouraging the invaders Isandlwana had made them all the more determined to exact revenge. The king was genuinely keen to avoid further fighting and sent the emissaries already referred to in an attempt to head it off. At the same time, however, the military threat posed by Chelmsford's new offensive could not be ignored. Sufficient forces were available in the Eshowe

Left: Wood's personal escort, Mounted Infantrymen drawn from the 90th Light Infantry. The MI wore regimental jackets and cord riding breeches, and carried Swinburne–Henry carbines.

Right: Colonel Weatherly of the Border Horse, killed at Hlobane.

area to harass Pearson, and the king and his council correctly decided that Wood's was the most dangerous of the surviving columns. Mblini and the Qulusi had been begging for support against Buller's raids, and a decisive victory in the region would have the additional advantage of neutralizing Hamu's defection and bringing waverers back into line. Accordingly the army had been sent from Ulundi a couple of days before, with instructions to destroy Wood's column.

On the summit, the approach of the main army was encouraging the Qulusi attacks. The FLH rearguard had not been sufficient to stretch right across the mountain and the Zulus had burst round its flanks, causing it to make a hasty retreat. Buller had sent thirty men of the FLH under Captain Barton to bury the men killed on the ascent and then to retire by the same route on the south side of the mountain. Barton's men had met the Border Horse, by now on the summit, and Weatherley fell in with the FLH men. It was soon clear to Buller that his own men would be unable to fight their way back to the pass and that the only feasible means of retreat was via the drop to Ntendeka. As he rode west, skirmishing with the Qulusi all the way, he scribbled a note and sent it after Barton, warning him of the main Zulu *impi* and ordering him to retire 'by the right of the mountain', meaning the northern side.

Meanwhile both Russell and Wood had spotted the Zulu approach. Wood sent a message to Russell telling him to abandon Ntendeka and retire to Zungwini *nek*. By this he meant the saddle connecting Ntendeka to Zungwini, but Russell misinterpreted the order and retreated miles away to the far side of Zungwini, nearer Khambula. He left behind him a few officers and others who had volunteered to help Buller descend the pass. Wood himself proceeded to the western foot of Ntendeka.

Buller's note, when it reached Barton, was also misunderstood with more tragic consequences. When he received it Barton was facing the opposite direction to Buller and took the direction 'by the right' to be a confirmation of his original orders to retire along the southern face of the mountain. He and Weatherley therefore descended the mountain and were riding across the plain when they ran smack into a Zulu column coming towards them. The Zulu army had detached a regiment – either the iNgobamakhosi or Khandempemvu – to support the Qulusi. Barton and Weatherley turned round and retreated rapidly across Ityenka *nek* only to find their way blocked by hordes of Qulusi streaming down the eastern end of the mountain. A running fight broke out which was brought up short at a line of cliffs running along the northern edge of Ityenka *nek*. Unable to descend, most of the FLH and Border Horse were wiped out. Weatherley and his teenaged son were killed; Barton was one of the few who managed to get down, and was chased for several miles before he was caught and killed.

Buller's own retreat was only marginally less disastrous. He reached the pass to Ntendeka safely, but

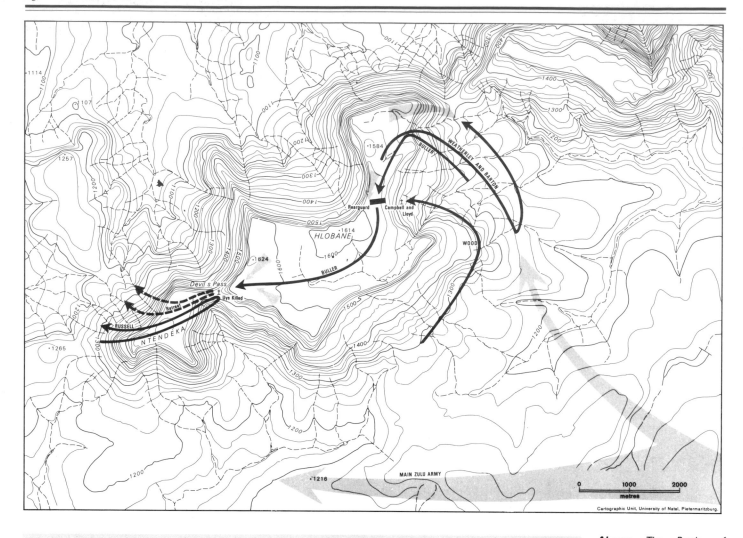

Cartographic Unit, University of Natal, Pietermaritzburg.

Above: The Battle of Hlobane, the running fight which took place throughout 28 March 1879.

Left: Buller's descent; the 'Devil's Pass', photographed from Ntendeka, 1989.

the sudden drop was a worrying prospect, especially as the Qulusi were now hovering close on his flanks. Wood's Irregulars were sent down first and somehow, jumping from stone to stone, they managed to get most of the cattle down with them. Buller then detailed a rearguard to keep the Zulus at bay, and ordered his mounted men over the precipice. The first few were able to pick their way down leading their horses, but the retreat soon lost any sense of order as the Qulusi slipped in among the rocks on each side and began firing into the troops or clambering across the rocks to spear them. By the time the last men began to descend all was frightful confusion, a struggling mass of wounded men and horses, the dead tumbling down the slope, white men and Zulus mixed up together and fighting hand to hand. The Zulus dislodged boulders and hurled them down the edge, crushing men and knocking the legs off horses. Buller was a tower of strength and his example inspired his officers; time and again they went up and down the pass to snatch wounded men to safety from under the noses of the warriors. Nor was Ntendeka a safe refuge, as the Qulusi pressed their attacks right down on to the lower plateau. The Boer leader Piet Uys saw one of his sons in difficulty and turned back to help him; a warrior ran up behind him and speared him in the back. Many of

the men who made it down the pass had lost their horses and Buller tried desperately to remount them since further retreat on foot would have been suicidal. The Volunteers began a disorganized retreat via the north of Ntendeka towards Khambula, many of them carrying wounded men doubled up behind them. Buller stayed to the last, then spent the rest of the day and night patrolling in search of stragglers.

The fight at Hlobane had been a shambles. No less than fifteen officers and seventy-nine men had been killed and many more wounded. The survivors were completely exhausted and Wood's Irregulars were so demoralized that they deserted that night. Piet Uys's followers, having seen their leader killed, were no more inclined to stay and rode out of Khambula the next morning. Yet there was no doubting the bravery of the troops concerned, and Hlobane was recognized by the award of five Victoria Crosses. Lysons and Fowler received the award for their dash into the cave; Buller, Lieutenant Browne of the MI and Major Knox Leet, an officer of the 13th attached to Wood's Irregulars, for rescuing men at what came to be christened 'The Devil's Pass'. Captain D'Arcy of the FLH was recommended for the award but was turned down on the curious grounds that he was a Colonial, not a regular officer. The Zulus remained in complete

mastery of the field, and their losses were unknown.

There was a curious sequel to the Hlobane affair. A Frenchman named Grandier, a member of the Border Horse, was found alive by the Zulus after the battle. Instead of killing him, they took him to Mbilini who sent him on to Ulundi. He was taken before the king and closely questioned, but otherwise treated with courtesy. Presumably deciding that he had little value, either as a hostage or as a source of information, Cetshwayo sent him back to Hlobane under guard. According to Grandier himself, he waited for his chance, then seized an assegai from one of his captors and killed him with it, and drove the other off. He was picked up by a patrol on 16 April wandering naked some miles from Khambula. Later, doubts were cast on his story. It seems likely that the Zulus had brought him as near to the British camp as they dared and set him free. In any case, he was the only prisoner of war taken by the Zulus during the entire campaign.

The Zulu *impi* spent the night of 28 March camped on the White Mfolozi River, a few miles west of Hlobane. They were in high spirits. Although only a few of them had been engaged in that day's battle, it was clear that the British had once again been routed, and they were eager to try the issue with the remainder of Wood's column. The hundreds of rifles captured at Isandlwana had been distributed among the *amabutho* and the warriors were convinced that, fighting in the open, they would have no difficulty in overwhelming the British force. Early the next morning their commanders, Mnyamana kaNgqengelele, Tshingwayo kaMahole and Zibhebhu kaMaphita, formed them into an *umkhumbi*, the traditional circle to receive instructions prior to battle. The king had been most specific in his orders and Mnyamana, Cetshwayo's Chief Minister, and one of the most important *izikhulu* in the country, addressed the warriors, reminding them that they were not to attack the British in fortified positions, but were to try to lure them out either by seizing their cattle or by feinting towards the town of Utrecht. Yet Mnyamana's words apparently had an unsettling effect as he stressed the great importance of the coming fight. The army then formed up into five columns and began to advance on Khambula.

It was equally clear to Colonel Wood that a further battle was imminent. He sent out patrols to scout the Zulu movements and prepared his camp for attack. His position was a strong one, running along the west/east crest of the Khambula ridge. On a slight rise at the eastern end Wood had built a narrow redoubt, a deep trench with the earth piled up inside to form a rampart. Just below the redoubt on a lip in the falling ground a cattle-kraal was formed by laagering and entrenching some of the wagons. The remainder of the wagons formed a main laager about two hundred yards west of the redoubt. The wheels of the wagons were chained together and a trench was dug around them, the earth being piled up between the wheels. The outside of each wagon had been further barricaded with sacks and boxes of provisions. To the north the ground fell away gently towards the headwater streams of the white Mfolozi and was open and largely free of cover for an attacking force. To the south it dropped in

Above left: 'Unspike the guns!' 'I'd die first!', runs the exchange in the original caption to this engraving, depicting Grandier at Ulundi. In fact, Grandier's interrogation at Ulundi was more mundane and his resistance less heroic than he claimed.

Above right: Buller's men retreated in disarray from Hlobane, harried by the victorious abaQulusi.

Above: An unidentified battery of 7pdrs in Zululand.

Right: Officers of the 90th Light Infantry with Wood's Column.

a series of terraces into a steep, narrow valley. There was a danger that this side might afford the Zulus some protection, but generally the field of fire was clear, and conspicuous white markers had been placed to indicate ranges. Wood had two infantry battalions and a battery of 7-pounders at his disposal. In addition he had the Mounted Infantry, the Edendale contingent, and Buller's Volunteers, whose morale was beginning to recover after a night's rest. Finally, there were about 100 black auxiliaries who had not deserted with their colleagues the night before. Official sources listed his total as 2,086 officers and men, including 88 sick. Two companies of infantry and two of the guns were positioned in the redoubt, and one and a half companies were detailed to guard the cattle-kraal. The remaining infantry were positioned around the main wagon laager and the other four guns were lined up in the open between it and the redoubt. The mounted troops were placed inside the laager until they were

needed. Shortly before noon the scouts came in with news that the Zulus were advancing on the camp. Wood let the men finish lunch, then struck the tents and stood them to. Ammunition boxes were opened and placed behind the lines.

The Zulu army came into sight shortly after, moving west. For a few agonizing minutes it looked as if it would indeed by-pass the camp and strike off towards Utrecht. Then it halted and at a leisurely pace began to deploy. The centre and left horn formed up about three miles south of the camp, while the right horn swung round to the north and halted about a mile and a half beyond the British left. Whatever the intentions of Cetshwayo or Mnyamana, the battle would take place on the ground of British choosing. The young warriors who made up the bulk of the *impi* had no patience for complex stratagems to lure the British out, and perceived it their duty to overrun the camp as quickly as possible. Wood noted coolly that the Zulu line, fully extended, covered about ten miles; to the troops it seemed as if there was no end to the masses. Wood's one concern was that the Zulus might attack his position from all sides at once, which would severely stretch his firepower. He was wondering how to prevent this when the Zulu right gave him a golden opportunity.

While the left and centre were still manoeuvring into position, the right horn, consisting of the iNgobamakhosi *ibutho*, suddenly broke into a run and formed up only a mile from the camp. Quite what prompted this action is unknown; there had been fierce disputes between the iNgobamakhosi and the Khandempemvu, on the left horn, as to who had been first into the tents at Isandlwana, and this may have had something to do with it, or it may be that the right horn thought the main body was already in position. Observing the movement, Wood ordered Buller and two squadrons of the Volunteers to sally and provoke the iNgobamakhosi to a full-scale, unsupported attack. Buller's men dismounted a few hundred yards from the Zulu line and loosed a volley. The manoeuvre worked perfectly; the warriors rose and charged. Buller's men fell back before them, now and then stopping to dismount and fire. The Zulus swept after them crying out, 'Don't run away, Johnnie, we want to talk to you!' and, 'We are the boys from Isandlwana!' As they came within range the guns fired their first salvo; the battle had begun in earnest. It was about 1.45 pm.

Buller's men retreated to the safety of the laager; the Edendale men retired further to the west, and remained outside during the battle. The artillery shells seemed to make little impression on the Zulus, but at about 300 yards they were caught by a terrible cross-fire which rippled in volleys down the northern side of the laager and redoubt. Some sections of the right horn pushed forward as far as the laager, but they were soon driven off. The bulk of the warriors had to throw themselves down behind the slender protection of ant-hills, the only cover available on the northern slopes. Time and again they tried to push forward, but the volley-fire cut them down. At last, realizing that there was no chance of coming to grips with the enemy, the iNgobamakhosi, sullen and angry, retired to the cover of a rocky outcrop to the east of the redoubt. Here they opened up a heavy fire on the camp.

Spurred on by the sight of the right horn in defeat, the left and centre came into action. The centre moved along the ridge east of the redoubt, keeping to what cover it could while the left horn massed in the valley to the south. Here they were virtually out of sight of the garrison and could push forward to within a few hundred yards, protected by the rocky ledges which rendered their position dead ground. Yet when they did break into the open the storm of fire was awesome, for the collapse of the right meant that Wood could turn his guns to each new attack as it developed. Nevertheless, there were several occasions when it looked as if the Zulus might carry the day. One of the charges of the Zulu chest, consisting of the uNdi

Above: *Crealock's sketch of Colonel Wood's position at Khambula. The Zulu right attacked on the left of the picture (marked 'C'), while the left horn massed in the valley on the right ('E'). The relative positions of the redoubt, cattle laager and main laager are well shown. Zungwini Mountain is on the right skyline.*

(uThulwana, iNdlondlo and iNdluyengwe *umabutho*) and Nodwengu (uDududu, iMbube and isAngqu *amabutho*) Corps, together with the uDloko *ibutho*, pressed right up to the wall of the redoubt before it was driven back. The uNokhenke regiment, on the left of the centre, massed in the dead ground then boiled out to attack the cattle-kraal from a few yards' range. There was a flurry of hand-to-hand fighting and the men of the 13th defending it were driven back. The kraal was still full of cattle which made it difficult for the Zulus to exploit their success fully, but they lined the ramparts and began a heavy fire-fight with the redoubt and wagon-laager. To the left of the uNokhenke, the uMbonambi regiment formed up in a dense column, preparing to launch itself up the slope between the two laagers, and the extreme left, the Khandempemvu, swept up to take possession of a small knoll used by the camp as a rubbish heap, which commanded the open ground about 200 yards from the main laager.

This was a most serious threat, perhaps the crucial point of the battle. If the uMbonambi could sustain its charge, supported on both flanks, there was a very real danger that it might burst into the laager. Wood had little option but to order a couple of sorties to break up the Zulu concentrations before they could charge. He ordered out two companies of the 90th under Major Hackett, who advanced with parade ground precision and formed up across the lip of the terrace from where they could see down into the valley. They opened a terrific fire which devastated the close Zulu ranks, and

the Mbonambi were driven back into the valley. Yet Hackett's men were also very exposed to Zulu enfilading fire from the rubbish heaps and from the cattle laager. Several men were killed, and Hackett himself was hit in the head and frightfully wounded, losing both his eyes. His subaltern, Lieutenant Arthur Bright, was shot through both thighs, and bled to death before the surgeons recognized the extent of his injuries. A company of the 13th was also ordered out to drive back the Khandempemvu threatening Hackett's right. The position was far too exposed to remain there, however, and as soon as they had dispersed the Zulus Wood pulled his men back to the laager. The Zulu riflemen on the knoll were causing serious problems for the southern face of the laager, and Wood directed his men to fire volley after volley at it until the fire was suppressed.

It was now about 3 pm, and the Zulus had reached their high-water mark. Bodies were strewn everywhere around the laager and it was increasingly difficult to exploit immediate tactical advantages. Armed for the most part with ineffectual firearms and spears, and carrying shields that were no protection against bullets, the Zulus were, in effect, attacking the camp both naked and bare-handed. Yet their raw courage was extraordinary. Time and again the different regiments surged forward, on one occasion coming close enough to be within reach of the artillery horses. On another the iNgobamakhosi advanced, only to be cut down as before as they ran up the steep final approaches to the redoubt. By late afternoon it was becoming obvious that the attacks were less well co-ordinated, and that the warriors were exhausted. At 5.30 pm, just as the sun was beginning to go down, Wood ordered a company of the 13th to re-occupy the cattle-kraal, and the Zulus were driven out at bayonet point. A company of the 90th was advanced to the lip of the terrace once more, and fired on the regiments still gathered in the valley. Gradually the Zulus began to fall back. Wood, choosing his moment, sent out his cavalry to turn the retreat into a rout. Buller's men were in no mood to be merciful – 'No quarter, boys, and remember yesterday!' urged D'Arcy of the FLH – and they pitched into the Zulus with a will. Most of the warriors were too tired to fight back and the volunteers shot them with impunity. When shooting became too slow a way to finish them, many seized spears and rode the warriors down with the point.

The pursuit after Khambula was undoubtedly brutal and would later cause some controversy at home, but Wood had the opportunity to destroy the Zulu army and was determined to make the most of it. In truth, he would have had difficulty in restraining his vengeful cavalry in any case. They chased the Zulu army for nearly ten miles, 'butchering the brutes all over the place', as D'Arcy observed. Buller was 'like a tiger drunk with blood'. Many of the Zulus simply stood, awaiting their fate, while others tried to hide in ant-bear holes and long grass. The British Infantry and the remains of Wood's Irregulars were sent out after the cavalry, and flushed out and killed those hiding or wounded. The Zulu retreat had begun in an orderly fashion, but the fierce pressure of the pursuit caused it to break up as it neared Zungwini. The abaQulusi

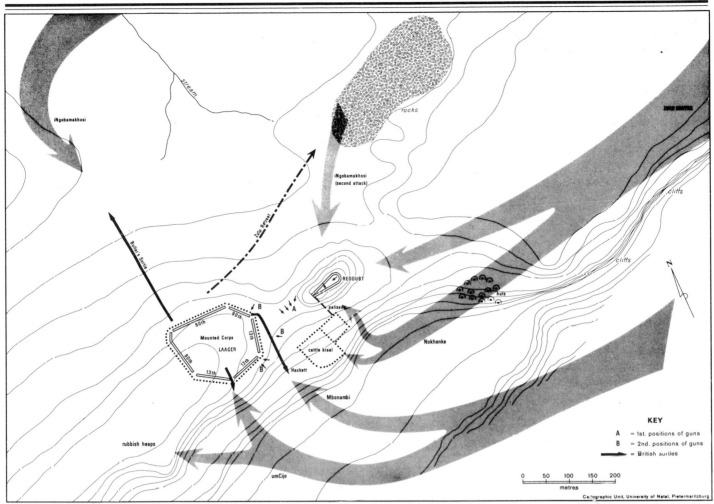

Map labels: iNgobamakhosi, stream, rocks, iNgobamakhosi (second attack), Zulu Retreat, Buller's Sortie, REDOUBT, cliffs, palisade, huts, 90th, Mounted Corps LAAGER, 13th, cattle kraal, Nokhenke, Hackett, Mbonambi, rubbish heaps, umCijo, N

KEY
A = 1st. positions of guns
B = 2nd. positions of guns
= British sorties

0 50 100 150 200
metres

Cartographic Unit, University of Natal, Pietermaritzburg.

Above: The Battle of Khambula; the climax of the battle, from the first Zulu attacks (about 1.30 p.m.) to the last British sorties (about 5.30 p.m.), 29 March 1879.

Top left: A Zulu sniper fires at Buller's cavalry as they emerge to pursue the fleeing Zulus.

Left: Orlando Norie's watercolour depicting a sortie by the 13th driving the Zulu left horn back into the valley. Note the position of the laagers and redoubt; this picture gives a good impression of how the Zulus were able to mass in the dead ground.

Right: The British pursuit at Khambula. Although this sketch has romanticized the appearance of Buller's men, it does give a good impression of their impact on the disheartened Zulus.

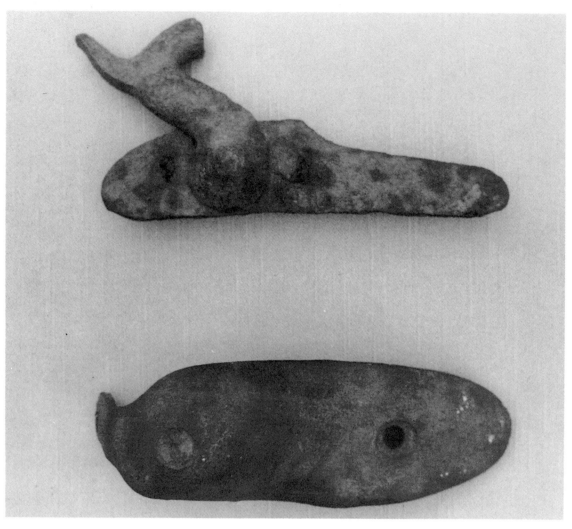

suffered particularly severely and fled as fast as they could towards the safety of Hlobane. Only when it was too dark to continue did the cavalry give up the chase and return, exalting, to Khambula.

The Zulu losses were indeed fearful. The next day Wood began the grim task of collecting the dead and burying them in mass graves. Wagon-loads were brought in, many horribly mangled by shell-fire. More than sixty were found near the rubbish heaps alone, and in all 785 were collected from close by the camp. Many more lay out on the line of the retreat where the slaughter had been heaviest, and hundreds no doubt left the field with dreadful wounds to which they would succumb within days. A week after the fight, border patrols reported the grim sounds of mourning songs being sung in the homesteads all along the Mzinyathi River. Perhaps as many as 2,000 died, among them a high proportion of *izinduna* who had exposed themselves a good deal to encourage their men. Mnyamana himself lost two sons, and Godide

kNdlela, who had commanded at Nyezane, also lost several members of his family. By comparison, Wood's losses were inconsequential: 3 officers and 25 men killed, and 5 officers and 50 men wounded. As usual, no one bothered to take a detailed roll of the black auxiliaries, although they too had suffered a number of casualties.

The effect on the Zulu army was simply shattering. Mnyamana tried to keep the regiments together and persuade them to return to Ulundi, but they had had enough. Their tremendous struggle had been in vain and their casualties stunned them. Most of the warriors simply drifted back to their own homes to attend to post-combat purification rituals and to rest. King Cetshwayo was appalled when Mnyamana told him the story of the fight; his men had behaved exactly as he had instructed them not to, and the nation as a whole had paid the price. The losses at Isandlwana had been bad enough, but this time there was nothing to show for it. The significance was obvious; at

Khambula the Zulu army had very probably lost not only the battle, but the rest of the war.

This was also immediately apparent to the British. A British army had at last met a Zulu army head on and had won an uncompromising victory. The ghost of Isandlwana had been laid to rest and Chelmsford was in a position to make a fresh start on his original objective, destroying the Zulu kingdom by forcing Cetshwayo to accept the terms of the Ultimatum. At Khambula Wood was content to clean up after the battle and to harass Zulu stragglers with his patrols. In this, too, he was to be rewarded with a notable success.

The abaQulusi spent the first few days after Khambula shut up on Hlobane, but by 3 April they had evacuated it, moving north towards the Phongolo and Ntombe once more. Mbilini went with them. In one of the battles he had sustained a light head wound, but this does not seem to have dampened his enthusiasm for raiding. Presumably he considered Luneburg a softer target than military concentrations like Khambula. On 4 April he led a force of 1,200 warriors into the Phongolo valley, rounding-up cattle and destroying the homesteads of Africans friendly to the Luneburg settlers. The next day patrols from Luneburg set out to harry their retreat. One patrol came across a small party of mounted men near the Ntombe. Two Zulus broke free from the rest and Captain Prior and Private Bowen of the 80th gave chase. There was an exchange of shots and both Zulus were wounded. One fell from the saddle and was promptly speared by black auxiliaries. He proved to be Tshekwane, a son of Chief Sihayo who had accompanied Mehlokazulu's raid into Natal. The other escaped, but he had been severely wounded by a bullet which had entered his right shoulder and come out below his waist. He died a few days later. He proved to be Mbilini kaMswati. The career of the most independent and aggressive Zulu raider of the war was over.

DESTRUCTION OF THE ZULU KINGDOM

*Chelmsford plans the **Second Invasion**; the reconstruction of the British forces. Border raids and sorties, and the visit to the Isandlwana battlefield. The start of the Second Invasion; the arrival of the **Prince Imperial**. The Prince is killed while on patrol; the Court-Martial of Carey and subsequent repercussions. The advance to the Upoko, and the death of Lieutenant Frith. Increased diplomatic activity. Chelmsford learns that he is to be replaced, and presses forward with his advance. The destruction of Zulu homesteads. Final preparations for confrontation; The Battle of **Ulundi**. The Zulus are broken, British troops withdraw, and Chelmsford resigns his command.*

I n the aftermath of Gingindlovu Lord Chelmsford, leaving the troops of his coastal command to secure themselves at Forts Tenedos and Pearson, returned to Durban and assessed the situation. In the two severe defeats the British had inflicted on the Zulus at opposite ends of the country and within a few days of each other, Chelmsford had totally regained the initiative. He found that the huge quantities of men and material sent out as reinforcements were unloading daily at the docks, and he would soon have more than enough troops to start his invasion afresh. This time he would be in a position to force the Zulus to accept whatever conditions he chose, or destroy them utterly. And, as subsequent events would show, Chelmsford's conditions were not **negotiable**; King

Cetshwayo must accept the terms of the Ultimatum unconditionally or take the consequences. Only by breaking up the army and deposing the king could Chelmsford and Frere regain the prestige they had lost at Isandlwana.

Planning the new invasion was a logistical nightmare, but Chelmsford was in no hurry. The troops fresh out from England, especially the two cavalry regiments, the 1st (King's) Dragoon Guards and the 17th Lancers, whose heavy English chargers had suffered badly on the voyage out, and refused to eat local grasses, needed time to acclimatize. It was no bad thing to let Cetshwayo ponder his fate, and after the appalling weather of the summer the onset of autumn at least offered the hope that the roads might

'We had a glorious go-in, old boy, pig-sticking was a fool to it.'
Anonymous NCO, 17th Lancers.

Below: *Ships bringing Chelmsford's reinforcements leave Cape Town for Natal.*

dry out. A new plan had to be thought out, officers allotted their appointments and troops marched to their starting-positions. By now the transport situation was in a terrible mess; there were insufficient wagons to support a rapid advance and, following Isandlwana, many transport riders were refusing to cross into Zululand and some even objected to using exposed stretches of the border roads, although it was clear to all by now that the danger of a major Zulu invasion was past.

Chelmsford's new invasion plan was shaped by the changed strategic situation. It was clear that the decisive confrontation would take place on Zulu soil and it was no longer necessary or practical to invade in a number of equally spaced columns. Instead, he would push forward with a main striking army from northern Zululand, supported by Evelyn Wood's column which would retain its separate identity and work in close co-operation. A further column would advance up the coastal strip, but its objectives would be limited and specific; its main function would be to secure the right flank of the striking arm. The coastal column was christened the First Division, the striking arm the Second Division and Wood's column was redesignated the Flying Column. To command these forces, Chelmsford had an embarrassment of riches, the four Major-Generals sent out by the War Office. The most senior, the Hon. Hugh Clifford, VC, was given the thankless but crucial task of guarding the garrisons and lines of communication in Natal.

Clifford's remit was far-reaching and reflected, ominously, the Home Government's concern about the expense of the transport crisis and the poor state of relations between the civil and military authorities. Clifford was ordered to find a new and thorough

transport system, and repair the damage between the Colonial administration and the Army. In that, he did not consider himself at all subordinate to Chelmsford, and a new twist was added to the saga of mistrust and rivalry between senior British officials in Natal. The jobs found for the other three were, mercifully, less controversial: H.H. Crealock, the brother of Lieutenant Colonel J.N. Crealock, Chelmsford's military secretary, was given command of the First Division, and Edward Newdigate that of the Second Division. Frederick Marshall was appointed commander of the Cavalry Brigade which was attached to the Second Division. It was the lot of most of the Dragoons to spend the war patrolling the lines of communication, but one squadron and all the Lancers were to march on Ulundi. Evelyn Wood was promoted to the local rank of Brigadier-General.

The exact route to be taken by the Second Division was the cause of some concern. For various reasons Chelmsford was reluctant to use the old Greytown – Helpmekaar – Rorke's Drift route. For one thing, his supply routes would have to run parallel to the border near the Middle Drift, an area where the difficult nature of the country made them vulnerable to even a small raid. Secondly, he had no desire to advance his fresh troops via the battlefield at Isandlwana, where the bodies of the dead still lay unburied. Instead, he decided to make the hamlet of Dundee, north of Helpmekaar, his base, with another camp at Landman's Drift where the road crossed the Mzinyathi. This route would mean crossing the Ntome River as well, and since there appeared to be no track running due east across the difficult country on the Zulu side of the Ntome, a long detour almost as far north as Khambula was thought necessary. In fact,

Below: The 17th Lancers encamped at Cato Manor farm, Natal, on their way to the front. Note the lances standing upright between the tents.

Left: *A Private of the 17th Lancers in the uniform worn during the Zulu campaign. In addition to the carbine and sword shown, Lancers were armed with a nine-foot bamboo lance.*

Right: *A Private of the King's Dragoon Guards in Zululand.*

once the troops began to mass at Dundee and Landman's Drift, scouts were pushed across the border who found an acceptable route across the Ntome at Koppie Alleen, which then veered south, skirting Isandlwana, before joining the Babanango heights. From there there was an established track over the Mthonjaneni ridge, dropping to the White Mfolozi valley and thence to Ulundi. Nevertheless, even this shorter route would stretch the transport services to the limits and supplies would have to be ferried first from Pietermaritzburg to Dundee – where the same iron sheds which had once been at Helpmekaar were now re-erected to house them – and thence by stages to fortified posts along the line of advance. The effort required to establish the Second Division had an immediate effect on the First, which was lower on the list of priorities. Although much easier to provision, and moving across easier country, the First Division's inadequate transport facilities meant that it, too, would have to advance in stages, halting regularly while its convoys made the return journey to Natal to stock up. Since it was close to the coast, it was suggested that it might be possible to land supplies from the sea, and in mid-April HMS *Forrester* put ashore a landing-party who were fired on by a party of Zulus in the bush. They made it safely back to the ship which lobbed several shells into the bush – surely the only time that a British warship had fired on the Zulus. The site at Port Durnford was less than ideal, but Crealock was instructed to push forward and make of it what he could. Towards the end of April his men built two strong forward posts; Fort Crealock, commanding the crossing of the Amatikulu and Fort Chelmsford on the Nyezane. A pontoon bridge was built across the Thukela and Crealock began accumulating supplies at Fort Chelmsford for his advance.

The start of the new invasion was scheduled for the end of May and it was heralded by a number of diversionary moves along the border. This small-scale raiding was a highly controversial matter since its advantages were a matter of heated debate. Sir Henry Bulwer was bitterly opposed to Natal volunteers or levies being used for actions that, he believed, would only provoke Zulu counter attacks, and were sure to engender lasting hostility. Chelmsford did not agree, however, and used every means in his power to manipulate the border garrisons until at last Bulwer was overruled, and it was decided that Chelmsford should have complete control of all troops in defensive areas. On 9 May levy leader Boast led the White Rock Border Guard upstream from the Lower Drift, in a raid across the river which rounded-up a handful of cattle. A few days later a party of Volunteers accomplished much the same thing, at the same spot. On the 20th, however, there was a much more serious incursion at the Middle Drift.

It was led by Major Twentyman of the 4th Foot from his advanced base at Fort Cherry which stood on the Kranskop escarpment, 3,000 feet above the winding Thukela. Twentyman was an enthusiastic

Left: Officers of the Flying Column: Evelyn Wood, centre, talking to his Staff Officer, Major Clery. Lieutenant Lysons sits on the ground with Lord Beresford behind him.

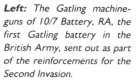

Left: The Gatling machine-guns of 10/7 Battery, RA, the first Gatling battery in the British Army, sent out as part of the reinforcements for the Second Invasion.

Right: A battery of 7pdr Rifled Muzzle-Loading guns with the Flying Column.

Right: Colonel Collingwood of the 21st, commanding the First Brigade of the Second Division. Note the headquarters flag.

Right: More new arrivals; the officers of the 21st Royal Scots Fusiliers.

Left: Fort Tenedos on the Zulu bank at the lower Thukela Drift.

Right: Men of the White Rock Border Guard, who crossed briefly into Zululand on 9 May, as part of the diversionary demonstrations which heralded the Eshowe relief expedition.

Left: Officers of the 88th (Connaught Rangers) at Fort Tenedos, awaiting the advance of the First Division.

Right: Major A. C. Twentyman, 4th Foot, who led the raid at the Middle Drift on 20 May. Photograph c. 1882.

believer in the policy of active patrolling and, at Chelmsford's request, he moved a force of Volunteers down the steep incline and into the Thukela valley. His attack was co-ordinated with separate thrusts by local Border Guards and levies. The Africans on the Natal bank had lost the son of their Chief in a minor skirmish with the Zulus across the river and were burning for revenge. Twentyman's party, about a thousand strong, mostly Africans, with only 37 Natal Volunteers, crossed the river at dawn. A small party of Zulus spotted their approach and lined the bush along the Zulu bank to fire at them, but they were driven out, only to take possession of a hill a few hundred yards away. Twentyman had several rocket troughs and three rockets fired at the hill silenced the Zulus. Twentyman's men then enthusiastically burnt every homestead they could reach before crossing back into Natal that afternoon. Twentyman himself had been the first across the river and was the last to leave. Farther up and down stream the African contingents had similar success, but they would not be allowed to retire with impunity; that night, as the exhausted men struggled back up from the valley, word spread that the Zulus had crossed in pursuit. No sooner had the troops begun to retreat than small parties of Zulus slipped across the river at a number of points and began destroying homesteads on the Natal bank. They retired having inflicted minimal damage, but their counter-attack had decidedly undermined Twentyman's moral victory.

There were two more sorties across the border before the invasion got under way. On the 15th Major Black – now promoted to Lieutenant-Colonel – led another patrol to Isandlwana and was fired on by Zulus who gathered to oppose him. The purpose of this patrol became obvious a few days later when Chelmsford announced his intention to visit Isandlwana. It was high time some attempt was made to bury the dead and, more pragmatically, there were still wagons in working order on the battlefield and

Isandhwana
May 21st

Above: *General Marshall's visit to Isandlwana, 21 May 1879; examining the wreckage on the nek.*

these were desperately needed by the Second Division. A large force comprising mostly the 17th Lancers, and led by General Marshall, crossed at Rorke's Drift, proceeded up the Batshe, past the ruins of Sihayo's homestead, and descended the Nqutu hills to the camp. Its path was marked by a line of burning homesteads as the troops set fire to every *umuzi* they could find. The old battlefield was a grim sight. The incessant rain meant that the area was covered with tall grass and some of the mealies had sprouted, even growing through the bones of the dead. For the most part these were now skeletons, although many were curiously mummified, the dry skin stretched tightly over the bones. On some the features were still recognizable and, with the help of tatters of uniform clinging to the bones, it was possible to identify a number of officers, among them Durnford and Lieutenant Scott of the Carbineers. The troops searched the camp area in silence, wrapped in their own thoughts, marvelling at the evidence of the tough fighting and collecting relics from the debris to send home to the families of the fallen. Colonel Glyn had asked for the bodies of his regiment to be left untouched so that they might receive a proper burial at the hands of their comrades, but many of the other bodies were gently tipped into shallow graves scraped

in the rocky ground, and stones were piled over them. It would take many more visits before the task was completed, and it was not until March 1880 that a patrol of the 60th Rifles was able to report that all the dead had at last been decently interred. The Zulus did not challenge the expedition, but Marshall, conscious that they might, ordered his men to retire to Rorke's Drift as soon as they had decided which wagons were still serviceable. Forty wagons were taken away by teams of horses brought along for the purpose.

Once the troops were back in their respective positions the invasion could begin in earnest. On 27 May the Second Division, of more than 5,000 men and 600 wagons, began its advance from Landman's Drift. A few days later it crossed the Ncome by Koppie Alleen and entered Zululand. Wood's Flying Column began to move down from Khambula and it was intended that the two should meet somewhere near the junction of the Itshotshozi and Tombokala Rivers. Chelmsford's preparations had been thorough and meticulous, yet within a few days of the beginning of the new invasion he would be dealt another severe blow.

On the evening of the 1 June Wood and Buller were patrolling ahead of the Flying Column looking for signs of the Second Division with whom they were

Above: A visit to Isandlwana in June 1879 to bury the dead. Many of the wagons are still in place and the troops appear to he breakfasting on the old camp site.

Right: The interior of Fort Chelmsford, one of the First Division's staging-posts in Zululand.

rapidly converging. They were approached by a number of riders, the survivors of a patrol sent out by the Second Division, and ambushed by the Zulus. The patrol had lost three men dead – an unfortunate occurence, but one which any army might expect when advancing into enemy territory. Except that among the dead was the young Louis Napoleon, the exiled heir to the Bonapartist throne in France.

Chelmsford must, by now, have been wondering what he had done to upset the Gods of War, since he had not wanted the Prince on the campaign in the first place. Louis had been born in 1856 and grown up during the giddy hey-day of the Third Empire. His father, Napoleon III, had imbued in him a deep sense of the Bonaparte tradition, and the boy had been filled full of romantic ideas of military glory. He had received something of a shock, however, at the battle of Sedan in 1870, when France's army was found woefully wanting in the face of steely Prussian efficiency. The Third Empire had collapsed overnight, and Napoleon III sent his wife, Eugénie, and heir, Louis, into exile in Britain. The Emperor himself joined them a year later, but did not long survive the ruin of his dreams. At first the presence of a Bonapartist pretender on British soil caused some

Left: *Stores accumulated at Fort Pearson for the Second Invasion – the pontoon bridge across the Thukela is visible in the distance.*

Above: *'Transport difficulties': Chelmsford's Second Invasion was shaped by the practical problems of supplying his men in the field.*

Below: *J. L. Knight's Border Levies in impressive formation. These levies were required to guard a section of the Mzinyathi down river from Rorke's Drift.*

political embarrassment, but Queen Victoria befriended Eugénie and a place was found for the young Prince at the Royal Military College at Woolwich, where officer cadets of the Royal Artillery and Engineers were trained. Louis' gallic charm and vitality endeared him to his fellow cadets, and he passed out seventh in a class of 34 in 1875. There was no question of his being given a commission in the Royal Artillery, however, and Louis seemed destined to live the empty lives of most leaders in exile, awaiting a call to resume his throne which would probably never come. When news of Isandlwana reached London Louis begged to be allowed to accompany the reinforcements being sent to Zululand. He managed to persuade his mother, the Queen, and the Duke of Cambridge to support him and, faced with such distinguished pressure, Disraeli reluctantly agreed. The war might at least provide the military experience the boy so yearned for, and an obscure war in Africa could surely have no European political repercussions.

Armed with a letter of introduction to Chelmsford, the Prince Imperial set sail at the end of February. Chelmsford was advised to let him see as much of the war as possible, but to keep him out of harm's way; Louis held no rank, and was officially no more than an observer.

Chelmsford was not overjoyed at being saddled with a celebrity tourist, but he took him on to his staff and, during the final weeks before the start of the second invasion, allowed him to take part in a number of supposedly safe patrols. The Prince proved too reckless and daring, however, and the proximity of even small groups of the enemy would provoke him to draw his great-uncle's sword and charge. Buller refused to take him out again and Louis was attached to the staff of Lieutenant-Colonel Richard Harrison, RE, the Second Division's Assistant Quarter-Master General. This at least allowed him to play a useful part in selecting the sites of future camping grounds while keeping him away from the enemy. In this post Louis

Below left: Louis Napoleon, the Prince Imperial of France, photographed on his arrival in Durban. He is wearing a Royal Artillery officer's uniform.

Below: This sketch by Lieutenant Fairlie captures something of the Prince's jaunty charm which won him so many friends in the Second Division.

befriended Harrison's deputy, Lieutenant Jahleel Brenton Carey of the 98th Regiment. Carey was 32, the son of a Devon vicar, and had been educated in France before attending the RMC and acquiring a commission in the West India Regiment. He had entered the Staff College at Camberley in 1877 and emerged just as the Zulu War broke out. He had applied for a Staff post and because of his expertise in map-making, had been attached to Harrison. He was a hard-working and talented officer and his knowledge of France attracted him to the Prince. Shortly before the invasion began Louis accompanied Carey and a strong escort, under the command of Commandant Bettington of the Natal Horse, on a patrol to scout the Second Division's line of advance. The patrol was fired upon by Zulu skirmishers and when Bettington's men rode forward to disperse the Zulus Louis immediately charged. The Zulus fled and the patrol returned without casualties, but Louis was becoming an increasing embarrassment.

Below: Lieutenant J. B. Carey, 98th Regiment who accompanied the Prince on his fatal patrol. This photograph appears to have been taken in 1879 as a souvenir for Carey's supporters, at a time when he was trying to clear his name.

Nevertheless, on 31 May, the day the column crossed into Zululand, Louis asked Harrison for permission to scout ahead to the confluence of the Itshotshosi and Tombokala. The area had been pronounced free of Zulus and Harrison reluctantly agreed, provided that Louis was accompanied by an escort of Bettington's men and Natal Native Horse. Bettington selected six reliable men: Sergeant Willis, Corporal Grubb, and Troopers Abel, Rogers, Cochrane and Le Tocq, a Channel Islander who spoke French. When he heard of Louis' plans Carey asked for and was given permission to join the party. A Zulu scout completed the group.

The patrol set off early the next morning and from the start there was a certain laxness and confusion about it. The NNH men failed to turn up, having reported to the wrong tent, and Carey was told to boost his escort from the advanced patrols they were sure to encounter. On the way out of the camp they passed Harrison who made a nonchalant remark to the effect that Carey should not interfere with the Prince's duties. In fact, no-one had thought to appoint a proper command structure; since Louis was no more than a civilian observer, Carey should have assumed control as a matter of course, but the Prince habitually wore an Artillery lieutenant's uniform, and everyone, Harrison included, treated him as if he were an officer. Carey did not think to question the matter and let Louis' natural air of authority dominate the patrol.

The patrol failed to meet any advance parties and pushed ahead on its own towards the Itshotshosi River. In the early afternoon they reached a low hill overlooking the river and Carey suggested a halt. The Prince pointed out a homestead at the bottom of the slope below them and suggested that they rest there, since the proximity of the river meant that the men could make coffee. Carey agreed and the party rode down and off-saddled at the *umuzi*. It was not, perhaps, the wisest of halting-places, since the homestead itself, a collection of half-a-dozen huts surrounding a stone cattle-pen, was surrounded by tall green mealie fields with a large donga about two hundred yards off to one side. However, it seemed to be deserted and Carey and the Prince rested in the shade while the escort brewed up. There was a dog skulking among the huts and one of the troopers noticed some freshly chewed sugar cane on the ground, sure indications of recent occupation. At about 3.30 Carey suggested that it was time to return, but Louis replied that there was no hurry. A few minutes later, however, the Zulu guide came in and said that he had seen a Zulu on the shoulder of the hill. Louis told the men to collect their horses which had been wandering freely about the huts. There was still no great sense of urgency and when at last the men were lined up, Louis gave the order 'Prepare to mount.' At that moment a terrific volley crashed from the mealies only a few yards away, and a party of between thirty or forty warriors charged forward, yelling the war-cry, 'uSuthu!'

Left: Commandant Bettington and a member of his Horse; Bettington's Horse provided the escort on the Prince's last patrol.

Left: The last bivouac; the Prince seated, foreground, with Carey standing centre.

Left: The donga where the Prince was killed. This photograph was taken by the party who erected the monument to him on the site.

Above: *The most accurate representation of Louis' death; Paul Jamin's 1882 painting depicts his final struggle. His right hand injured, Louis fires his revolver with his left as the Zulus close in. The patrol flees across the donga in the background.*

The Zulus were men of the iNgobamakhosi, uMbonambi and uNokhenke *amabutho*, a scouting party who had presumably been shadowing the advance of the column. They had seen the Prince's party dismount and had moved down the donga until they had reached the river, then worked up under its steep banks until they could slip undetected into the mealies. They were scarcely in position when Louis' order to mount was given, and, afraid that such a perfect opportunity should slip through their grasp, had decided to attack. They burst out of the undergrowth just as the patrol were mounting. The sudden crash of their volley startled the horses which immediately bolted towards the donga. Trooper Rogers did not make it to his horse; he was seen running off towards the huts, raising his carbine at a Zulu chasing him. Trooper Abel was riding off when a bullet hit him square in the back and he slumped sideways to the ground. In those first few panic-stricken seconds, no-one had a very clear idea of who

was where. Not until the riders crossed the donga did the Zulus give up the chase, and breathlessly Carey looked round to see who was missing. The Prince was down.

Louis' horse was a large, spirited grey called Percy, and Louis had just gripped the saddle when the Zulus attacked. Percy reared up, then galloped after the other horses with Louis clinging to the saddle, trying to haul himself up. Le Tocq, the French speaker, passed him and called out encouragingly 'Dépêchez-vous, s'il vous plait, Monsieur.' but a few yards from the donga Louis' luck ran out. Most of his weight was dragging on his saddle-holster, and a leather retaining strap gave way. The Prince fell heavily under Percy's hooves and his right arm was trampled. Stunned for a second, he picked himself up to see about a dozen Zulus just yards behind him. Louis grabbed his revolver with his left hand and there was a brief flurry of fighting, but it was all over in seconds. A warrior named Xamanga of the uMbonambi was the first to

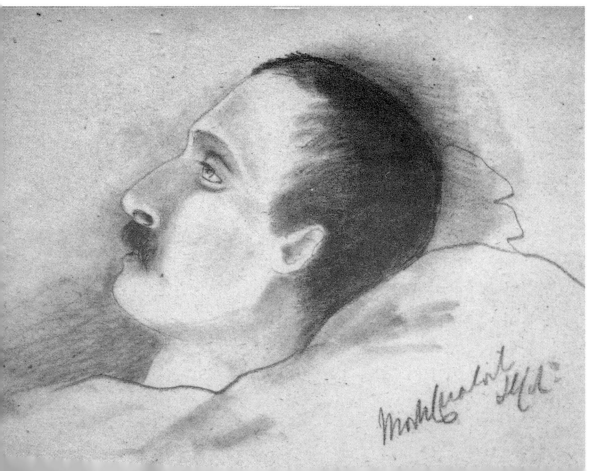

Above: Exultant Zulus crowd around Louis to stab his corpse in a ritual known as ukuhlomula; the artist has depicted Zulu costume accurately enough, but it is unlikely that so much would have been worn in action.

Left: The Prince's death mask, drawn by J. N. Crealock.

stab him, the Zulus pressing round to thrust at him until he was dead.

Beyond the donga the patrol could see the Zulus running across the ground where the Prince had been, and Percy galloping riderless. There seemed no point in rallying; they kept riding until they met Wood and Buller. News of the incident soon reached the Second Division camp where it was greeted with shock and horror. It was too late to organize a search-party that evening, but the next morning a strong force was sent out to recover the body. Louis was found where he had fallen, stripped naked except for a religious medallion around his neck, lying on his back with his left arm across his body in an attitude of self-defence. There were eighteen spear-wounds in all, including two that had passed clear through his body, and others in the right eye, chest and neck, any of which would have

proved fatal. The searchers took some comfort in the fact that all the wounds were in front. Troopers Rogers and Abel were lying nearby, naked and mutilated. Louis was gently lifted on to a stretcher improvised by draping a blanket over two lances, and brought back to camp in an ambulance wagon. Many amongst the escort were moved to tears by the sight.

Wearily, Chelmsford arranged for a funeral service to be held that day in camp. Louis' body was drawn past the lines of troops on a gun-carriage, with Chelmsford walking behind. The news of his death was taken by galloper to the nearest telegraph, then passed to Pietermaritzburg, then Durban, and on to a ship for Britain. When it broke, it caused more furore than the massacre at Isandlwana. The Empress Eugénie collapsed and Queen Victoria was mortified. Louis' body was passed back down the line with

ceremonies of increasing solemnity. In Pietermaritzburg it lay in state in the small Catholic church, before being drawn through the street between lines of troops. At Durban crowds turned out in mourning to watch the coffin loaded aboard ship. It arrived in England to a wave of public sympathy and was finally laid to rest with Napoleon III at Eugénie's house at Chislehurst in Kent. Months later, when the fighting was finished, a large stone cross was erected on the site where he fell, and trees were planted in a walled enclosure around it. Eugénie herself later made a pilgrimage to the site, accompanied by Evelyn Wood and Ronald Campbell's widow. They traced and interviewed Zulus who had fought in the war, and a stone cross was placed over Campbell's lonely grave on the shoulder of Hlobane, but Eugénie was horrified to find that the wild and remote spot where Louis had died had been transformed into a miniature European park.

Carey's career was blighted by the incident. In the first few days after the skirmish he found himself the subject of muted accusations of cowardice and was obliged to ask for a Court of Inquiry into his conduct. It recommended a Court Martial on the charge of deserting the Prince in the face of the enemy, and this took place less than a fortnight after Louis' death. Carey defended himself well, pointing out that all the

decisions throughout the patrol had been made by Louis and that if he was guilty of abandoning the Prince, he was equally guilty of abandoning the two dead troopers: all the witnesses from the patrol supported his claim that nothing could be achieved by rallying. The court was not convinced, however, and found him guilty. He was sentenced to be cashiered and was relieved of his appointment and sent home.

By the time he returned home, however, Carey had become something of a public hero. The press smelt a scapegoat in the making and championed his cause, pointing an accusing finger instead at Harrison, for failing to organize the patrol properly, and Chelmsford for allowing Louis too near the front in the first place. Eugénie, whose sense of loss was overpowering, wanted no more suffering and induced the Queen to intervene. The findings of the Court were overturned, and Carey was allowed to return to his regiment. The public acclaim had perhaps gone to his head, however, and he continued to protest his innocence long after it was politic to do so. He even tried to arrange a meeting with Eugénie, a public reconciliation to clear his name. Eugénie, tired of his pestering, passed on his letters to the Queen who, appalled by his insensitivity, mentioned the matter to Disraeli. Snubbed, Carey sank back into obscurity within his regiment. He died of peritonitis in Karachi in 1883.

Top: The first of many funeral services. Lord Chelmsford follows the body, strapped to a gun carriage, past the 17th Lancers and men of the 2nd Division.

Above: British troops destroying the homestead where the Prince was killed. Note the man posing, about to cast down a stone, and the flattened huts and mealie fields.

Right: The band of the Maritzburg Rifes, with black-draped instruments, leads Louis' funeral cortège through the streets of Pietermaritzburg.

Right: A Guard of Honour lines the streets of Pietermaritzburg for the passing of the funeral procession.

Right: Curious crowds watch as the Prince's coffin is loaded aboard a tug at Durban, to be ferried to HMS Boadicea, *lying beyond the bar. The Boadicea transported it to Cape Town, where it was transferred to HMS Orontes, which completed the journey to England.*

Tragic as Louis' fate was, to Lord Chelmsford it was little more than a gloomy side-show, since his main concern was to continue his advance to confront Cetshwayo. By 5 June both the Flying Column and Second Division had reached the Nondweni River where Chelmsford intended to establish his first supply depot. That day he had his first significant encounter with the Zulus since the second invasion began. The night before, scouts had reported Zulu concentrations along the line of advance, and at dawn Buller had set off with the irregular cavalry to clear the way. The Zulus were on the slopes of a hill known as eZungeni, across the shallow uPoko River. Buller's men splashed across the stream, dismounted in the tall grass on the far side and opened fire on the warriors moving down from eZungeni. While this fire-fight was in progress the 17th Lancers, led by their Colonel, Drury Curzon Drury-Lowe, came up and, eager for the fray, crossed the stream. Buller, noticing that the Zulus were infiltrating the grass in large numbers on his flanks, recalled his men, but the Lancers lined up and proceeded to charge backwards and forwards through the grass. The Zulus promptly retreated to the hills again and opened fire on the Lancers. Drury-Lowe's adjutant, Lieutenant Frith, was just turning his horse next to his Colonel when he threw up his arms and fell dead, shot through the heart. Drury-Lowe called off the attack and Frith's body was taken back to the camp across his saddle and buried the same evening. The next day Chelmsford began to build a fort at the camp, Fort Newdigate, but despite this increased security there was a serious alarm that night. African troops on outlying picket fired shots at what they thought were approaching Zulus, then fell back on their supports. The officer in charge of these ordered two volleys to be fired, then retreated to the fort. The whole camp stood-to in its defensive posts and began firing volleys into the night. Even the artillery fired two rounds before the cease-fire was called and order restored. There were no Zulus in the vicinity and the only casualties were five soldiers wounded. These had been on outpost duty and had not been able to get back to the camp before the firing started. Coming so soon after the death of Louis and Frith, it was a potent reminder of the terror the Zulus still inspired in troops who had yet to face them in battle.

Yet the truth was that King Cetshwayo no longer had faith in the military option and realized that his only hope of survival was to stave-off the advance through negotiation. As it became obvious during May that a new British offensive was imminent, the king had tried to call up his army once more, and for the first time there was some resistance. The warriors were not ready and the crops still had to be gathered from the delayed harvest. The king gave permission for the warriors to remain at their homesteads for a few more weeks, but insisted that they muster in June. This time he summoned them from right across the country. There was no point in leaving troops along the coast or in the north; it was apparent that the army had the

Above: Wood's Column, the newly designated Flying Column, marches to the River uPoko. Notice the cased Colours in the centre of the infantry Battalion.

Left: Lieutenant and Adjutant F. J. Cockayne Frith, 17th Lancers, killed in the skirmish at eZungeni. He is wearing the 17th's dress uniform; on active service he would have reversed the white plastron front of his tunic to show the less conspicuous blue side, and the ornate plumed cap would have been replaced by a white foreign service helmet.

Right: A sketch of the skirmish at the River uPoko. Although the artist has incorrectly shown the dead Lancer as a Private, the picture otherwise gives a good impression of the incident in which Frith was killed.

capacity for only one more struggle and that would take place near Ulundi. Large numbers of warriors did not answer the call, but it is astonishing, given the huge losses they had sustained, that so many did. By the end of June Cetshwayo had mustered more than 20,000 men in the *amakhanda* around Ulundi. Perhaps even more remarkably, their will to resist was scarcely diminished and they remained convinced that they would be victorious if only they could lure the British away from their laagers and entrenchments.

It is unlikely that Cetshwayo shared their conviction, and as the British columns came nearer he stepped up his efforts to obtain a negotiated settlement. His chief emissary, Mfunzi, it will be remembered, had been detained at the Middle Drift after crossing on the same day that the battle of Hlobane had taken place. He had been released in May and had returned to Cetshwayo, only to be sent back again. A further stream of messengers were sent to Crealock's First Division. Their advance had been so laborious that it had been dubbed 'Crealock's Crawlers'. Few Zulus had been encountered so the division had not had the chance of any major fighting, but it had been achieving significant success in other fields, and this is why the king had singled it out for attention. As it advanced up the coast the First Division had been accepting surrenders from a number of important local chiefs. Chelmsford's policy had always been to try to prise the *izikhulu* away from the king and thus weaken the bonds which held the Zulu state together. Any chief who surrendered was offered lenient terms, while no terms at all were to be offered to the king. As early as 21 April Prince Magwendu kaMpande surrendered near Gingindlovu. He was one of the lesser princes and had very little influence within the kingdom, but he had been at Isandlwana and was a member of the Royal House, so his defection was an important propaganda *coup*. Rumours had it that Prince Dabulamanzi who had commanded at Rorke's Drift, been present at Gingindlovu and who lived near Eshowe, was considering surrender. So too was Mavumengwana

kaNdlela, one of the senior commanders at Isandlwana, who also lived near the coast. It is difficult to judge these defections too harshly; the men had fought bravely and were increasingly convinced that they could not win. The impressive First Division was occupying their territory in such numbers that they were clearly there to stay. Furthermore, there were no Zulu reserves in the district anyway, all those willing to fight having gone up to Ulundi. By sending his messengers to Crealock, Cetshwayo hoped to halt his advance and at the same time remind his men in the south of his authority. Crealock merely referred the messengers to Chelmsford, and the coastal chiefs continued to prevaricate.

In fact, Chelmsford held all the cards in these negotiations. When three messengers, Mgcwelo, Mtshibela and Mphokothwayo, arrived at Nondweni on 4 June and were taken before the General the next day, they were told that Chelmsford would, on the whole, prefer to negotiate with individual chiefs. If the king wished to express his good will he must surrender the oxen at his royal homestead, the two guns taken at Isandlwana and all the firearms within the kingdom. In addition, an *ibutho* to be named by Chelmsford would have publicly to lay down its arms. These terms were so harsh as to be almost flippant. Chelmsford knew there was no possibility of Cetshwayo accepting them, nor did he want him to. Chelmsford was still intent on inflicting one last military defeat on the Zulus.

The messengers trudged disconsolately back to Ulundi carrying a written dispatch outlining Chelmsford's terms. This was a cynical touch for the record, because the Zulus, of course, could not read.

Ironically, however, the king was able to call upon the services of someone who could. A young Dutch trader, Cornelius Vijn, had been hawking trade goods around Zululand when the outbreak of war overtook him. After a few dangerous days he was taken into custody by the Zulus and treated with courtesy. Cetshwayo now ordered Vijn to be brought to Ulundi where he translated Chelmsford's letters and penned the king's replies.

In the meantime, however, Chelmsford was beginning to press home his advance with more urgency since he had just learned that he was about to be replaced. When the political storm over Isandlwana broke in Britain in February, the Duke of Cambridge and the military establishment had rallied to Chelmsford's support. British pride and Disraeli's reputation required the Zulus to be defeated. Chelmsford had been given due chance to redeem himself, but, despite the victories at Gingindlovu and Khambula, the war seemed no nearer a conclusion. Clifford's dispatches indicated that relations between the civil and military authorities in Natal were at an all-time low, and the continued transport débâcle was adding hugely to the war's cost. Everywhere the Confederation policy was in tatters. The Transvaal Boers, encouraged by the failure of British arms in Zululand, were poised to reject annexation. The Pedi were undefeated, the Basotho were stirring and there was no immediate sign of an end to Cetshwayo. Whatever his military faults, it was his inability to master the Commissariat and keep costs within bounds that Chelmsford's political masters were unable to forgive. It was decided to replace him with a Special Commissioner who would take charge of all military,

political and administrative decisions across the whole area; Frere was allowed to remain in sole charge of only the Cape Colony.

There was an obvious choice for such an appointment – General Sir Garnet Wolseley. Then only 46, Wolseley was regarded as something of an upstart by the military establishment to whom his insistence on radical army reform was anathema. He had, however, made himself a public hero by his swift and efficient campaigns in Canada in 1870 and Asante in 1873 – 4. Modesty was not his strongest point, and he tended to agree when the Press dubbed him 'Britain's only General'. Nevertheless, Wolseley did seem to have a political flair and military vigour sadly lacking in South Africa at the time, as well as experience of the country, where he had served briefly as Lieutenant Governor of Natal in 1875. What is more, he was desperate for an appointment, having been kicking his heels in the decidedly dull post of Governor of Cyprus. He had begged to be allowed to join the fighting then raging in Afghanistan, but had been turned down. When he heard the news of Isandlwana he immediately asked to be transferred to South Africa. This time he got his wish; Hicks Beach commissioned him to bring the Zulu war to a successful conclusion, and sort out the political complications. In Natal, Zululand and the Transvaal Wolseley was to be the senior British representative; both Frere and Chelmsford would have to take their orders from him. His appointment was announced at the end of May and he embarked immediately. On 23 June he arrived in Cape Town. With characteristic energy he immediately conferred with Frere, then set sail for Durban. He was determined to reach the front in time to take charge of the final advance on Ulundi. Chelmsford, of course, once he heard that he was to be superseded, was equally determined to bring the war to a close himself.

By this time the combined Second Division and Flying Column advance had moved down the Babanango spur and was in distant sight of Ulundi. The advance had been a particularly destructive one. Throughout the war, the British considered Zulu homesteads fair military targets and now, keen to reduce the Zulu will to resist by every possible means, Chelmsford had ordered his patrols to destroy as many *imizi* as they could, and particularly any supplies of the newly harvested grain. If necessary the Zulu people would be starved into submission. The advance was therefore screened by a great wave of scouts who burnt and looted everything before them. On 26 June a major raid was made into the emaKhosini valley, 'the place of kings'. This was the traditional birth-place of the Zulu nation and a number of graves of old chiefs were situated there, including that of Shaka's father, Senzangakhona. There were also a large number of important *amakhanda* in the valley. Three were destroyed by the 17th Lancers on the 26th, and a further six as the columns passed by during the next few days. This act had one dire spiritual consequence for the Zulus. Housed at one of the *amakhanda* –

esiKlebheni – was the *inkatha yezwe yakwaZulu*, a coil of grass rope, bound in python skin, which had been handed down by Shaka himself. This was a highly sacred object which was believed to embody the spirit of national unity itself. When the *inkhata* was burnt, the omens for the future of the Zulu kingdom were appalling.

On 27 June, Chelmsford reached the Mthonjaneni ridge. From here the ground dropped steadily down into the thorn-bush of the White Mfolozi valley, on the far side of which the Mahlabathini plain, with its cluster of *amakhanda*, including Ulundi itself, was clearly visible. That same day Buller's patrols, pushing down towards the river, came across the same three messengers who had come into the camp on 5 June. They had arrived with two enormous elephant's tusks and a herd of 150 cattle taken at Isandlwana. They

Below: General Sir Garnet Wolseley; appointed to supersede both Frere and Chelmsford, he arrived too late to command all but the pacification and withdrawal from Zululand, and his post-war settlement was a disaster.

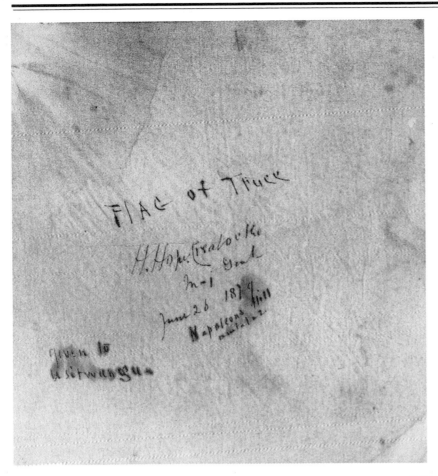

FLAG of Truce

H. Hope Crealock
2nd
June 26 1879
Napoleons shirt

given to
Usirwangu

Above: *A poignant souvenir of King Cetshwayo's hopeless peace missions; a white flag carried by Zulu envoys when they approached Crealock's First Division on 26 June.*

Right: *Zulu emissaries entering Chelmsford's camp on 27 June, carrying elephants' tusks as a peace offering; a final attempt to ward off the impending catastrophe – they were destined to be disappointed.*

indicated that Cetshwayo could not comply with Chelmsford's earlier demands, but had sent the gifts as proof of his earnest desire for peace. Chelmsford replied that he could not accept the tusks at this time; that his terms still stood, but that he would accept the cattle and would not cross the Mfolozi for the time being. The messengers left with the comment that now they 'would have to fight', because the British gave them no choice.

In fact, it cost Chelmsford nothing to promise a delay in his advance, since he wanted to prepare a major camp at Mthonjaneni. This was to be the final base for his dash on Ulundi, and it consisted of three wagon-laagers large enough to contain all the tents and stores. When the troops moved down towards the river they would take no kit or tents with them, only supplies for ten days and the ammunition carts. An unlucky garrison, the draft sent out to replace the 1/24th, would be left at Mthonjaneni, while the rest of the army would have the glory of wreaking the final revenge for Isandlwana.

The descent into the Mfolozi valley began on the morning of 30th June. The more experienced men of the Flying Column toiled down the slope first with the Second Division behind, but the sight of large bodies of warriors moving about across the distant river, and the apparent inevitability of an imminent battle, was beginning to prey on the soldiers' nerves. At midday, they met yet more Zulu envoys, this time including Mfunzi, carrying the Prince Imperial's sword. Chelmsford agreed to modify his terms slightly;

Left: Soldiers of the 80th Regiment cutting wood in one of the camps during the march to Ulundi.

Right: The 17th Lancers crossing a river on the advance to Ulundi.

Left: Although damaged, this photograph shows officers of the 80th Regiment, photographed during the final stages of the Flying column's advance into Zululand.

Right: The descent through the thorn-bush into the White Mfolozi valley; the final approach to Ulundi. The British laager is visible in the centre of the picture, with the bluff overlooking the drift beyond. The great amakhanda can be seen on the Mahlabathini plain on the far side of the river.

instead of the surrender of an *ibutho*, he would accept a thousand rifles taken at Isandlwana. In order to allow the king time to comply, he would delay his advance across the Mfolozi until 3rd July. This offer was, of course, a sham – Chelmsford knew Cetshwayo could not agree to his terms. Throughout the negotiations, Chelmsford's sole intention was to manipulate the deplorable situation to allow himself time to destroy the Zulus in battle at a time and place of his choosing. Cetshwayo's peace initiative was doomed before it began since the General was not acting in good faith.

In the meantime, as the axe poised threateningly over Cetshwayo's head, Sir Garnet Wolseley was frantically trying to reach the front. He had reached Durban on 28 June and had sent a stream of messages to Chelmsford instructing him to halt all operations and wait for Wolseley to take command. But Chelmsford was a long way from Durban, and even Pietermaritzburg, and it took time for the messages to reach him. As Frere had once exploited the slowness of

communications with Britain to precipitate the Zulu War before the Government could object, so Chelmsford now exploited them to bring it to a close before Wolseley could intervene. Wolseley was faced with a dilemma: should he try to join the First or Second Divisions, and which of them would allow him to influence events the quickest? Deciding that the Second Division in the heart of Zululand was out of reach, he opted for the First. He set sail up the coast only to be prevented from landing at Port Durnford by the surf. He had to return to Durban and make his way to Crealock overland. By the time he had done this, Chelmsford had gained his victory and the war was over.

The final advance to Ulundi had been accomplished in the face of a severe jitteryness on the part of the troops of the Second Division. As they moved down towards the river, Zulu *amabutho* could be seen marching from one *ikhanda* to another across the Mahlabathini plain. The veterans of the Flying

Column guessed – correctly – that this was just part of the doctoring ceremony for the coming fight, but at one point the Second Division opened fire blindly, the bullets whistling unpleasantly close to the Flying Column men in front. It was decided to camp on the banks of the Mfolozi, in a bend in the river overlooking the drift. The wagons were just coming up and being allotted their positions when a Zulu force moved closer to the river. Chelmsford ordered the laagers to be formed in half an hour – an impossible task – and the Second Division troops milled about in great confusion, expecting an immediate attack. It did not materialize, but that night a picket fired a warning shot at someone who failed to answer his challenge and the Native Contingent, sleeping outside the laager, panicked and rushed in, trampling the troops. The next day Chelmsford set about building a secure post, a combination of linked laagers and a stone redoubt, to reassure his men.

At last, the Zulus had grown tired of the diplomatic charade. Cetshwayo himself seems to have been anxious to keep talks open until the last minute, but his chiefs and generals had realized that they were being made fools of. When Mfunzi returned with Chelmsford's final demands, the chiefs had not even allowed him access to the king. Cetshwayo had ordered that his *amabutho* should prevent the British crossing the Mfolozi drift, but should on no account launch an attack. His commander on the spot, however, the Mandlakazi chief, Zibhebhu kaMaphita, took matters into his own hands and placed snipers on a long bluff on the Zulu bank overlooking the Drift. From here they regularly harassed the British parties collecting water and bathing in the drift. On 2 July Cetshwayo made one last gesture and sent a herd of his own white cattle to the British camp; the Khandempemvu *ibutho* intercepted it and refused to allow it to cross. The Zulu army had become as

Right: A blemished photograph of Chief Zibhebhu kaMaphita who commanded the Zulus guarding the Mfolozi crossings at Ulundi.

Far right: Captain Cecil D'Arcy and Sergeant Edmund O'Toole of the Frontier Light Horse both of whom won the VC for their part in the skirmish on 3 July. Like many mounted Volunteer officers, D'Arcy is wearing a blue patrol jacket; O'Toole appears to be wearing the FLH's black uniform.

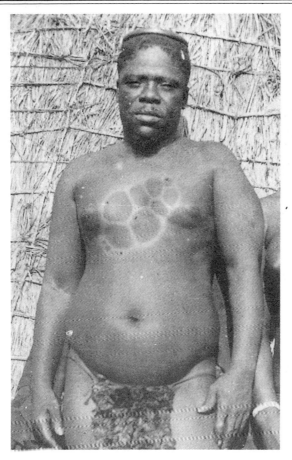

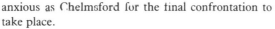

anxious as Chelmsford for the final confrontation to take place.

At noon on the 3rd, the time allotted for Cetshwayo's reply ran out and the British drove the cattle, delivered by the envoys on the 27th, back across the river to symbolize the end of negotiation. Immediately, Chelmsford went on to the offensive. Buller was ordered to make a foray with a force of mounted men with the joint purpose of clearing the snipers from the bluffs and locating a spot on the Mahlabathini plain for the coming fight. The Volunteers crossed the river in two sections: one party under Commandant Baker, crossing at the drift opposite the bluff; the other, led by Buller, crossing farther down stream. The snipers, caught between the two scattered, and Buller's men chased them out on to the plain. Buller had already espied a gentle rise to the west of Ulundi as being the best position for a British force to occupy, and now his men, still pursuing the Zulus, were led over the same ground. Unbeknown to them they were being led into a trap, carefully planned by Zibhebhu. As the patrol moved towards the Mbilane stream, which separated them from Ulundi, about 4,000 Zulus suddenly rose out of the grass in front of them, and loosed a volley at only 70 yards' range. Two other Zulu groups of about the same strength then sprang up on each side. The fleeing warriors had led the patrol between the Zulu forces towards the far end by the stream, where the long grass had been carefully plaited to trip the horses. A few

more yards and the patrol would have ridden to its death. As it was, the volley emptied a number of saddles and several of Buller's men – Lord William Beresford, Buller's Staff Officer, and Captain D'Arcy and Sergeant O'Toole of the Frontier Light Horse – had to rescue unhorsed troopers from right in front of the charging warriors. All three were subsequently awarded the Victoria Cross. Buller was able to extricate himself thanks to his own foresight; he had left a body of men close by the Nodwengu *ikhanda* and their fire slowed the Zulu advance. Alternately firing and retreating, Buller's men made it back to the drift, but not until they were fired upon by some of the guns and troops in the camp did the Zulus give up the pursuit. Buller had been lucky to escape with only three dead and four wounded.

That night was not a comfortable one in the British camp. It was a cold, clear, moonlit Zululand winter's night, and the coming fight preyed on the men's minds. Moreover they were kept awake by the mournful chants of the *amabutho* across the river who, at one point, marched down to the drift, causing an alarm. Dawn must have come as something of a relief; when the troops were roused and had taken a sparse breakfast of coffee and biscuits it was clear to all that the long and trying campaign would be decided that day. Several companies were told off to guard the camp and the rest were marched down to the river. There was still a fear that the Zulus might contest the crossing, but Buller's men spurred across and occupied the bluff without opposition. The advancing column was the largest to have been assembled for any of the Zulu War battles – 4,166 white and 958 black soldiers, twelve guns, two Gatlings and a rocket battery. The men were carrying their greatcoats and two days' rations, but the only baggage train consisted of the ammunition carts. As they moved out on to the edge of the Mahlabathini plain, Chelmsford formed his men into a huge hollow square. The sides were composed of ranks of infantry, four deep, with the artillery at the corners and along the sides. The Flying Column troops were given the place of honour at front and sides, with the Second Division completing the sides and sealing the rear. There would be no scattered firing lines as at Isandlwana, and no wagon laagers. The Zulus would be fairly faced in the open. As the square marched through the tall green grass, beginning now to turn brown, the cavalry hovered on the flanks. The NNC and ammunition carts were safely positioned inside the protective box formed by the infantry. Chelmsford was aiming for the low rise Buller had reconnoitred the day before, and as the cumbersome formation passed close by the Nodwengu *ikhanda* it turned to the right. The Colours were flying and the band of the 1/13th were playing martial airs. When it reached the appointed spot Chelmsford halted the square and dressed the ranks. The men faced outwards and the first two ranks knelt. The guns unlimbered. It was now about 8 am, and the front of the square was facing Ulundi, about a mile and a half away. Nodwengu lay much closer, on the right rear, and several other *amakhanda* were on the slopes of the surrounding hills. Until now there had been little sign of the Zulus, but when the square halted they began to come over the crest of the hills, out from the *amakhanda* and up from the dongas where they had been gathering, and began to form up on three sides of the square.

The Zulus were surprised at the British deployment. They were convinced that the troops would not dare emerge from their laagers and had planned to draw Chelmsford on to the very spot where he now stood. As a consequence the general opinion was that the British had played right into the Zulus' hands. Even those who had suffered so severely at Khambula and who were reluctant to attack defended positions were confident of victory. The king, however, did not share their optimism, and he had scolded them that by their defiance during the previous days they had brought about the destruction of the kingdom. They clamored to fight, however, and Cetshwayo gave them what advice he could before retiring to one of his homesteads away from Ulundi. His favourite brother, Prince Ziwedu kaMpande, stayed to watch the fight on his behalf, and a number of important men were present including Zibhebhu. In all, the Zulu army, drawn from all the regiments in the kingdom, numbered between 15,000 and 20,000 warriors with a further 5,000 in reserve. Its plans were to repeat the tactics of the previous day and to surround the British formation and find its weak spots.

Left: J. N. Crealock's sketch of Lord Chelmsford on the morning of the battle of Ulundi suggests something of the tension he must have felt on confronting the Zulus on his own terms at last.

Above: The band of the 1/13th who played as the square marched into position.

Right: Prince Ziwedu kaMpande who watched the battle as the king's representative.

As the Zulus moved down on to the plain those British officers who had not faced them before were amazed by the precision with which they deployed in extended companies, screened by skirmishers. Chelmsford was anxious to draw them on and the irregular cavalry were sent out to skirmish. They set fire to the great circle of huts at Nodwengu and rode to within a few hundred yards of the advancing Zulus. The Natal Native Horse coolly traded taunts with the warriors as they fell back just ahead of the advance. 'Gallop in,' shouted the Zulus, 'but we will overtake you. We are going to kill every one of those red men. Perhaps some of you wild men may escape. But go quick, for we will chase you to the Mzinyathi!' This was not work for the regular cavalry, the 17th Lancers

and one squadron of Dragoons, and they had already retreated to their appointed place inside the square. The NNH thought for a moment that they were expected to remain outside throughout the battle, as they had done at Khambula, and they were resigning themselves to the prospect of a glorious, if pointless death, when the 13th opened a gap for them and they rode in. As the scattered parties of horsemen retreated to the square, the artillery opened fire, showering the converging *amabutho* with shrapnel. It was 8.45 am and the battle had begun. The Zulus responded with a great shout of 'uSuthu!' and broke into a charge.

The Zulus came on at a run all round the square, making what use they could of any natural cover afforded by grass or a few scattered trees. When they were within about 400 yards range the infantry opened up with crashing volleys that rippled round the square by sections. The Gatlings of 10/7 Battery, the first Gatling Battery in the Royal Artillery, opened up with a steady chatter from the centre of the front line, which ripped great holes in the Zulu ranks. Major Grenfell of the 60th Rifles, on Chelmsford's staff, watched fascinated as a Zulu *induna* mustered a group of warriors and led them straight at the Gatlings. The Battery commander, Major Owen, was working one gun himself and a single turn of the crank served to cut the warriors down. A year later different duties would bring Grenfell past Ulundi again and he visited the site of the battle. He found the skeleton of the dead *induna* lying where he had fallen, and brought away his skull as a souvenir.

The hail of fire presented a barrier which the Zulus could not penetrate. A few rushed to within twenty or thirty yards, but they were easily gunned down. One young warrior ran in closer to fling a spear, but it missed its target and he was killed immediately. Most of the charges faltered a hundred or more yards from the lines, and the Zulus dived into the grass and opened a terrific volume of fire on the square. Chelmsford's formation was particularly vulnerable to

Above: Shepstone's Native Horse skirmish with Zulus to draw on the attack; the start of the battle of Ulundi.

Left: Men of 'C' Company, 1/13th Light Infantry, who took part in the battle.

rifle-fire, and it says much for Zulu inaccuracy that he did not sustain heavier casualties. Even at this range the Zulus were firing high and bullets whizzed and hummed over the heads of the infantry. Chelmsford refused to dismount during the action, so his staff were also obliged to remain mounted and, being higher than anyone else, their position was particularly vulnerable. A couple of them received minor grazes, but none was seriously hurt.

After the initial rush stalled the Zulus made determined attempts to seek out and attack British weak spots. They were disappointed to find that surrounding the square had given them no obvious advantage, but they soon realized that the corners, where the infantry fire was less concentrated, were the weak spot. The iNgobamakhosi and Uve *amabutho*, on the Zulu left horn, rushed in a mass into Nodwengu, and opened a terrific fire on the rear right corner of the square. The smoke from the burning huts billowing across in front of them gave them some protection, and several times throughout the battle Chelmsford ordered the cease-fire to be sounded to allow the smoke from the volleys to clear. From Nodwengu the Zulus launched a determined attack which pressed right up to the corner. Seriously alarmed, Lord Chelmsford ordered up a company of Royal Engineers who had been posted inside the square to support the infantry, and rode over calling out 'Men fire faster! Cannot you fire faster?' The guns on the corner, 9-pounders of N/6 battery, had to fire seven rounds of case shot, and the infantry officers drew their swords and revolvers in preparation for hand-to-hand combat. But the charge collapsed. Afterwards the leading corpses were found just nine paces from the line.

All around the square the Zulu advance had been pinned down. At this juncture a solid body of men, apparently married warriors from senior *amabutho* and so far held in reserve, was seen to move out of Ulundi

Right: Ulundi, showing the position of the British camp on the White Mfolozi, Buller's reconnaissance on 3 July and the climax of the battle at about 9.00 a.m. on the 4th. The inset shows Chelmsford's square: the right face pointed towards Ulundi. The ammunition carts were placed in a protective square around the N.N.C., and at the start of the battle two guns were moved to cover the top right corner.

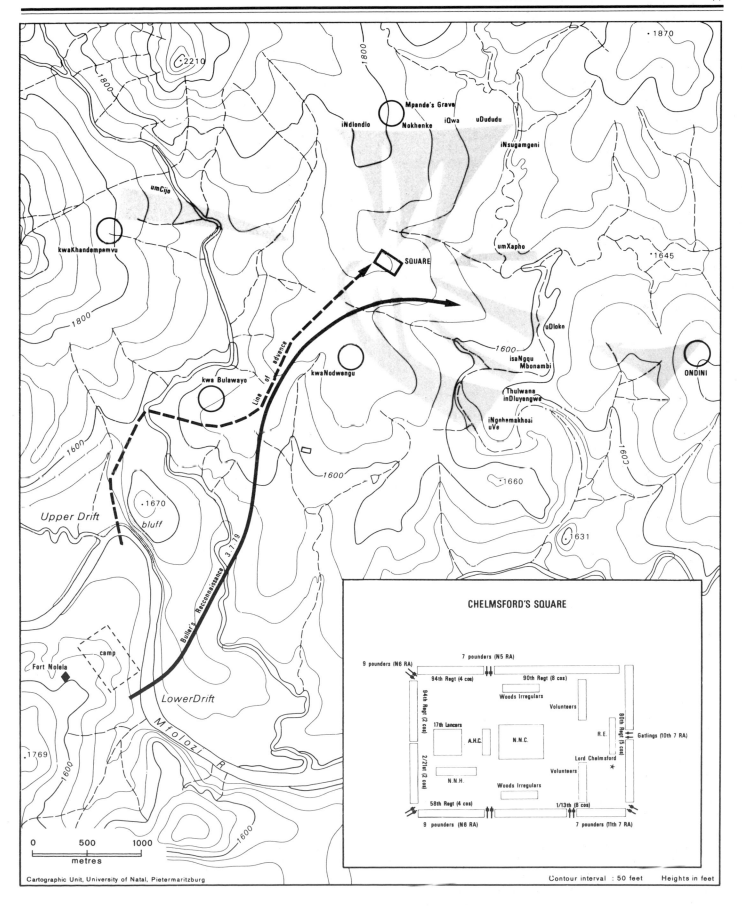

- 1870

- 2210

1800

1800

1800

Mpande's Grave

iNdlondlo   Nokhenke   iQwa   uDududu

iNsugamgeni

umCijo

kwaKhandempemvu

umXapho

- 1645

SQUARE

Line of advance

Buller's Reconnaissance 3.7.79

kwa Bulawayo

kwaNodwengu

uDloko

1600

isaNgqu
Mbonambi

ONDINI

Thulwana
inDluyengwe

iNgnhamakhosi
uVe

1600

- 1660

- 1631

Upper Drift

- 1670
bluff

1600

camp

Fort Nolela

LowerDrift

Mfolozi R.

- 1769

1600

1600

CHELMSFORD'S SQUARE

9 pounders (N6 RA)   7 pounders (N5 RA)

94th Regt (4 cos)   90th Regt (8 cos)

Woods Irregulars

94th Regt (2 cos)   Volunteers

17th Lancers   80th Regt (5 cos)

A.H.C.   N.N.C.   R.E.   Gatlings (10th 7 RA)

2/21st (2 cos)   Lord Chelmsford

N.N.H.   Volunteers

Woods Irregulars

58th Regt (4 cos)   1/13th (8 cos)

9 pounders (N6 RA)   7 pounders (11th 7 RA)

0   500   1000
metres

Cartographic Unit, University of Natal, Pietermaritzburg

Contour interval : 50 feet   Heights in feet

Top left: Chelmsford's square during the battle, the infantry on one side have moved to allow the Lancers to emerge. This picture gives a good impression of the British formation. Note the Zulus pinned down in the foreground.

Left: The right face of the square; N/6's 9pdrs foreground, the 13th with Colours flying, beyond.

Above: 10/7 Battery's two Gatlings with Major Owen, who commanded them at Ulundi, in front of the one on the left.

Right: Major Grenfell, 60th Rifles, Chelmsford's Deputy Assistant Adjutant-General and a participant in the battle of Ulundi.

towards the front of the square. The Gatlings had jammed – the bolts had slipped out and were difficult to find in the long grass – and the 9-pounders on the right front corner were directed to break up the attack. As their first shells burst above the Zulus the warriors fanned out into battle formation, but each manoeuvre drew well-placed shots from the guns. The Zulu column stalled, then began to retreat without pressing home its attack.

Indeed, many of the Zulu reserves on the hills were still uncommitted and were clearly reluctant to face the fire. Soldiers who had fought at Khambula later claimed that the Zulu attack was not pressed home with the same determination at Ulundi, and no doubt their previous experience must have disheartened many warriors. Yet the attacks continued for more than half an hour, despite the fact that it was clear as soon as the first charges were cut down that there could be no hope of victory. At about 9.20 the Zulus began to slip away in significant numbers and, noticing them go, the British infantry raised a cheer and threw their helmets in the air. Now was the moment the regular cavalry had been waiting for. Chelmsford turned to the Colonel of the 17th Lancers and said, 'Go at them, Lowe!' The infantry were hastily moved aside and the Lancers rode out, dressed their ranks briefly, then charged.

Their first charge took them across a stretch of ground in front of Nodwengu where they rode down a concentration of warriors still lurking in the grass. Seeing that there were few remaining Zulus in front of them, they turned to the right and plunged into a mass of retreating warriors. If the pursuit after Khambula

Left: A spectacular view of the Zulu charge. The Zulu numbers are probably exaggerated, but this sketch does give a good impression of the battle from their perspective. The flashing bayonets around the square and the apparent invulnerability of the British troop led many warriors to believe that Chelmsford's position was protected by a temporary fort of corrugated iron.

Below left: Carbines found among the Zulu dead on the battlefield of Ulundi. The Martini-Henry (rear) had probably been captured at Isandlwana. Zulu fire at Ulundi was heavy but inaccurate.

Above: The Zulu rush presses to within a few yards of the 90th Light Infantry.

Below: The charge of the 17th Lancers, a water-colour by C. E. Fripp, who was present during the battle as a war correspondent. Probably the most accurate version of the scene; the square is centre rear.

had been severe, that at Ulundi was more so, since it was exactly the work for which the Lancers were suited. Yelling their war-cry 'Death! Death!' they spitted the fleeing warriors through the back. Some Zulus threw themselves on the ground to escape, but the nine-foot bamboo lances had the reach to skewer them where they lay. The heavy British chargers bowled many warriors over and trampled them under their hooves. Here and there the Zulus turned to stand, flinging spears or firing, or crouching down to slash at the bellies of the horses as they rode past. Some of the troopers found that their lances fouled on Zulu shields and they were forced to draw their swords. Yet even then the Zulus stood little chance and they were cut down without mercy. Only when the charge reached a donga, beyond which was a rise, from which a body of warriors rose and loosed a volley, shooting Captain Edmund Wyatt-Edgell through the head, did Drury-Lowe halt the charge. By now Chelmsford had unleashed the irregular cavalry, who were following behind the Lancers, shooting wounded Zulus with their carbines, or streaming out across the field breaking up any remaining Zulu concentrations. The Natal Native Horse found themselves chasing the same group of warriors who had taunted them at the beginning of the fight, and they yelled 'Well, are you going to the Mzinyathi now?' All around the square the Zulus were in full flight and the artillery began lobbing shells on to parties still lingering on the hill tops.

Above: Volunteers pursuing Zulus in the wake of the 17th's charge. Note the Nodwengu ikhanda burning (right), and Ulundi itself beyond the square. Sketch by Lieutenant W. Fairlie, NNH, who was present at the battle.

Left: Colonel Drury Curzon Drury Lowe, who led the 17th Lancers' charge at Ulundi.

The Zulus generally gave no quarter in battle and they were to receive none now. One eye-witness noticed a Basotho horseman dismount to question a wounded Zulu. After carefully gleaning everything the man knew, he conversationally asked if there was more; when the Zulu replied 'No', the Basotho shot him, then mounted up and joined in the pursuit. The NNH, indeed, were particularly efficient at killing off any Zulus they came across. A party of 70 warriors trapped in a donga was wiped out to a man, and when the pursuit was called off the NNH rode around the battlefield shooting every wounded Zulu they found. When the cavalry had broken what little resistance remained Chelmsford allowed the black auxiliaries to scour the field. They were so utterly ruthless that some officers, despite the jubilation of victory – and most of the British were glorying in the revenge they had exacted for Isandlwana – were embarrassed by the enthusiastic way the auxiliaries speared wounded Zulus. None were safe; the regimental dog of the 17th Lancers distinguished itself by running round the square barking at any Zulus who moved. They were soon finished off, and the slaughter was complete.

When the firing ceased Chelmsford counted the cost. He had lost two officers and ten men killed, 19 officers wounded – one later died – and 69 men wounded. The dead were buried in the centre of the square while the Chaplain read a service over them. Then once the wounded could be moved, Chelmsford advanced the square to the banks of the Mbilane

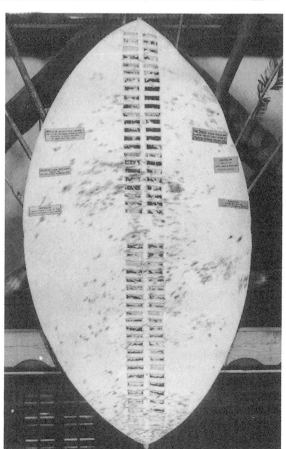

Above left: *The destruction of Ulundi; officers watch King Cetshwayo's isigodlo, including his European-style building, go up in flames.*

Above: *Smoke from the battlefield and burning Ulundi drifts across the Mahlabathini plain, photographed from the camp on the White Mfolozi.*

Left: *Crealock's sketch of a dead Zulu after Ulundi; Zulu losses during the battle were heavy. Note the obsolete firearm and powder-horn.*

DESTRUCTION OF THE ZULU KINGDOM 185

stream. The men were allowed to rest and eat their dinner. Out on the surrounding plain the cavalry patrols had already started setting fire to the great *amakhanda* and Chelmsford now gave permission for his officers to ride to Ulundi. There was a desperate race to be the first among the huts which was won by Lord Beresford. Cetshwayo's *isigodlo* was eagerly searched, but there were no great treasures, just three ivory tusks found in the square, European-style building. They were promptly seized by eager souvenir hunters, before the whole royal complex was put to the torch. Souvenir hunting was the order of the day and, now that the campaign was clearly over, the troops desperately collected Zulu weapons and shields, lamenting the fact that there were not more valuable or attractive items to be had.

As Ulundi slowly went up in flames Chelmsford and Newdigate spoke to their men, congratulating them on their conduct. At about 2 pm the troops began to march back to their camp on the far side of the Mfolozi. By 5.30 there was not a white man on the far side of the river. Ulundi would burn for four days and the great pall of smoke hung over the Mahlabathini plain. Quite how many Zulus died is a matter of debate, but hundreds were strewn around the site of the square – in one place sixty were sprawled in front of a Gatling – and they lay in clumps where the volley fire had caught them. So thorough had been the pursuit that many of the wounded had been overtaken and killed before they could escape, and perhaps as many as 1,500 had died in all. The British made no attempt to bury the Zulu dead and months later their bones could be seen whitening in the grass.

At Khambula, the British burial details had noted the fine physiques and youth of the Zulu dead, and it was the same everywhere, since it was the men of the young *amabutho* who had taken up the challenge of the war with all the naive truculence of a proud warrior tradition. They had offered their naked bodies against the world's most sophisticated military technology, and now scarcely a family in Zululand did not feel the loss. The army was gone and the great national centres plundered and destroyed, together with countless ordinary homesteads. Dispossessed, impoverished and grieving, the civilian population could only look to the ruin of the late harvest and the remains of their looted herds to ward off the further horror of famine. The King was powerless, and the nation was on the verge of collapse. That night, in their camp across the river, Chelmsford's soldiers slept easy, freed forever from the spectre of Isandlwana. For them, the months of hardship and privation, the forced marches in baking heat or drenching downpours, the poor food, bad water, disease and sudden frights, were coming to an end, and they viewed the prospect with satisfaction. Frere's dirty work was done at last.

On the day after Ulundi Chelmsford made his first official reply to Wolseley's appointment. Inevitably he chose to regard it as a censure and tendered his resignation. Ulundi would vindicate him and he could return home victorious. He ordered the Second Division to retreat by the way it had come, via Mthonjaneni, and sent Wood's Flying Column across country to join up with the First Division.

Sir Garnet was welcome to whatever remained of the war.

Below: The Ulundi battlefield nine months after the fight, still strewn with Zulu skulls and bones. This view, coincidentally, is across the same ground as that on page 176.

LAST SHOTS

Wolseley takes command; the pacification of Zululand and the hunt for the king. **Cetshwayo Captured.** *Wolseley's post-war settlement; mopping-up; the suppression of Manyanyoba and the abaQulusi. Final British withdrawal from Zululand. Zululand collapses into civil war.*

'All what is mine in Zululand has been overturned and spoiled.' King Cetshwayo kaMpande.

Sir Garnet Wolseley heard the news of Chelmsford's victory at Ulundi from Archibald Forbes, the correspondent of the *Daily News*, who had ridden across country to scoop his rivals. Wolseley was at Fort Pearson and was no doubt bitterly disappointed at being cheated of the kill. He took his revenge in his private diaries where Chelmsford's officers are singled out for caustic personal abuse. Nevertheless, he pressed on to Fort Chelmsford and within a few days had reached Crealock, whom he galvanized into action. From here he pushed on with his staff to the deserted mission at St. Paul's on the road to Ulundi, where he had arranged to meet Lord Chelmsford and the withdrawing Flying Column. Chelmsford was relieved to hand over his command. He made one last speech to his troops then, accompanied by Wood and Buller, travelled down the line to Durban and sailed for home. He was greeted with all the acclaim and honours Victorian Britain reserved for its conquering heroes, but he never quite escaped the mournful field of Isandlwana; he was never given an independent command again.

Wolseley applied himself to the pacification of Zululand with characteristic vigour. Along the coastal strip the great chiefs had now been fully detached from their allegiance to the king. On 4 July, after protracted negotiation, many of the district *izikhulu* 'came in', including Somopho kaZikhala, the commander-in-chief at Gingindlovu, Phalane kaMdinwa, also a commander at Gingindlovu, and Chief Somkhele kaMalanda, the powerful and influential leader of the Mphukunyoni clan who dominated the northern coastal plain. These surrenders had been made before news of the battle at Ulundi could have been known, and the chiefs were lured by the easy British terms which simply required them to hand over their firearms and royal cattle. Even Dabulamanzi, who had achieved the reputation of a *bête noire* among the British who knew him from his role at Rorke's Drift

Left: Major Marter, 1st King's Dragoon Guards – the man who captured King Cetshwayo.

Above: A typical incident in the skirmishing in northern Zululand; Commandant Schermbruker of the Volunteers rescues Captain Moore, 4th Regiment, whose horse has been killed in a surprise attack by Manyanyoba's warriors.

and imagined him the fiercest and most daring of the Zulu commanders, surrendered on the 12th.

And yet the country as a whole was by no means at peace. Even Wolseley accepted that the Zulu army had ceased to exist after Ulundi, but the gradual erosion of Cetshwayo's authority which had led to many chiefs holding men back from the muster, also meant that those men were at large in the country, often under arms. As early as June, long before Chelmsford gave up his command, there were a series of ugly incidents which hinted that a formal victory might not be enough to end the fighting, and which suggested that several chiefs might be prepared to prosecute a guerrilla war on their own account. Early in the month Manyanyoba's supporters, having recovered from the death of Mbilini and encouraged by Wood's moving out from Khambula, began raiding the Ntombe valley once more. These raids became so frequent that those Africans friendly to the British abandoned their homesteads and crops, and took to caves for refuge. On one occasion a white civilian was killed. The garrison at Luneburg proved too weak to curb the Zulu depredations. There had been a serious flare-up at the Middle Drift, too, apparently a belated response to Twentyman's raid of 20 May. As the war had moved further and further into Zululand, the border districts had seemed to be returning to a more normal, peaceful existence, so the Zulu raid on 25 June took the garrisons along the Thukela completely by surprise. A

party of several hundred Zulus crossed the river at dawn at several points where the water was lowest and, under cover of a dense mist, brushed aside the local Border Police and began burning and looting the homesteads of Natal Africans. By the time Twentyman had mustered his levies to stop them, they were on their way back to the river, driving off a herd of captured cattle. Despite some skirmishing at the drifts, the Zulus managed to extricate themselves in good order. One Border Policeman and several black civilians had been killed. On 30 June Lieutenant Scott-Douglas of the 21st and his orderly, Corporal Cotter, 17th Lancers, had taken a message from Chelmsford to one of the forts back down the line of advance. On the way back they had cut across country and become lost near the deserted mission of KwaMagwaza. Here they were surprised by a party of 500 warriors, apparently heading for Ulundi. Scott-Douglas managed to fire off five rounds from his revolver before he was speared through the chest. The bodies of both men were found some days later by Evelyn Wood and were buried where they had fallen.

To Wolseley, it seemed that such incidents would only stop once Cetshwayo had been captured, and the recalcitrant chiefs brought into line by force. Chelmsford's old Divisions had been disbanded and in their place Wolseley organized two fresh columns. One, under Lieutenant-Colonel Clarke, drawn from troops of the old First Division, was sent to re-

Above: *King Cetshwayo emerges from his hut to surrender to Major Marter (right), while the Dragoons surround the homestead.*

Left: *A heavy guard is mounted on the king's hut during the march to Wolseley's camp at Ulundi.*

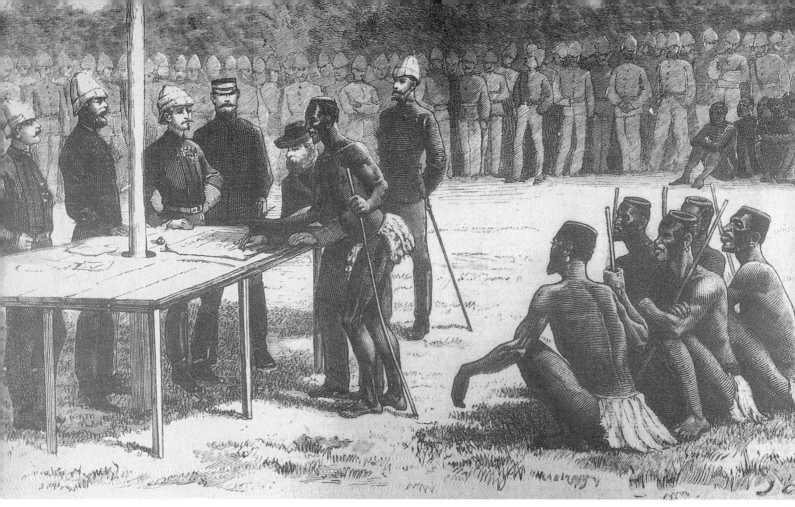

Above: Sir Garnet Wolseley accepting the surrender of the izikhulu at Ulundi on 1 September 1879.

Right: In this sketch by an eye-witness, King Cetshwayo stares wistfully over the hills of Zululand for the last time.

Far right: Mkhosana Zungu, King Cetshwayo's attendant, captured with him. Mkhosana shared the king's exile and accompanied him on his visit to England in 1882.

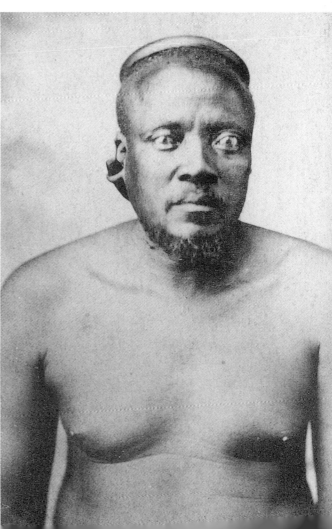

establish a British presence at Ulundi and organize the hunt for the king. The second, drawn from the Flying Column and commanded by Lieutenant-Colonel Baker Russell, was sent off to northern Zululand to suppress Manyanyoba and persuade the abaQulusi to submit. In the meantime Wolseley called a new meeting of the coastal chiefs at Mhlatuze on 19 July and informed them of his intention to break up the kingdom into a number of independent Chiefdoms. The military system was to be disbanded and king Cetshwayo – once he had been found – would be deposed. Wolseley promised to outline his plans at a meeting of all the important men at Ulundi in August.

The capture of the king offered one last chance for adventure in Zululand and the British approached the task with all the gusto of the hunt. In fact, Cetshwayo had stayed in the vicinity of the Mahlabathini plain just long enough to hear the news of his final defeat, then struck north to the principal homestead of his Prime Minister, Mnyamana. He was inconsolable. From the first he had been reluctant to fight the British, but they had allowed him no option and his army had gone willingly to its destruction. Now he had only a handful of personal attendants and all his chiefs were deserting him. He toyed briefly with the idea of moving north and building a new capital on the Swazi borders, as Dingane had once done, but when he tried to regroup several *amabutho* to perform the task, they ignored him and stayed at home. Nothing was left to him but to try to negotiate the best possible deal with the British. But if Wolseley was prepared to offer the

izikhulu their independence, he was prepared to offer Cetshwayo nothing but his life. Accordingly, at the beginning of August he went on the run, moving from one homestead to another, among those ordinary Zulus who stayed loyal to him. Once Clarke's column had established its headquarters at Ulundi it organized a large patrol under Major Barrow and accompanied by the trader, Vijn, to scour the countryside to the north in an attempt to track the king down. Cetshwayo easily eluded the patrols, however, and Barrow returned to Ulundi leaving only a small party under Major Lord Gifford to continue the pursuit. Gifford had earned a reputation as a dashing leader of scouts during the Asante War, where he won the VC, and he was determined to have the honour of bringing in the king. For ten days Gifford and his men patrolled the wild, sparsely inhabited country north of the Black Mfolozi, following every lead and trying to bully local Zulus into revealing the king's whereabouts. Then on 26 August a rumour reached Clarke at Ulundi that Cetshwayo was making for the Ngome forest and he sent a party of Dragoons under Major Marter to head him off. Marter's party were close on his heels when they intercepted a message from Gifford suggesting that he, too, knew of the king's intentions. Thus two parties were converging on Cetshwayo from different directions and the race was on to see who would reach him first.

Marter won. On the morning of the 28th his guides led him to a steep precipice and pointed out a small homestead nestling in the bush 2,000 feet below. That,

Right: Officers of the 4th
Regiment engaged in the final
suppression of Manyanyoba
and Mbilini's followers. Left to
right: Captain Crofton, Lieutenant Bonomi, Major Law-
rence and Captain Moore.

they said, was where the king was hiding. The slope
was too steep for his Dragoons to descend, but Marter
sent down a party of auxiliaries with orders to hide
themselves in the bush at the bottom. He then led his
men on a wide detour, descending into the valley by a
less steep approach. There he formed them up and led
a dramatic charge to surround the homestead. The
inhabitants were taken by complete surprise and,
although someone panicked and fired a shot, there was
no resistance. Once he was assured that he was not to
be killed, the king came out of his hut and wearily
surrendered to Marter. He had with him his personal
friend and confidant, Mkhosana Zungu, and a few
attendants. As Marter led his prize away, he was met
by the disappointed Gifford, who had been only a few
miles distant. Cetshwayo spent that night under guard
at a homestead on the road to Ulundi and one last act of
bloodshed marked his passing into captivity. Some of
his attendants tried to bolt for the bush and the escort
opened fire, killing two of the men. On 31 August the
king was marched into Wolseley's camp at Ulundi,
and by 4 September he was at Port Durnford where he
was taken into a surf-boat and embarked for Cape
Town, where he was destined to be exiled.

Wolseley had already disposed of his kingdom.
Throughout the second half of August the great chiefs
gathered at his camp at Ulundi and signified their
desire to surrender. Among them were Mnyamana and
Tshingwayo, the king's principal commanders, and
Zibhebhu kaMaphita. On 1 September Wolseley held
a great meeting and announced his plans for the

country. He had decided to split it up into thirteen
small Chiefdoms, each ruled by his appointees. Most
of these proved to be *izikhulu* who had 'behaved
themselves' and surrendered in time. Hamu was
rewarded with a large tract of land, and so was John
Dunn, whom Wolseley privately wanted to make the
'white king' of all Zululand. Hlubi, the Tlokwa chief
who had fought so well for the British, was allocated
the strategic strip of territory on the Zulu bank of the
Mzinyathi, where Sihayo had once ruled the Qungebe.
The plan showed a superficial understanding of the
nature of the kingdom by attempting to exploit the
izikhulu's desire for autonomy, and by attempting to
revive some of the pre-Shakan clans. But it under-
estimated the complex relationship between the king
and his chiefs, and a bloody and destructive civil war
would result almost as soon as the British troops
withdrew.

All that remained was to squash the last traces of
resistance in the north of the country. Baker Russell's
column had marched north to Zungwini with the
intention of intimidating the Qulusi. Still ardent
supporters of the king, they prevaricated until news
reached them of Cetshwayo's capture and then on 1
September their chief commander, Mahubulwana
kaDumisela, surrendered on behalf of his people.
Manyanyoba was still holding out with some of
Mbilini's old supporters in the Ntombe valley and on
the 4th Wolseley ordered Russell to get him. That
same day a force was dispatched to try to winkle him
out. Several Zulus surrendered and were placed in the

charge of black auxiliaries while negotiations went on with Manyanyoba himself. One of the chief's followers fired a shot and the auxiliaries promptly massacred the prisoners in their care. The Zulus decided they did not trust the white man's word and swore to fight on. The next day the British tried to smoke the Zulus out by piling up wood at the entrances of the caves and setting it alight. They were unsuccessful. Then, on the 8th, they made a determined effort to finish the business. One party returned to Manyanyoba's caves which were found to be deserted, and blew them up. Another, consisting of men of the 4th Foot, proceeded to Mbilini's caves. There was a slight skirmish in which two men were killed, and when the troops threatened to blow up the caves the Zulus merely swore at their interpreter. Charges were placed around the caves and they were blown up with a number of people still inside. Resistance ceased. A fortnight later Manyanyoba surrendered.

The fighting over, Wolseley supervised the evacuation of Zululand. Clarke's column was marched back to Natal by way of the Middle Drift where its presence had a salutary effect on those Zulus who had launched the raid on 25 June. By the end of September the chains of forts were empty, the regulars on their way back to Durban and home, and the Volunteers disbanded. Zululand was left to its own devices.

It is hard to see who benefited from so much brutality and bloodshed. Certainly, the Confederation policy, as executed by Frere, had been destroyed at Isandlwana. In 1880 Disraeli's government fell, given a sharp push by Gladstone's attack on the South African situation. The new Liberal Government wanted no further involvement in Zululand. In late 1880 the Transvaal Boers rose and threw off British rule by their victory at Majuba in 1881. Zululand swiftly slid into chaos, aligning itself with either pro- or anti-royalist factions. In an attempt to restore some sort of order, Cetshwayo was allowed to return from exile, after first being allowed to visit London to argue his case, and was given back some portion of his old lands. How bitterly he must have felt that irony; he, who had appealed for Britain's support in 1873, was abandoned and broken by them in 1879, and was now expected to extricate Zululand from the mess they had made of it. His return was not a success and merely provoked a civil war. Zibhebhu's Mandlakazi had waxed fat in the king's absence and had no intention of returning to the royal fold. Cetshwayo was defeated by Zibhebhu in 1884 and died shortly afterwards, a sad, broken, hopeless man. The Royalist cause fell to his son, Dinuzulu, who tried unsuccessfully to throw off British interference by a minor uprising in 1888. The years of violence and chaos broke up the old order and discipline more effectively than Chelmsford's military campaign ever had, and at last the area was drawn into the mainstream of South Africa's economic development. So perhaps, in the end, Shepstone, and those who shared in his vision of Zululand as a large pool of cheap migrant labour, had won; and yet, with an irony worthy of the whole sorry saga, Natal was cheated of its pre-eminent economic role within South Africa when the world's largest gold deposits were found beneath the Witwatersrand in the Boer republic of the Transvaal. Against the resultant bloody struggle between whites for those riches, the subjugation of the black kingdoms would be reduced to the level of a sideshow, though their bitter legacy has born fruit in the troubles which beset the country today.

There are now six million Zulus in South Africa and their role within the contemporary drama is a complex one. Once it was only the British who built monuments to past victories and defeats, the crosses, obelisks and poignant clusters of graves and whitewashed cairns which mark the progress of Chelmsford's army in 1879. But a new sense of cultural pride has encouraged the commemoration of Zulu heroes by the people themselves, and archaeologists have restored part of King Cetshwayo's Ulundi homestead. A phoenix rising, perhaps, from the ashes of past glories.

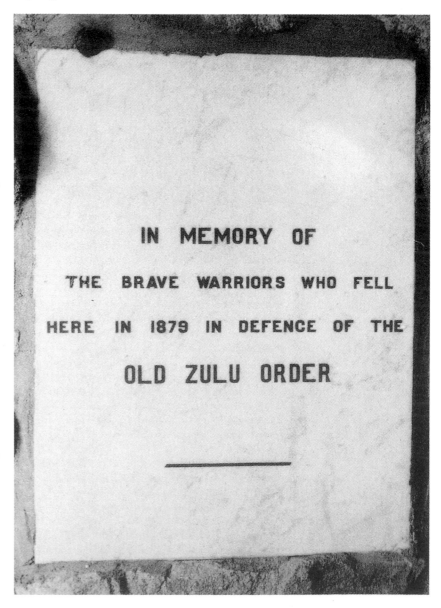

Below: A poignant memorial on the Ulundi battlefield monument to the thousands of Zulus who died in the war.

GLOSSARY

ibandla: the council of important men within the kingdom who advised the king on matters of national importance.

ibutho (pl. *amabutho*): age-grade regiment, also a member of such a regiment, a soldier or warrior.

ikhanda (pl. *amakhanda*): a large homestead belonging to the king; a state barracks where *amabutho* were quartered when in service.

ikhehla (pl. *amakhehla*): a married man who had donned the *isicoco* headring.

ikholwa (pl. *amakholwa*): a Christian convert.

iklwa: the prototype stabbing spear introduced into the army by Shaka. The original pattern had a blade eighteen inches long and 1½ inches wide and a thirty-inch haft; considerable variation on this pattern was evident by 1879.

ilobolo: cattle or goods given by a groom's family to the father of the bride as a guarantee of status and good standing.

impi: a body of armed men, an army, a battle or war.

impondo zankomo: 'the beast's horns', the Zulu battlefield formation.

inceku (pl. *izinceku*): a personal attendant of the king or chief.

induna (pl. *izinduna*): a civil or military officer of the state, appointed by the king.

inkhosi (pl. *amakhosi*): a king or chief.

insizwa (pl. *izinsizwa*): a youth, or young man not yet married and granted the full status or adulthood.

inyanga (pl. *izinyanga*): a practioner of traditional medicine, a doctor or herbalist.

iphovela (usually pl. *amaphovela*): a type of headdress worn by some of the younger *amabutho* on ceremonial occasions, consisting of upright strips of stiff cowhide, worn above the temples, with cowtails attached to the tips.

isangoma (pl. *izangoma*): diviner; person in touch with the spirit world, able to detect supernatural evil and 'smell out' its perpetrators.

isicoco: ring of fibre and gum worn on the crown of the head by married men.

isigodlo (pl. *izigodlo*): the fenced-off area at the upper end of an *ikhanda*, which housed the king or his household; girls of the king's household, given to him in service as 'tribute' and disposable by him in marriage.

isihlangu (pl. *izihlangu*): large war-shield, approximately five feet tall by two feet six inches wide, introduced into the Zulu army by Shaka and still carried in 1879.

isikhulu (pl. *izukhulu*): a man of power and influence within the kingdom, usually the head of an important clan or lineage.

iviyo (pl. *amaviyo*): a company within an ibutho.

ka: the son of, e.g., King Cetshwayo kaMpande.

umbumbuluzo: smaller warshield, approximately forty inches by twenty inches, introduced by King Cetshwayo among his faction in the civil war of 1856 and used, together with the larger isihlangu type, in 1879.

sakabuli: a long-tailed finch, whose glossy black tail feathers were a popular component of warriors' headdresses, particularly those of the younger *amabutho*.

umkhonto (pl. *imikhonto*): the general name for a spear.

umkhosi (pl. *imikhosi*): the annual First Fruits ceremony, a national gathering of great importance ritually to strengthen the kingdom and usher in the new harvest.

umuzi (pl. *imizi*): a homestead, an ordinary collection of huts under one headman or patriarch. Also the members of that homestead.

uSuthu: the name of King Cetshwayo's victorious faction in the civil war of 1856, also the war cry of that faction and the national war-cry in 1879.

BIBLIOGRAPHY

In a work of this nature, it would scarcely be appropriate to give detailed text notes. Although I have consulted many primary sources, most have already been analysed and interpreted by other historians, and anyone seeking to read further on the campaign may find the following review useful. The list is by no means exhaustive, but it does include those works that were found to be particularly helpful.

The first attempt at a narrative history of the Anglo-Zulu War was the official *Narrative of Field Operations Connected With the Zulu War of 1879* (London, 1881, reprinted 1907 and 1989). Inevitably, its summary of the causes of the war reflect the opinion of the Home Government, and it skirts round the more contentious issues of the campaign itself, but it is concise and detailed and includes exactly those tables of facts and figures that one would expect from such a record. Its maps, drawn from surveys made by officers in the field, are particularly valuable, although necessarily weak on Zulu dispositions. *The South African Campaign of 1879* by J. P. MacKinnon and S. H. Shadbolt (London, 1882, reprinted 1973) has a similarly official air, but confines its history of the campaign to the first chapter. The bulk of the book is taken up with photographic portraits and biographical details of the officers who died in the war, together with an invaluable list of service details.

In the decades following the war many of the participants wrote books about their experiences. All, of course, are valuable to a greater or lesser degree; C. L. Norris-Newman's *In Zululand With the British Throughout the War of 1879* (London, 1880, reprinted 1988) is the account of the only journalist to accompany the Centre Column during the Isandlwana campaign. Although its coverage of the rest of the war is less satisfying, it does include many valuable first-hand accounts and statements, including Pearson's report of Nyezane, Wood's account of Khambula and a transcript of the Court of Inquiry's investigations into the death of the Prince Imperial. Volume Two of Wood's autobiography, *From Midshipman to Field Marshal* (London, 1906), gives a résumé of his experiences in the field. Wood was conscientious in Intelligence matters, and he paid closer attention than most to Zulu movements, but his map of Khambula is marred by a curious reversal of the Zulu dispositions. Captain H. H. Parr's *A Sketch of the Zulu and Kaffir Wars* (London, 1880, reprinted 1970) is also important, but stops short after Rorke's Drift. Two NNC officers left accounts of the Isandlwana campaign:

Commandant G. Hamilton-Browne, whose scurrilous yarn, *A Lost Legionary in South Africa* (London, 1912), is nevertheless an important source for the events of 22 January; and Lieutenant H. Harford, whose diary was later edited by Daphne Child and published as *The Zulu War Journal of Colonel Henry Harford* (Pietermaritzburg, 1979). George Mossop's virtually unobtainable *Running The Gauntlet* (London, 1937) contains a graphic account of Hlobane and Khambula from the viewpoint of a trooper of the Frontier Light Horse. D. F. C. Moodie's *The History of the Battles and Adventures of the British, Boers and the Zulus in Southern Africa* (Adelaide, 1879) presents a curious hotch-potch of contemporary accounts not found elsewhere. The relevant sections were edited by John Laband and republished in 1988 as *Moodie's Zulu War*. Major Ashe and Captain the Hon. E. V. Wyatt Edgell's *The Story of the Zulu War* (London, 1880) mixes personal experiences with more general history. F. E. Colenso and Lieutenant-Colonel E. Durnford's *History of the Zulu War and its Origins* (London, 1880, reprinted 1970) also includes much useful material, although it is fiercely partisan, attacking Frere's policies and castigating Chelmsford for the Isandlwana débâcle while exonerating Durnford.

Press coverage of the war has been re-packaged in S. Bourquin and Tania Johnston's compilations: *The Zulu War of 1879 as Reported in 'The Graphic'* (2 vols., Durban, 1963 and 1965), and *The Zulu War of 1879 as Reported in 'The Illustrated London News'* (Durban, 1971). There have been more recent attempts to use contemporary material, notably Frank Emery's excellent *The Red Soldier: Letters from the Zulu War, 1879* (London, 1977) which collects many eye-witness accounts, previously published in obscure local newspapers, and presents a fascinating picture of the war as seen by those who waged it. Norman Holme's *The Silver Wreath* (London, 1979) includes a long letter written by Lieutenant Chard, at Queen Victoria's request, describing the battle of Rorke's Drift in great detail, together with Chard's sketches of the mission station, other accounts of Isandlwana and Rorke's Drift, and brief biographical details of the men of the 24th who fell at Isandlwana or fought at Rorke's Drift. Sonia Clarke's *Invasion of Zululand 1879* (Johannesburg, 1979), and *Zululand At War* (Johannesburg, 1984) comprise a number of important diaries and collections of letters relating to the campaign.

The first popular histories of the war began to appear in the 1930s. W. H. Clements' *The Glamour and Tragedy of the Zulu War* (London,

1936) is not highly regarded, nor is Rupert Furneaux's *The Zulu War: Isandlwana and Rorke's Drift* (London, 1963). The Hon. Gerald French's *Lord Chelmsford and the Zulu War* (London, 1939) has more to offer, since it made use of the General's military papers, though they had been first edited by a member of his staff. Katherine John's *The Prince Imperial* (London, 1939), and E. E. P. Tisdall's *The Prince Imperial* (London, 1959) are popular biographies more concerned with the drama of their story than military detail. Donald Featherstone's *Captain Carey's Blunder* (London, 1973) is better, but is marred by the author's occasional apparent flights of fancy, including the story that Carey's death resulted from a kick from a grey horse which I have not been able to substantiate. R. Coupland's *Zulu Battle Piece: Isandlwana* (London, 1948) was the first look at the subject by a trained historian, and is a concise battle account still worth reading. C. W. DeKiewiet's *The Imperial Factor in South Africa* (Cambridge, 1937) was one of the first to set the causes of the war within a broader imperial and economic context, paving the way for subsequent revisions.

The major work on the war appeared in 1966. Donald R. Morris's monumental *The Washing of the Spears* (London), running to 600 pages, is a superb work of scholarship, beautifully written. It inspired a new generation of historians to study the war, and, if their subsequent researches have challenged some of its interpretations, it remains a bench-mark and essential reading. A greater study of Zulu sources has questioned its understanding of Zulu polical systems, and Morris's account of Isandlwana, with its emphasis on ammunition failure as the root cause of the disaster, has now been challenged, but this cannot detract from the nature of the author's achievement. Subsequent popular accounts – A. Lloyd's *The Zulu War* (London, 1973), David Clammer's *The Zulu War* (London, 1973), and Michael Glover's *Rorke's Drift: A Victorian Epic* (London, 1975) merely re-work Morris's material and add little or nothing new. Michael Barthorp's *The Zulu War: A Pictorial History* (Poole, 1980) benefits from the large number of previously unpublished illustrations. R. Egerton's *Like Lions They Fought* (New York, 1988) adds little beyond a curiously dated and stereotypical analysis of the British Army, and has many factual inaccuracies. James Bancroft's *Rorke's Drift* (London, 1988) has much to offer in an imaginative use of illustrations, but the text is similarly flawed. A. McBride's *The Zulu War* (London, 1976) and C. Wilkinson-Latham's *Weapons and Uniforms of the Zulu War* (London, 1978) both attempt to describe and depict the uniforms of the combatants, but both are in need of revision. Philip Gon's *The Road to Isandlwana* (Johannesburg, 1979) follows the 1/24th through the Cape Frontier War and on to its demise, and is a valuable insight into the closed world of an Imperial infantry battalion in the 1870s, but its account of Isandlwana does not address the areas of controversy.

Even before the impetus of the centenary in 1979, a new wave of writers, many of them professional academic historians, began to re-assess the Anglo-Zulu War and question many of its accepted truths. F. W. D. Jackson's three-part article 'Isandlwana: The Sources Re-Examined' in the *Journal of the Society for Army Historical Research* (London, 1965) is a meticulous and thorough re-assessment of the primary sources, and its conclusions have influenced many subsequent works, including this one. Jackson also contributed an article on the 24th to the Victorian Military Society's booklet, edited by I. Knight, *There Will Be An Awful Row at Home About This* (Shoreham-by-Sea, 1987). The same booklet includes a number of essays reflecting the current understanding of the War in the field. Jackson and Morris defended their respective views on Isandlwana in

an issue of *Soldiers of the Queen*, the Journal of the Victorian Military Society. Jeff Guy's *The Destruction of the Zulu Kingdom* (Bristol, 1979) broke new ground with its perceptive analysis of Zulu political and economic structures, but it is primarily concerned with the Zulu Civil War of the 1880s, and its academic style may not appeal to the general reader. A collection of papers presented to a Conference on the Anglo-Zulu War at the University of Natal in 1979, and published as *The Anglo-Zulu War: New Perspectives* (Pietermaritzburg: eds. A. Duminy and C. Ballard) outlines the current thinking on the causes of the war. *John Dunn*, by Charles Ballard (Johannesburg, 1985) is a sound biography of the famous 'White Zulu Chief,' again marred by an inaccessible style and a preoccupation with academic jargon.

Pre-eminent among the new historians specializing in military aspects of the War are John Laband and Paul Thompson of the University of Natal. Their *Field Guide to the War in Zululand and the Defence of Natal 1879* (Pietermaritzburg, 1983) is not only an excellent collection of battle maps – invaluable to those seeking to visit the historic sites – but also an excellent concise history of the campaign. Their subsequent work together, chiefly *War Comes to Umvoti: The Natal Zululand Border* (Durban, 1980) and *The Buffalo Border* (Pietermaritzburg, 1983), has done much to focus attention on lesser known aspects of the fighting, and in particular the role of Colonial Volunteer and Natal African units. Both have contributed a number of crucial papers to academic journals such as *The Journal of Natal and Zulu History* and *Theoria*; at the time of going to press, some of these papers are being collected for publication in book form by the University of Natal Press. John Laband has also written three booklets for the KwaZulu Monuments Council: *Cetshwayo kaMpande* (with John Wright, Durban, 1983) *Fight Us in the Open*, a collection of Zulu accounts of the War (Durban, 1985), and *The Battle of Ulundi* (Durban, 1988), a carefully researched and detailed account of the last great battle of the War.

A Zulu perspective has, indeed, been lacking until recently. Bertram Mitford's charming travelogue, *Through the Zulu Country* (London, 1883, reprinted 1975), includes a number of important Zulu eye-witness accounts of battles, particularly Isandlwana. C. T. Binns' *The Last Zulu King* (London, 1963) is a useful popular biography, now in need of revision, while the King himself explains his military strategy in *A Zulu King Speaks: Statements Made by Cetshwayo KaMpande on the History and Customs of His People* (Pietermaritzburg, 1978), edited by C. de B. Webb and J. B. Wright. This is a crucial collection of interviews given by the King during his captivity after the War, and upon which much of our knowledge of the Zulu position is based. An insight into conditions within the country during the War can be found in Cornelius Vijn's *Cetshwayo's Dutchman; Being the Private Journal of a White Trader In Zululand during the British Invasion* (London, 1880, reprinted 1988). Bishop Colenso's additional notes to this provide not only a useful contemporary account of the Zulu military system, but also descriptions of incidents not readily found elsewhere. F. B. Fynney's Pamphlet, *The Zulu Army and Headmen*, published at Chelmsford's request at Pietermaritzburg in April 1878, has long been the standard source of information of the Zulu army, though it is now recognized to be incomplete and at times inaccurate. R. C. Samuelson's *Long, Long Ago* (Durban, 1929) contains details on Zulu dress and weapons, as observed by one who grew up among them as the son of a missionary. By far the most important collection of Zulu primary evidence, however, can be found in the *James Stuart Archive*, edited by C. de B. Webb and J. B. Wright, published by the University of Natal and currently standing at four thick volumes (1976, 1979, 1982 and 1986). Stuart was a Natal civil servant who, at the turn of the century, collected the statements of surviving Zulus who remembered the old kingdom, and their testimony covers a phenomenal range of historical and cultural topics. *Paulina Dlamini: Servant of Two Kings* edited by S. Bourquin and H. Filter (Durban, 1986) is the autobiography of one of King Cetshwayo's *isigodlo* girls, and includes revealing character studies of important historical figures. *The Zulus* by Ian Knight (London, 1989) is an introductory study of the Zulu army from Shaka to the 1906 Rebellion, and includes many rare illustrations.

Finally, tying up loose ends, Major G. Tylden's *The Armed Forces of South Africa* (Johannesburg, 1954) contains a list of all the Volunteer units that fought in the War, though much work still needs to be done in this area. Ian Bennett's *Eyewitness in Zululand* (London, 1989), being based on the journal of Assistant Commissary Dunne, contains much on the transport problems which shaped Chelmsford's strategy. Currently in preparation, Ian Knight's *The British Army In Zululand, 1879*, a companion to *The Zulus*, will cover British organization and uniforms for the general reader. J. Y. Gibson's *The Story of the Zulus* (London, 1911) is a general history, enriched by the author's contact with Zulus during the latter part of the century. T. V. Bulpin's *Shaka's Country* (Cape Town, 1952) is an excellent introduction for those new to the subject, with a keen sense of place and illustrated by evocative drawings. For those wishing to visit the sites, there is *Historic Natal and Zululand* by H. C. Lugg (Pietermaritzburg, 1949), a collection of notes on battlefields and people, and valuable because of the author's personal associations; his father had fought at Rorke's Drift. J. L. Smail's *With Shield and Assegai* (Cape Town, 1965) is a scrap-book of photographs of battlefields and monuments which was revised and expanded as *From the Land of the Zulu Kings* (Durban, 1979). Although not without occasional mistakes and misidentifications, it is ideal for those seeking to explore the green hills of Zululand, either in the field or through their imagination from the comfort of an arm-chair.

INDEX

ILLUSTRATION
ACKNOWLEDGEMENTS

S. BOURQUIN: 21 (top), 25, 27 (top), 28 (top), 33, 36 (left), 40, 57, (top), 68, 70 (bottom), 71, 74 (centre), 76, 79 (top), 81, 83, 85, 86, 90 (top), 91 (top), 94 (bottom), 96 (top), 97 (top), 101, 105 (top left & bottom right), 107 (bottom), 112 (top), 113 (bottom), 115 (bottom), 117, 118, 119, 121 (top), 122 (bottom), 126, 130 (bottom), 135, 138 (top), 148, 149, 150 (top), 151 (top), 153 (bottom), 155 (top), 158 (centre), 162 (top), 163 (centre), 169 (bottom), 170 (top), 171 (top), 175 (top), 176 (bottom), 179 (top), 184 (top right), 185.

KILLIE CAMPBELL AFRICANA LIBRARY: 36 (right), 44 (top), 100 (top), 106 (bottom), 110 (centre), 145, 173 (right), 190.

LOCAL HISTORY MUSEUM, DURBAN: 19 (top), 27 (bottom), 41 (bottom), 46 (top and bottom), 77 (top), 116 (bottom), 156 (left), 163 (top and centre).

AFRICANA MUSEUM JOHANNESBURG: 19 (bottom), 22, 42/3, 55, 122 (bottom), 160 (top), 181 (bottom), 189 (bottom).

NATIONAL ARMY MUSEUM: 38 (top), 45, 53 (top), 58 (top), 111, 120 (top), 146, 147, 150 (bottom), 156 (right), 158 (top), 176 (top), 182 (top), 188 (top).

BY KIND PERMISSION OF THE TRUSTEES OF THE SHERWOOD FORESTERS'
MUSEUM: 127 (top), 137, 160 (bottom), 184 (bottom).

CANTERBURY CITY MUSEUM: 17, 26, 32, 38 (bottom), 41 (top), 49, 50, 84 (top), 87 (bottom), 90 (bottom), 93, 154 (top), 166 (bottom).

AUTHOR'S COLLECTION: 2, 7, 18, 20, 21 (bottom), 23 (bottom), 28 (bottom), 30 (top), 51, 54 (top), 58 (bottom), 59 (bottom two), 61, 62, 64/5, 67, 69 (bottom), 72, 74 (top and bottom), 78 (bottom), 80, 91 (bottom), 94 (top), 100 (bottom), 102 (bottom), 103, 105 (bottom left), 107 (top), 108/9, 110 (bottom), 113 (top), 115 (bottom), 116 (top), 121 (bottom), 122 (top), 123, 124, 125 (top left), 127 (bottom), 129 (bottom), 130 (top), 132, 133 (left), 134, 136 (top), 139, 140/41, 143, 152, 161 (top), 164, 165, 166 (top), 167, 170 (bottom), 171 (bottom), 172, 178 (top), 180 (top), 183 (top), 184 (top left), 187, 188 (bottom), 192.

BRYAN MAGGS: 29.

IAN CASTLE: 66, 87 (top), 125 (bottom), rear cover.

SOMERSET LIGHT INFANTRY MUSEUM, TAUNTON: 120 (bottom), 138 (bottom), 178 (bottom).

LORD CAWDOR: 129 (top left).

NATAL ARCHIVES DEPOT: 31, 37, 44 (bottom), 46 (centre), 70 (top), 77 (bottom), 79 (bottom), 84 (bottom), 89, 144, 155 (bottom), 173 (top left).

GEORGE ROBINSON/PARKER GALLERY: 164 (bottom).

ROYAL HIGHLAND FUSILIERS MUSEUM: 39 (top right).

ZULULAND CULTURAL HERITAGE MUSEUM, ONDINI: 175 (bottom).

KEITH REEVES COLLECTION: 60, 69 (top), 82, 95, 99.

CAMERONIANS REGIMENTAL MUSEUM: 181 (top right).

J. WEBB COLLECTION: 53 (bottom), 157.

KENNETH GRIFFITH: 73, 169 (top), 174.

CARDIFF CASTLE: 180 (bottom).

OSBORNE HOUSE/ENGLISH HERITAGE: *Photo Frank Taylor*: 183 (bottom).

KING'S OWN REGIMENTAL MUSEUM: 78 (top), 151 (bottom), 191.

LA REUNION DES MUSEES NATIONAUX (Versailles Collection): 159.

ROYAL ENGINEERS MUSEUM: 92 (top), 158 (bottom).

ROYAL GREENJACKETS MUSEUM: 102 (bottom).

ROYAL COLLECTION: 23 (top), 24, 30 (bottom two), 35, 39 (top left), 54 (bottom), 75 (top), 114, 125 (top right), 128, 129 (top right and centre), 131, 133 (right), 136 (bottom), 161 (bottom), 179 (bottom), 182 (bottom), 186.